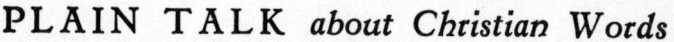

BY THE SAME AUTHOR . . .
Plain Talk on Acts
Plain Talk on Luke
Plain Talk on Matthew

PLAIN TALK
about Christian Words

---

by Manford George Gutzke, D.D., Ph.D.

ZONDERVAN PUBLISHING HOUSE
GRAND RAPIDS, MICHIGAN

PLAIN TALK ABOUT CHRISTAIN WORDS
© Copyright 1964 Royal Publishers, Inc.
Johnson City, Tennessee
Assigned to Zondervan, 1965

First printing — 1964
Second printing — 1965
Third printing — 1967

Printed in the United States of America

Dedicated to

W. A. WAGNON

whose personal encouragement and generous help meant so much to me in producing this book.

Preface

WITHOUT words we cannot think, understand or communicate ideas. No one is born with language. We are born with capacities but we must learn all we know. This is true with our vocabulary. Whatever we know and can share with others is largely limited by the words we can use. This is also true in Christian life and experience.

Before I became a Christian I understood practically none of the words in which the Gospel is expressed. Even when I wanted to believe, I had no real idea what there was to believe. When I went to the public worship of God my mind and my heart were actually dumb; I could not think nor understand anything. I heard the praying, singing and preaching but everything was just so much jargon to me. Even when deeply stirred in the service, I remained ignorant and helpless because I did not know the meaning of the words which I heard.

I have long been convinced that many do not worship, praise, pray nor witness as they would like to because they do not have the words which will express what they have in their hearts. In this book I try to explain the meaning of common words and phrases which are used to express the Christian Gospel as it is set forth in the Bible.

In a very real sense we cannot use any word or phrase unless we have an idea of what it means in our conversational language. There are certain terms and expressions used in the Bible to refer to certain aspects of the truth revealed in Jesus Christ for which there can be no substitutes. We need to learn the meaning of such words so that we can use them in our worship and our witness.

There are many more words and expressions used in the Bible which are not mentioned in this book. I have selected these largely from my own experience in coming to faith. I trust the plain talk I have used will serve to make clear the basic meaning of the Christian words I have discussed.

Contents

PREFACE

One — GOD 11
    GOD IS A SPIRIT 11
    GOD IS A PERSON 12
    THE TRINITY 12
    GOD IS INFINITE 16
    GOD IS ETERNAL 19
    GOD IS HOLY 21
    GOD IS JUDGE 23
    GOD IS SAVIOUR — REDEEMER . . . 25
    GOD IS FATHER 26

Two — MAN 28
    MAN IN THE IMAGE OF GOD . . . 28
    MAN IS BODY, SOUL AND SPIRIT . . 31
    MAN NEEDS COMMUNION WITH OTHERS . 33
    MAN MUST RULE 36
    MAN IS RESPONSIBLE 39
    MAN CAN BE LOST 42
    MAN HAS A CONSCIENCE 45
    MAN SUFFERS IN DISTRESS . . . 48

Three — SIN 52
    THE LAW OF GOD 52
    THE NATURE OF SIN 55
    THE COURSE OF SIN 58
    FORGIVENESS OF SINS 61
    SACRIFICE FOR SINS 64
    THE SIN OFFERING 66
    THE LAMB OF GOD 69
    THE HIGH PRIEST 71

Four — THE PRIESTHOOD	74
THE TABERNACLE	74
CLEANSED BY THE BLOOD	77
CONSECRATION	80
BEING SANCTIFIED	82
BEING HOLY	85
THE ATONEMENT	87
THE PRIESTS	90
THE SHEKINAH GLORY	93
Five — JESUS CHRIST	97
THE SON OF GOD	97
THE INCARNATION	99
HIS EARLY MINISTRY	102
HIS DEATH	105
HIS RESURRECTION	107
HIS ASCENSION	110
THE HEAD OF THE CHURCH	113
HIS COMING AGAIN	116
Six — THE GOSPEL	120
REPENTANCE	122
BELIEVING	123
BORN AGAIN	126
RECEIVING CHRIST	129
ABIDING IN CHRIST	132
SERVING THE LORD	135
THE BLESSED HOPE	139
THE RESURRECTION	142
Seven — THE HOLY SPIRIT	146
THIRD PERSON IN THE TRINITY	147
IN THE OLD TESTAMENT	150
PENTECOST	153
RECEIVING THE HOLY SPIRIT	156
BRINGING MEN TO CHRIST	159
IN BELIEVERS	162
IN THE CHURCH	165
FRUITS OF THE SPIRIT	168

Eight — THE CHRISTIAN	172
HIS FAITH	172
REGENERATION	175
JUSTIFICATION	177
SANCTIFICATION	179
GLORIFICATION	181
COMMUNION	184
GROWING IN GRACE	187
SERVICE	190
Nine — THE CHURCH	194
ECCLESIA	195
THE BRIDE OF CHRIST	198
THE BODY OF CHRIST	202
MEMBERS ONE OF ANOTHER	205
THE HABITATION OF GOD	209
THE TEMPLE OF THE HOLY SPIRIT	212
AGAPE	215
NOT OF THIS WORLD	218
SCRIPTURE REFERENCES	223
INDEX	229

PLAIN TALK *about Christian Words*

CHAPTER ONE

God

THE word *GOD* has many meanings. Anything which a man considers to be most important in his life, whose power he thinks is the greatest, and whose favor he would do anything or give anything to win, is properly called his "god." A man may have many gods. When a man worships anything else than the God of the Bible, we say he is worshipping an "idol."

An idol may be attractive or ugly. An idol may be a concrete thing, a mythical character, or a mental ideal. But it is always something a man will serve with all he is or has. Some men worship drink, pleasure, money, power, or even other persons. Whatever or whoever I put first in my heart is a god to me. Sometimes a man will worship himself (2 Thess. 2:4).

When Christians speak of God, they mean the God of Abraham, Isaac and Jacob, the God and Father of our Lord Jesus Christ, *the God of the Bible.*

God has different names in the Bible. He is called the "Lord," the "Almighty," the "Lord God," the "Creator," our "Maker," our "Heavenly Father." Sometimes the word "Jehovah" or "Yahweh" is used, but such names have the same meaning as "Lord." The first statement in the Apostles' Creed is still the Christians' faith:

> "I believe in God the Father Almighty, Maker of heaven and earth."

GOD IS A SPIRIT

When we say that God is Spirit, we mean He does not have a physical body such as we have. He may have a body, but not like ours. He is not material which can be seen, or heard, or smelled, or tasted, or touched by us. He cannot be measured. He is not so long, so wide, so thick, or so heavy. We should not let ourselves picture God with head, shoulders, arms, and face like our own.

God made the rocks and trees, stars and creatures; but God is not in these things, nor a part of these things. They are His creation. He is their Creator—somewhat like an inventor and his machine.

Men can think of God only in terms of what He does, not what He looks like. He is the invisible God. But He is the Creator, the Giver of life, the Keeper of Israel, the Ruler, the Judge of all the earth, the Saviour, the Redeemer, the eternal Father.

> "God is a Spirit: and they that worship him must worship him in Spirit and in truth" (John 4:24).

GOD IS A PERSON

God does not have a body like ours, so He is not limited to time and space, and He can be anywhere, everywhere, any time, every time, all the time! But He is a *Person*. By this we mean He can *think, feel* and *will* to do as He is in Himself.

God understands and knows all things. He sees what is in our hearts better than we do, before we do. He feels joy, sorrow, pleasure, anger as He looks upon us. For example, "God is *angry* with the wicked every day" (Ps. 7:11). He chooses to act according to His holy, just and wise will. In all things any little child can say "Thou, God, seest me"—"He knoweth the way I take." The Psalmist writes, "I sought the Lord and He heard me" (Ps. 34:4). It is always true that "The eyes of the Lord are in every place, beholding the evil and the good" (Prov. 15:3).

The God of the Bible is a Person in whom we can put our trust and confidence because He knows about us, cares about us, and intends to do us good.

THE TRINITY

The idea that God is a Person is not too hard to grasp, because this implies that God in Himself is a Being who *is* in some way similar to the way a man *is*. This is confirmed by the Scriptures when they say that God made man in His own image (Gen. 1:27). The Hebrew word for *image* is the word used for *shadow*. So the Scriptures imply that man was made in the likeness of God—the way a shadow on the grass is in the likeness of the man casting the shadow.

The grass in the shadow is not the same kind of stuff as the man who casts the shadow; but the general shape of the shadow is made up by the shape of the man who casts it. Just as you could look at the shadow and get some true idea of the man, so it would seem that you could look at man and get some true idea of God.

This is not at all to claim that God has any human limitations, or sin, or weakness; nor does it claim that man has in himself any of the holiness, or grace, or power that belongs to God. It does not mean that God has arms, legs, nerves, and muscles like a man. But it does mean that there is a likeness between God in Himself and man in his being.

This truth seems to be involved in the Incarnation. When God manifested Himself in this world so that man could see Him and know Him, He "was made in the likeness of men" (Phil. 2:7-8 and Heb. 2:14-18). Apparently, "being found in fashion as a man" enabled Him to show what God is like.

Philip said to the Lord Jesus, "Lord, shew us the Father, and it sufficeth us" (John 14:8). Jesus of Nazareth replied, "Have I been so long time with you, and yet hast thou not known me, Philip? he that hath seen me hath seen the Father..." (John 14:9).

God is like the Lord Jesus Christ. It has been pointed out that perhaps the most complete word about God in Scripture is Jesus of Nazareth, who is spoken of as "the express image of God" (Heb. 1:3).

The Bible further speaks about God as in three persons. The Christian Church has long used the expression "three persons in one Godhead." This idea is called the *Trinity* and involves the most difficult line of thought in the Scriptures. The human mind finds it almost impossible to conceive three persons in "One."

The Trinity is God the Father, God the Son, and God the Holy Spirit. God the Father is One who knows, cares, and wills. God the Son is One who knows, cares, and wills. God the Holy Spirit is One who knows, cares, and wills. Each is a distinct person, and yet the Three are One.

This distinction is indicated by the Scriptures. They strongly imply that God the Father manifests Himself especially in heaven,

God the Son manifested Himself on earth as Jesus of Nazareth, and God the Holy Spirit manifests Himself especially in the church in the spiritual experience of believers.

It should always be kept in mind that each of the three Persons in the Trinity is God. The church has learned to say they are each equally God: equal in power, equal in glory, and equal in might. Each is equal to the others and is entitled to the same worship, the same devotion, the same trust and faith.

From the Scriptures we may deduce that God the Father functions as the *executive director;* God the Son functions as the *activator,* the performer, the doer; God the Holy Spirit functions in bringing the will of God into realization so far as actual human experience is concerned. It is stated that the Father sends the Son; the Son serves the Father and sends the Holy Spirit; the Holy Spirit shows the things of the Lord Jesus Christ to believers honoring the Father. The distinctions between the functions of these three Persons are not always specifically spelled out in Scripture. All three work together as One, and yet these distinctions are definitely implied.

Although there is no absolute statement in the Bible that God is three Persons and yet one God, the idea is plainly there. The three Persons in the Godhead are mentioned as distinct from each other at the baptism of Jesus of Nazareth (Matt. 3:16-17). The Lord Jesus gave His disciples explicit instructions to baptize "in the name of the Father, and of the Son, and of the Holy Ghost" (Matt. 28:19). *Holy Ghost* is another expression for *Holy Spirit.* When Paul gave his apostolic blessing, he said, "The grace of the Lord Jesus Christ, and the love of God, and the communion of the Holy Ghost be with you all" (2 Cor. 13:14). Such Scripture verses as these cannot be understood to mean anything else than the existence of three distinct Persons in the Godhead.

While the doctrine of the Trinity names three distinct Persons, the *unity* in God is real and basic. The Scriptures say, "The Lord our God is one Lord" (Deut. 6:4). The "one" used in this statement is not the numerical digit "1" in the number series 1, 2, 3, 4, 5, 6, 7. It is the "One" used to refer to a state of unity.

The Bible says about husband and wife, "And they twain shall be *one* flesh" (Gen. 2:24). Thus when a man and a woman marry, they become unified as *"one* flesh." Yet each still has his own body and her own body. When the Tower of Babel was being built, God said, "Behold, the people is one" (Gen. 11:6). The *people* is plural, but they were knit together into *one* unit. This is the meaning of the "one" used in the Scripture—"The Lord our God is one Lord." God is a unified Being.

Unity in function is even more clearly set forth when Paul writes, "I have planted, Apollos watered." And he goes on to say, "Now he that planteth and he that watereth are one" (1 Cor. 3:6-8). Paul is one man, and Apollos is another man. In what sense then can Paul and Apollos be "one"? Obviously, they are *one* in performance and intention. In this sense we can think of God as *One:* the Father, the Son, the Holy Spirit working as one performing unit. These Three are One in performance in the way in which Paul and Apollos are one, when the first plants and the second waters in the raising of the one crop.

The same idea is brought out in Galatians 3:28 when Paul writes, "There is neither Jew nor Greek, there is neither bond nor free, there is neither male nor female: for *ye* are all *one* in Christ Jesus." Paul means to say *many* are *one* in unity in Christ Jesus.

Again, in John 17:22 the Lord is praying, "That they may be *one* even as we are *one*." The Lord Jesus Christ on earth is talking to the Father in heaven. He is saying "and *we* two are *one* that they may be one"—meaning that they (believers) may be united, that they may come together in *one* communion.

Christians do not believe in three Gods, but in one God who exists in three persons.[1]

> "The grace of the Lord Jesus Christ, and the love of God, and the communion of the Holy Ghost, be with you all. Amen" (2 Cor. 13:14).

---

[1] This belief in a God who is three and yet one should not be referred to as "tri-theism," which would teach the essential separateness of the three Persons. The early Church fathers judged this view to be out of accord with Scripture and condemned it as error. Orthodox Christian thought rejects "tri-theism" but embraces the term "Trinity" when attempting to describe the distinctions of Persons within the Godhead without doing violence to the essential unity in God Himself.

GOD IS INFINITE

It is important in trying to understand what the Bible teaches about God to remember that He is held to be *infinite*. This is related to the fact that He is Spirit and so does not have a physical body like men. With human beings on earth, two or more persons cannot be in exactly the same place at the same time. In the spirit, however, two or more *can be* in exactly the same place at the same time.

This is because spirit has no spatial dimensions. So with God there is no limit—large or small. He is *infinite*. Thus the three Persons of the Godhead can be in one place at one time.

Luke 24 records the appearance of the resurrected Lord Jesus Christ in a room where the doors were closed. He did nothing like this before His resurrection. The fact that this was done after the resurrection implies that His body was changed from what it was prior to His resurrection. After His resurrection He had a body, but the "stuff" of which it was composed was different. His body was now "spiritual" (1 Cor. 15:44). In this *spiritual* body, He could appear and disappear at will. This is the form—so far as we know—of the Spirit, for which there is no limitation as to space.

Infinite simply means having no limit or end. God is immeasurably great in extent and duration. The important point here is that nothing is too big for God; nor is anything too small for God.

You may say, "I wouldn't want to bother God about this; it is so little." The truth is that God is smaller than that. He is *infinitely* small. Or you may say, "I wouldn't want to bring this before the Lord; it is such a big thing." The truth is that God is bigger than that. He is *infinitely* big. In other words, the whole matter of size or amount simply does not apply when we are talking about God. Nothing can possibly be *too* big or *too* small.

Because God is infinite, His judgment is not affected by size. Consider honesty. It would be dishonest to steal a thousand dollars. It would also be dishonest to steal one cent. In the eyes of God, it is just as dishonest to take a pin as an automobile. Humanly speaking, this is not the case. Men are inclined to judge by the amount of money involved, while God is not.

God is concerned about the principle of the thing—the attitude. And in addition, God is able to give full and complete attention to everything, any time, anywhere, without becoming weary. He is infinitely great, infinitely strong, infinitely wise, infinitely good, infinitely merciful.

Omnipresent is closely allied with *infinite*. *Omni* means "all" and *present* means "he is here." When we say God is omnipresent, we mean He is here and there, everywhere and anywhere. Paul quoted a great poet as telling the truth when he said, "For in him we live, and move, and have our being" (Acts 17:28).

The Scriptures record a man's saying that when he goes up into heaven, down to the lowest hell, to the islands of the sea, to the crowded streets of the city, into some forest, or into a mountain cave—he will find God there. It would be impossible to go any place God is not!

Although it is true to say that God is everywhere and anywhere, it must be noted that He is not everywhere in the same sense. There is a very definite sense in which heaven is His home. The Lord prayed, "Our Father, which art in heaven" (Matt. 6:9).

One can be in God's presence anywhere, although the Scriptures say He dwells in heaven. Heaven is *not* a locality. Heaven is not a place north of something, east of somewhere, up or down from some place. Perhaps, in a real sense, heaven is where God is.

Certainly believers are seated in the heavens while they are here in this world. The Lord Jesus said, "And no man hath ascended up to heaven, but he that came down from heaven, even the Son of man which *is* in heaven" (John 3:13). Wherever heaven is located, it is a place. Christ said to His disciples when He was leaving them, "Let not your heart be troubled; ye believe in God, believe also in me. In my Father's house are many mansions: if it were not so, I would have told you. I go to prepare a *place* for you" (John 14:1-2).

There is a sense in which God is in heaven in a way He is not in other places. But He is *omnipresent* and His presence can be felt in every place.

The Apostles' Creed begins by stating, "I believe in God the Father Almighty, Maker of heaven and earth." *Omnipotence* is the characteristic of God which is called here "almighty" and is also part of being *infinite*. He is so almighty, so powerful that He is able to do anything.

The New Testament emphasizes that nothing is impossible with

God (Matt. 19:26; Mark 10:2; Luke 18:27). All nature is subject to Him. Storms, earthquakes, events—as they happen—are under His control. All men are subject to Him. They do not all do what He wants them to do, but He has His hand over their limits. They can go only so far and no farther. They can live only so long and no longer. God has fixed "the bounds of their habitation" (Acts 17:26). He is Almighty God over men.

The angels do His will. They cannot do anything He does not permit them to do. Satan is subject to His will. Although Satan does not do what God wants him to do, he cannot go beyond what God allows Him to do.

The Bible says that God is infinitely powerful but exercises His power according to His will (Eph. 1:11). God is holy, just, and good; and He will *not* do anything contrary to His nature. To realize that God is *all-powerful* and yet *altogether good* helps us in the vital matter of prayer. To say that God is almighty does not mean that men should go to Him to ask anything and everything as it may please them. God will not act in a way that is contrary to His infinite wisdom and love. He is infinitely wise and will not do a foolish thing. He has infinite love and will not do a hateful thing. If a man asks God to do something that is not in His will—even though it might be argued that he *could* do it—there is a certain sense in which that argument would not be true.

When I was in high school, someone talked to me about God's omnipotence. I was puzzled by this, because I doubted it at that time. The question came up: "Can God make a five-year-old steer in a minute?" That bothered me. I thought about it a long time; I decided He could not.

When we speak of a five-year-old steer, it is implied that God made him in five years. God would not violate His own dealings with things. He would not make a five-year-old steer in a minute; He would make him in five years!

Once—when I needed money—I was depending upon the Lord to provide it. The question then came up: could He make dollar bills grow on trees? Then I realized He makes trees, and He makes leaves grow on trees. That is consistent with God. He is not going to do anything foolish.

He makes dollar bills come out of printing presses, and He makes leaves grow on trees. He may induce the woodsman to cut

God

down the trees and ship them to the sawmill so that he receives money for his labor—and then move him to give the money. But God does not make money grow on trees.

God is infinite in wisdom, goodness and strength.

> "Great is our Lord, and of great power: his understanding is infinite" (Ps. 147:5).

GOD IS ETERNAL

The word *eternal* points to something that we cannot fully understand.

When the Bible says God is *eternal,* it is saying that—with God—there are no yesterdays or tomorrows. As far as God is concerned, there is no passing of time. God is not old. Things are not a thousand years old to God. Everything is "right now" with God. People sometimes speak of eternity as "the Everlasting Now."

Eternal also means that—with God—there is no beginning and no end. When we speak of something with no beginning or ending, it is almost impossible to grasp the idea. God always was, He is, and He will always be. God was before time began. When time ends, He still will be. All this goes beyond our human understanding. That is one reason that the name God revealed to Moses was "Jehovah."

The word we translate as "Jehovah" is really *Yahweh.* The word *Yahweh* is a form of the Hebrew verb *to be.* When Moses asked God what he should call Him, God said, "I am that I am" (Ex. 3:14). Some say that what God really told Moses is, "I am, I am becoming, I am being." We might say also that God is telling us, "I am being your Saviour, I am being your Protector, I am being your Father."

He is the *Living God.* God is our Eternal Contemporary in the sense that He is right here—involved all the time in everything that is going on. Psalm 102:27 states, "But thou art the same, and thy years shall have no end." He is "The everlasting Father, the Prince of Peace" (Isa. 9:6). He is never young and never old.

Because God is eternal and everlasting, He is *unchangeable.* Another word for that is *immutable.* In Malachi 3:6 we read, "For I am the Lord, I change not." Someone might say this makes God a "static" Being. Oh, no! Static means "not moving." No one would say that God is not moving. God is a living Being, but God is unchangeable in that He does not change direction. He does not change His character, nor does He change His manner.

He is always faithful. "He that keepeth Israel shall neither slumber nor sleep" (Ps. 121:4). James 1:17 says, "With whom is no variableness, neither shadow of turning." God is not strong one day, weak the next; alert one day, and indifferent the next. God is steadfast, regular, and consistent.

Men are often afflicted with the sense of uncertainty and fickleness. Some days they are anxious; other days they are careless. Sometimes men are interested and concerned. Then again they are indifferent. But God is not like that. His attention does not shift. He started out to do us good. He intends to do us good. He will not fail or be discouraged in doing us good.

God is what He is, and He is always the same. He does not change. In 1 Samuel 15:29, we read these words, "For he is not a man, that he should repent."

This leads to a question of understanding what is meant when the Bible says that God repented. For instance, in the days of Noah, when God saw how man was sinning, the Bible reports "It repented the Lord that he had made man on the earth" (Gen. 6:6). When Nineveh had sinned, God told Jonah that in forty days that city would be destroyed. Jonah preached this message to the city, and the Ninevites changed their ways. "And God saw their works, that they turned from their evil way; and God repented of the evil, that he said that he would do unto them; and he did it not" (Jon. 3:10). The way these records read, it does seem that God changes His ways. But this is more apparent than real.

Consider a very simple illustration. Suppose a man is on a train coming to a railroad station. As the train approaches, the station may be to the north of it. Then, as the train goes on, the station is to the south. Did the station act in a fickle manner? Did it move around? First, it was north; and then, it was to the south of the train. Yet the station had not moved. It was the train that moved. And so it may be with God.

God is angry with the wicked every day; yet He will comfort the broken heart. When a man sins, God is angry with him. But when the sinner listens to God, comes to Him, yields to Him—then God is merciful. Does this mean God changed His ways? Has God become fickle in the matter, or did the man change *his* ways? Then God would act differently to be consistent in His attitude toward man.

While the sinner was opposed to God, he was on God's anger side! When the sinner turned to Him, he was on God's mercy side; yet God was really always the same. The sinner was the one who changed. And in every instance where the Bible says, "God repented," or implies that He changed His mind, you will find that the people had changed *their* ways.

When God created the world, He looked on it and said it was very good. But when He saw, just before the flood, all the sin of man, He said it was very bad. Had God changed His mind? No, but the people had changed their ways! In this way we can understand how God can be eternally consistent in Himself, and yet deal in various ways with men in differing situations. God is "the same yesterday, and today, and for ever."

When little children ask, "Who made God?"—tell them the truth. "Nobody!" The little child says, "I don't understand." Adults don't understand either because the finite cannot comprehend the infinite. He always was. He always will be. He is the Eternal God.

> "The eternal God is thy refuge, and underneath are the everlasting arms" (Deut. 33:27).

GOD IS HOLY

One of the central ideas which the Bible reveals about God is that God is holy. The word *holy* is used with reference to God so much that it is scarcely ever questioned. But what does it mean to say, "God is holy"? Many people have the feeling that to be holy means not to do anything wrong. In a negative way, that may be true; but what does it really mean? When it is said that God is holy, reference is being made to His character. There is nothing crooked about God. He is not two-faced. God is genuine, sincere, dependable.

The English word *holy* is closely related to the idea of being *whole*. One hundred cents is a whole dollar. Three feet is a whole yard. God is absolutely everything He sets Himself out to be. The essence of God is truth. God, in His holiness, is without any reservations or restrictions. He is totally dedicated to His plan, not half-hearted about anything. If He takes in hand to do something, He will see it through.

The Bible says that God is benevolent. This means that He wills to do good to His creatures. He will advance welfare, sustain life, and make things more agreeable. It is part of God's holiness to be that way. He is not selfish; He is not holding back something for Himself, nor is He careless. "He that keepeth thee shall not slumber" (Ps. 121:3).

God is faithful at all times. Man may falter; God will not. Man may somehow deteriorate in his attitude and intention to obey. God never deteriorates in His attitude and intention to bless. This is the nature of God.

Men speak much of the love of God. He is altogether, entirely, and totally committed to the purpose that He will do good to His people. In so doing, God is fair at all times. "God is no respecter of persons" (Acts 10:34). There is singleness of heart and sincerity about Him. At no time does He favor one and not the other. He can be trusted in the dark. He invites men to put their trust in Him because He is dependable. He is holy.

How ignorant a person is when he criticizes God! Things happen to a man in a certain way on a given day, and he finds fault. Maybe he doesn't realize it, but what he has done is to criticize God. He has said that God did not play *fairly*. That is a slander on the holiness of God. He has said that God did not care about him. That is a slander on the love of God. He may have the feeling that God did worse with him than He did with someone else. That is a slander on the justice of God. This is why it is so important to understand that God is holy in all His dealings with men.

Merciful is a helpful word at this point. It is to the glory of God that He is merciful. It is our salvation that He is merciful. The greatest hope any human being can have is that the Judge of all the earth, Almighty God, is a God of mercy. He delights to show mercy, especially to the repentant. "A broken and a contrite heart, O God, thou wilt not despise" (Ps. 51:17). The Bible indicates that the Lord is interested in the poor (Matt. 11:5; Luke 4:18; Jas. 2:5). He is also interested in the weak, and is merciful toward them.

There will be times when we will wonder whether God is compassionate toward the poor, the weak, and the helpless. Why did

He ever make them? God has arranged conditions that will challenge the mercy of men. The Rich Young Ruler was advised by Jesus to "... give to the poor" (Matt. 19:21). God would have men to be merciful. If you never met a person who was weaker, there would be no challenge to mercy. If you never met anyone who was helpless, there would be no chance to show mercy.

God surrounds you with people who—compared to you—are poor and weak and helpless. Thus He challenges you to act with mercy toward them the way *He* acts toward such unfortunate persons. We are to show mercy to people the way God shows mercy.

It is written, "He maketh the sun to rise on the evil and on the good, and sendeth rain on the just and on the unjust" (Matt. 5:45). Our Lord said, "Be ye therefore perfect, even as your Father which is in heaven is perfect" (Matt. 5:48). Believers are to be kind to their enemies and "do good to them that hate you, and pray for them which despitefully use you, and persecute you" (Matt. 5:44). Certainly God is this way at all times in dealing with us. God is holy and merciful.

"The Lord is righteous in all his ways, and holy in all his works" (Ps. 145:17).

GOD IS JUDGE

God is spoken of in Genesis as "judge of all the earth" (Gen. 18:25). Deuteronomy 32:36 states, "For the Lord shall judge his people." This really means that God cares about His creation.

The Bible teaches that God created the world and all things in it, and He is vitally interested in the creatures He has made. For that reason, He provides all they need for living.

God did not create man as an experiment to see how man would come out. He made man in His own image. He planned to provide for every need that man had. He gave him air to breathe, water to drink, and sunshine to keep him warm. Man was to "Be fruitful, and multiply, and replenish the earth and subdue it, and have dominion over the fish of the sea, and the fowl of the air, and over every living thing" (Gen. 1:28). God provided for man; and man was to be responsible to God. Since man failed to live up to his opportunity, it was necessary for God to exercise judgment over him.

God judges all things that He makes. It can be seen that He judges animals and trees, since some of them live and some of them die.

The outstanding illustration in the Old Testament of God as Creator and Judge is the one shown to the Prophet Jeremiah (Jer. 18:2-4). Jeremiah was taken to a potter's shop where he saw the potter take the clay on his wheel and turn it to make a certain vessel. If it suited him, he kept it. If the vessel did not suit him, he crushed it and made it over again. The potter was both creator and judge. In such a sense this is a true figure of God.

It is easy for the human mind and spirit to feel offended that God would treat human beings as the potter treated the clay. If this kind of feeling is examined, it may be noted that it is generated by a sense of pride. The Scriptures say, "Shall the thing formed say to him that formed it, Why hast thou made me thus?" (Rom. 9:20). That is being impudent. God made man, He keeps man, and He is the Judge approving or disapproving man's conduct. This is fair enough.

So far as man has any capacity to judge his own actions, he becomes responsible. This means he can be called to account for his actions. God judges a man's conduct by the choices he makes.

God knows what men think and how men feel when they do things. The Bible says that when God completed His creative acts on the first day, He saw "that it was good" (Gen. 1:4). On the second day, He saw that it was "good," and so on for six days. The word *good* shows He appraised it, and evaluated it. What He had made coincided with what He had in mind; and so it was *good*.

God judges all His works and His creature, man, who was made in His image. In the days before the flood, God saw that the thoughts of men's hearts were only evil continually. "It grieved him at his heart" (Gen. 6:6). This language seems to imply that God was sorry He had made man, who was not doing what He had planned for man to do.

The Bible teaches that God can and will do as He pleases when He judges what He has made. We do not know all He has in mind, and so we cannot always understand what He does. But we can be sure "The soul that sinneth, it shall die." God condemns sin and will destroy the wicked. This is the reason man feels guilty when he does wrong. The judgment of God is according to the truth about man's actions. And the man who sins, feels God will judge him.

"Shall not the judge of all the earth do right?" (Gen. 18:25).

GOD IS SAVIOUR — REDEEMER

In our study we have seen God as Creator, Keeper, and Judge. In fairness, justice, and truth—God deals with man as he is. Because of the sin of man, death entered the world (1 Cor. 15:21-22). Now comes the good news; God is also our Saviour (Isa. 63:16). He is not only almighty, just, holy, and true, but He is merciful. God is merciful and gracious even as He judges the sinner. There is a loving kindness about God. He can and will save man. As the hymn writer has stated it:

> There is a wideness in God's mercy,
> Like the wideness of the sea;
> There's a kindness in his justice,
> Which is more than liberty.

In saving man, God does more than redeem him from his folly and wrongdoing. He *changes* him! This is the whole idea in God's plan of salvation. Man tried to live as a natural human being and failed. God now offers to give man an opportunity to unite with Him—that is, to let God live His life in man. God will make His own power, even His eternal life, available to men because of His own grace and mercy. He will save man, but in His own way. Man must yield himself to God and let God change him. That is what God does through Christ Jesus.

Suppose a young lad is going to swim across a lake. While he is swimming, he gets cramps. He is about to drown. A man comes along in a boat, pulls him in, and takes him across the lake. The man does not take him out of the water just to revive him, and then put him back in the water to swim the rest of the way across the lake. He takes him out of the water, revives him and transports him *safely* to the other side of the lake. This is an illustration of what God does for man when He saves him.

God is our Redeemer; He is merciful and kind. "Like as a father pitieth his children, so the Lord pitieth them that fear him" (Ps. 103:13). "For God so loved the world, that he gave his only begotten Son, that whosoever believeth in him should not perish, but have everlasting life" (John 3:16). God will pardon us, He will redeem us, He will deliver us from bondage. God will save us from sin because He is our Salvation.

This is the meaning of the name *Jesus*. God will save us. God saves us by changing us, through His grace, into His children. "He is able to save them to the uttermost that come unto God by him (Christ)" (Heb. 7:25).

GOD IS FATHER

When the Lord Jesus Christ taught His disciples to pray, He said, "Our Father which art in heaven" (Matt. 6:9). Of all the names given to God in the Bible, no doubt the most familiar is *Father*. Thoughout the New Testament the word *Father* is used for God, even as Jesus is called His "only begotten Son." Jesus said, "Neither knoweth any man the Father, save the Son, and he to whomsoever the Son will reveal him" (Matt. 11:27).

The Bible uses the word *father* in its most essential meaning; a father is the one who begets the child. This is especially true when we speak of the Lord Jesus as the Son of God. Paul calls God "The Father of our Lord Jesus Christ" (2 Cor. 11:31; Eph. 1:3; Col. 1:3). In the Old Testament, God is called the God of Abraham, Isaac, and Jacob—and also the God of Moses, the God of Elijah, and the God of David. He is called in the New Testament "the God and Father of our Lord Jesus Christ," because our Lord was identified as the "only begotten Son of the Father" (John 1:14) while living on earth. Jesus in His human nature is the one who reveals God as Father, as the Begetter, and as the Source of Life.

When we are born again, our Father is a Heavenly Father. When I was born the first time, I had an earthly father; my first birth was physical. When I was born again, my second birth was spiritual; in this way, I have a Heavenly Father. I was begotten in my first birth by the will of man. In the second birth, I was begotten by the Word of God and the will of God; and this was done through the person of Jesus Christ.

While the Lord Jesus Christ is the only begotten Son of God, all Christians are the adopted children of God. Christians do not call God "Father" because He is their provider, but because He is the true Father of those who believe and are born again. God the Father regenerates believers as they are born again of His Spirit.

It is quite true that God is a provider. He provides for all the people in the world, and mankind should be grateful for what God does. The Bible reveals God as the Creator and as the Keeper of life. He is the Provider of man's needs, and He is the Judge of man's conduct. He is also the Saviour from the consequence of sin. In all this, He is "like a Father." However, to *become* the spiritual children of God we must be begotten by Him through Jesus Christ. The Apostle John wrote, "But as many as received him (the Lord Jesus Christ), to them gave he power to become the sons of God" (John 1:12). We are "born again" into this new relationship with God. In this way He *becomes* truly our *Father*.

God wants all human beings to have the opportunity to enter the family of God. They can become the children of God through faith. "Behold, what manner of love the Father hath bestowed upon us, that we should be called the sons of God" (1 John 3:1).

It is the wonderful truth of the Gospel that salvation brings believers into this relationship with God, in which they are *children of God* and He is their *Father*.

CHAPTER TWO

Man

THE whole of the Bible concerns man. When it speaks of the soul, it means the soul of man. When it speaks of sin, it means the sin of man. When God became incarnate, He came in the form of man. When the Gospel is preached, it is preached to man. Salvation means the salvation of man. Resurrection means the resurrection of the body of man. The blessing of God means the blessing of God upon man.

The Bible teaches that man was created by God. Man lives in a world made by God. Man is what he is because God made him that way. What man does, matters to God. What happens to man matters to God. God wants to save man (John 3:16) from the consequences of man's sin and to eternal fellowship with God. The Bible shows how God will save man through Jesus Christ, who was God in the form of man.

The real meaning of a man is not seen by looking at the human being in himself as he is. The truth is revealed in the Bible, which shows man as he is in relation to God and His plan for all things.

"What is man, that thou art mindful of him? . . ." (Ps. 8:1).

MAN IS IN THE IMAGE OF GOD

The Bible teaches that man was created "in the image of God" (Gen. 1:27). As discussed in Chapter One, the Hebrew word of *image* means *shadow* and is generally translated by the English word *likeness*. Here it would help to think of a person's shadow on the ground. The shadow has a likeness to the man, but the shadow is not exactly the same as the man. The man is a great deal more than the shadow. The shadow can fall on sand, but that dark area seen on the ground remains sand. This does not mean that the man standing there is sand, but it means that the shadow on the sand is shaped in the likeness of the man.

When we make the statement that man is created in the image of God, we are saying that the Bible sets forth very definitely that there is more to a man than there is to an animal. This can be seen when we compare various things in the natural world. Think of objects such as stones. A stone has size and it has weight. When the sun shines on a stone, it gets warm; when the rain falls on it, it gets wet.

Now, let us think of trees. A tree has what a stone has. A tree has size like a stone. When the sun shines on it, the tree gets warm; and when the rain falls on it, the tree gets wet. You cannot poke your finger through a stone; you cannot poke your finger through a tree. In many ways a tree is like a stone, yet it is different. The tree can take elements into itself. It has a process going on by which it grows. It gets bigger and it can reproduce its kind. It can produce fruit. A stone cannot do that. A tree is a plant, and thus is more than a stone. It can grow, bear fruit, and reproduce itself into other trees.

Now let us move from plants to animals. Think of horses. A horse has many of the characteristics that the stone has—such as size and weight. When the sun shines on a horse, it gets hot just like a stone or a tree. The rain falls on it, and the horse gets wet the same as the stone and the tree. The horse is like a tree in that the horse can take in food. The horse can grow like a tree; however, there is more to a horse than to a tree. The horse can go places. It can move around. The horse can see. So we can see that a horse has some features that a plant does not have—just as a plant has some features that a stone does not have.

Now let us look at man. Man is in some ways like a stone. He has size and weight. When sun shines on him, he gets hot; and when rain falls on him, he gets wet. He is also like a tree in that he can eat and grow; but he is more than the tree. Now compare him with a horse. Man can move; he can look and see where he is going. He can feel things and have certain reactions to them like a horse. Many seem to think this is all there is to man; that he is just some kind of "improved" animal. But the Bible does not stop here.

Man has certain creative capacities. A man can make things

different from anything that has ever been made before. Animals do not. Birds do not. The first time a robin builds a nest, it is a robin's nest; and the last time it builds a nest, it is a robin's nest. The first nest is just as good as the last. It has not learned anything in the process. It has a certain pattern that it can produce, and it produces that pattern.

Bird psychologists are unable to account for the fact that you can take a sparrow and let that sparrow hatch out in a robin's nest, so that it never sees a sparow's nest. But when it is big enough to build a nest, it will not build a robin's nest—it will build a sparrow's nest. It will never have seen one before, but it will build a nest that is characteristic of all sparrows.

Man has the ability to change things and is akin to God in his capacity to create. His creative ability is much more limited than God's. Christian theology teaches that God created the world *out of nothing*. Man must confine himself to using the matter that God has created when he engages in any creative act. It cannot be denied, however, that man has the capacity to create, build, and make things that would be impossible for any animal to do.

No theory of evolution that considers man as having come from the animal kingdom is satisfying to the Bible. The Bible simply does not accept any such view of mankind. The Bible does not consider man as being an animal that has improved. The Bible considers man distinct and unique among the creatures of the earth. Although the image of God has been disfigured in man because of sin, it has never been wiped out. Man is the crown of God's creative acts. When the Bible says that man was created "in the image of God," it seems to point to certain ways in which man can act which are like God.

Man can be "self conscious." He knows himself as a person and can think of himself as being somebody, always the same person from the cradle to the grave. This means that man sees himself as a person who has dealings with other persons. He can plan and work for himself and his loved ones.

He feels "responsible" for what he does. Man feels he "ought" to do this, and "ought not" to do that. When he does wrong, he feels "guilty." Thus we say he has "moral responsibility."

Man can think of new things, new ways of doing things, new

things to do. We say that man can be "creative" in that he can change his ways to do better than he was doing before.

Also man can take some of what he has, and give it to others who may need it. He can exercise "grace."

Man can find his greatest values in his loved ones. He can consciously deny his own desires in order to help someone else.

In all these ways we get ideas of what it means to say "Man was created in the image of God." While all these capacities can be abused to man's own hurt, they still mark him as being the highest creation of God.

> "For thou hast made him but a little lower than the angels, and hast crowned him with glory and honour" (Ps. 8:5).

MAN IS BODY, SOUL AND SPIRIT

The Bible speaks about the nature of man in two ways. Sometimes it refers to man as having body, soul and spirit. Then again it speaks of man as having body and soul. The Bible does not maintain a clear-cut distinction between these two views, but always refers to the body as being *material* and to the soul and spirit as being *spiritual*.

In telling how the world was created, the Hebrew record uses three different words. First we read, "In the beginning God created the heavens and the earth." For this the word *bara,* meaning "create," is used. This word means "to bring into existence out of nothing."

The word most commonly used is *asah,* meaning "to make," which implies taking raw material and making something new out of it. But when the Bible tells about the creation of man a different word is used: the Hebrew verb *yatsar,* which means "to form or fashion." In English we read "God formed man out of the dust of the ground" (Gen. 2:7). The word *fashioned* could be used instead of *formed*. In fact, we could well say, "He built man out of the dust of the ground."

The Bible says of man, "For dust thou art; and unto dust shalt thou return" (Gen. 3:19). This "dust" is actually the various chemical elements that make up the physical body of man. The Bible goes on to say that God "breathed into his nostrils the breath of life" (Gen. 2:7). The word *breath* is the same as the word *wind* and the same as the word *spirit*. "The breath of life" could as correctly be called "the spirit of life" or "the wind of life."

The interesting thing is that in the Greek a similar word is used in speaking about the Holy Spirit. The Lord Jesus said, "The wind bloweth where it listeth, and thou hearest the sound thereof, but canst not tell whence it cometh or whither it goeth; so is everyone that is born of the Spirit" (John 3:8). In the Greek, the word *wind* and the word *spirit* are very closely related. The same is true of the word *breath*.

So what we have in the record is that God breathed into this material structure—called the body—the *breath* of life, the *spirit* of life. This could very well be the origin of the spirit of man given to him from God. We read ". . . and man became a living soul" (Gen. 2:7). Here the third word *soul* is used.

The order of the creation seems to be this: when the spirit comes from God into the body, which comes from the ground, man becomes a living soul. The word *soul* refers apparently to man's emotional consciousness, the word *spirit* to his intellectual consciousness, and the word *body* to his material being.

The devil tempted Jesus of Nazareth to make the stones into bread to feed His body. The Lord Jesus answered in this way, "Man shall not live by bread alone, but by every word that proceedeth out of the mouth of God" (Matt. 4:4). For many years I stumbled at this statement. I could understand the saying that man does not live by bread only, but I did not see how he could live by the Word of God.

My trouble was that I did not know of the spiritual aspect of man. It helped me a great deal when I found that the Greek could be understood to say "man shall *not* live by bread *only* but also by every word that proceedeth out of the mouth of God." I now take a little liberty with that and I say to myself as I read, "man shall not live by bread only—though he does live by bread surely in the body—but also by every word that proceedeth out of the mouth of God spiritually." This is a way of saying man is both body and soul: as the body of the man feeds in the flesh on the things of this world, so the soul of man feeds on the Word of God.

The body and soul are both in man, but they are not of equal importance. The Lord Jesus is the one who said, "For what is a man profited, if he shall gain the whole world and lose his own soul? or what shall a man give in exchange for his soul?" (Matt. 16:26). What physical thing on earth is worth as much as the soul, which is spiritual? Keep in mind that in our culture the body is very well taken care of, and the soul is commonly neglected. One thing we must be very careful about is that we not go by popular opinion about the body and soul. The public will take care of the body but will neglect the soul. People usually take care of the bodies of their children very carefully, and neglect their souls and never worry a bit about it. That is *not* true about God. He thinks the soul is more important than the body.

MAN NEEDS COMMUNION WITH OTHERS

The Bible tells us one thing about man that is easy to believe. "It is not good that man should be alone" (Gen. 2:18). Of course, most everybody will smile at first and say that is the reason all men get married. But there is a lot more than marriage involved in this idea about man.

When the Bible says that "it is not good for man to be alone," it is saying in a very simple fashion exactly what the social scientists say when they tell us that man is a social being. Man develops normally to his greatest capacity in association with other people, and that is just the way the Bible puts it. Not only is it true that it is not good for man to be alone in any way, but it is also true that he needs to have communion and fellowship with someone who is his equal.

The story in Genesis tells us that when God saw man as He had created him and realized it was not good for man to be alone, He called all the creatures and the animals before man—that man should name them. Have you ever realized how much intellectual ability man would need to be able to name the animals? Have you ever tried to name something you have never seen before? It is not easy. Usually we name a thing we have not seen before by saying, "Give me that thing-a-ma-jig," or "that dingus you've got over there," or "whatever it is." It is an exceedingly difficult thing to give a name to anything.

In our modern time, we give names to things in scientific or functional fashion according to what a thing does—telephone, telegraph, automobile, etc. When Adam faced these creatures, he named them. This means he evaluated them; he estimated them. The Scriptures then say, "But for Adam there was not found an help meet for him" (Gen. 2:20). In his estimating the animals, he did not find one that was *meet,* meaning no one that would meet him on a level that was equal to him. The companion of man needed to be equal to man to provide the fellowship and communion man needs. This is very important in trying to understand the nature of man.

"And the Lord God caused a deep sleep to fall upon Adam, and he slept: and he took one of his ribs, and closed up the flesh instead thereof; and the rib, which the Lord God had taken from man, made he a woman, and brought her unto the man" (Gen. 2:21-22). This is language and description which baffles us, but it is not any more bewildering than the idea that He took the dust from the ground and formed man. Both descriptions go beyond anything we understand. It is quite interesting to note that when God made woman, He did not take her from man's head as if she were to rule over him. He did not take her from his feet as if he were to step on her. She was taken from his side in order that she might be his equal.

At the time Genesis was written other nations around Israel held a very low estimate of woman. Even to this day many pagan cultures treat women as if they were something less than human. Certainly woman was not considered the equal of man. The Bible, however, emphasizes that when woman was created she was equal to man.

As a matter of fact, man would not be at his best if he did not have fellowship with an equal. If a man at any time treats other people as less than himself, he is hurting himself and ruining his own experience. Just as surely as he despises other people as less than himself, he has reduced himself with those people. He can no longer be what he could have been. We need to be with people who are our equals if we are going to be what we could be.

Let us consider the matter of isolation. Have you ever seen people who live a lot to themselves for any reason? If you have seen such people, I want to ask you, don't they get to be queer? Think back on any member in our larger families—an uncle, aunt, or cousin—who for one reason or another lives off by himself or herself. Doesn't that person get to be odd? They all do. It is

natural. Any of us would be queer if we were left to ourselves.
What many a man does not know is that the one thing that is keeping him from being queer is that good wife, who forever keeps harping at him about his peculiarities, and rubbing off those queer spots. As far as women are concerned, if they are left to themselves, they can become peculiar, too. Being alone is not good. Mind you, we all need fellowship with other persons.

If people are left to themselves—and as a consequence, they do not have contact with other people's minds—things happen to them in various ways. They don't talk with people; and if they do talk, they don't listen. They live to themselves. They don't read; they don't listen to the radio; they have no contact whatsoever with other people's minds. They begin to have hallucinations and illusions. Some of these poor unfortunate people get beset with delusions until life is a misery for them. They do not have contact with other people who could knock those crazy ideas out of their minds by laughing at them or by showing how ridiculous they are. Without the benefits of fellowship with others, a human being is not normal.

If you are asked to go into the house or the room of one of these lonely people, you will often discover a certain untidiness. The argument may be raised that once in a while you will come across a woman or man who lives alone, where everything is neat and clean. But you will come to find out they do not live alone. In their minds, they have their relatives, they have their friends, and they are fixing things up for their people. Although their friends may live 500 miles away, they are keeping them in mind. Consider a person, however, who lets his mind get completely loose from other people. There will be a lost sense of values, no pride in one's appearance, and a loss of ambition. This is what we mean when we say such a person will not be normal.

Many a boy in high school who worries his teachers to death because he has neither interest nor ambition is a lonely boy. That boy is not having any personal dealings with anybody. Somehow his family is not having any association with him. He is in the same house, he eats the same food, and he sleeps in the same rooms; but somewhere, the contact with his family has been broken. It is evident that this boy has become shiftless and strange, for it is not good for a person to be alone as this boy is.

Anything which promotes good will among people from two up to two million is good. Anything that promotes or injects alienation and causes enmity and hostility is evil. No worse thing can be done to a person than to take away his friends. This can be done by gossip—the most devilish thing on earth. Through gossip, a person's status with his friends may be ruined. Shakespeare put it, "He who filches from me my good name hath robbed me of something that does not make him rich but leaves me poor indeed." Oh, yes, tremendously poor. Loneliness is man's worst fate. Nothing in the world will be so corrosive to human personality as loneliness.

It is a wonderful thing that the Gospel is a Gospel of *reconciliation*. The Lord Jesus came to people who were like sheep without a shepherd (Mark 6:34) and gave Himself to win them back to God, to bring them back into the family of God. He did this to reestablish them in communion that they might be normal. And so it works in the Gospel. The person who accepts Christ as Saviour and Lord becomes a member of the church in communion with Christ, and will never be alone again.

MAN MUST RULE

The Bible says it is in God's plan for men to rule over things (Gen. 1:28). Having dominion over something is to have the right to put it here or there or to dispose of it. To rule over anything is to have the right to say what it will do and where it will go. This may seem very simple to us, but it shows something about man that is quite important.

To be able to rule, man must have the power of choice. Man can see different things to do and different ways of acting. He must be free in himself to take it or to leave it as he wishes. He must be free to decide whether to turn to the right or to the left. Unless a person is free to make choices, he will not feel he is living normally. He will experience a sense of frustration. Only as a person is able to make decisions and act upon them can he fulfill his role as a man. It is only in this way he can be at his best. This is the nature of man.

Many human beings do things largely because circumstances force them. As long as a person is doing what he does because he has to do it, he is not really living in the way originally intended for him to live. It is when he controls things that he is like a man.

If he does not control—if he is being pushed from place to place, pulled by this or that, and crowded into doing things—he can never be satisfied. If man lets the things around him control and boss him, he is in for a miserable time. It is only when he manages them that he can have a feeling of fulfillment.

Everyone can apply this to his or her particular situation. The lady of the house may have only a kitchen in view. A man may have only an office in view. He must, however, "subdue the earth and have dominion over it" if he is going to be happy. If he cannot in some way manage it, if he cannot in some way have it in hand so that he can dispose of it, he will not in himself feel that he has accomplished what he can. And he will not be all that he could be.

What has been said about subduing the earth is also true about man himself. It is a very proper thing for us to recall that in our bodies we have a certain amount of the earth. I generally consider myself with over 200 pounds of it; and I go around with this day by day. For me to be at my normal best, I must take charge and control my body.

The wise man in the Book of Proverbs says, "He that is slow to anger is better than the mighty; and he that ruleth his spirit than he that taketh the city" (Prov. 16:32). Paul battled to have this control over himself. He said, "But I keep under my body, and bring it into subjection; lest that by any means, when I have preached to others, I myself should be a castaway" (1 Cor. 9:27). This is of great importance with reference to the living of life as a whole. We must be able to control and have mastery over the things that are of this earth.

In this connection, we can understand why slavery and bondage are so distressing. There are some people not really able to do what they want to do, because they are in bondage to their own desires. Some people have certain emotions that carry them away. Others may have fanciful ideas; or still others may have habits. In any case, where there is a person who is not in himself free to choose right or wrong due to some kind of compulsion or pressure, there we find a man in distress.

Man is happiest when he is in a position to respond to God's command and rule over the earth. Part of man's trouble comes when he tries to rule over his fellow man. Nothing in the Bible tells him that he should do that, and yet this tendency is in man all the time. He is trying to rule somebody else. This is related to the natural drive that he must be boss of something. If any human being is ever to amount to anything, he must have something to be boss over.

The trouble comes when he tries to manage the folks who are in his house or the people he works with. His disposition to want to manage is not unusual; it is a matter of properly directing his efforts. If he would remember to subdue the earth—to go out and work in the yard—he would be a lot better off than trying to manipulate the lives of others.

Man's ability to rule over the earth and his control of it is commonly called *science*. With man contriving so many technical ways of controlling the earth, it is hoped he won't develop something that, like Frankenstein's monster, will ultimately destroy him. As long as he can control it, it is all right for him to have it. Any human being who wants to live with some degree of happiness and satisfaction would like to do things, to accomplish things, to achieve things. The doing, accomplishing, and achieving of things is *exercising dominion over*.

Children are not very old before they like to manage things. Maybe what they are managing is just throwing their rattle on the floor, but they want to manage it for themselves. They have an urge from within to subdue something and to have control over it—run it, manage it. This is the thrust and drive in man that moves him on to achieve the things that he does in life as a whole.

One of the basic flaws in the communist ideology is the attempt to deny this inborn desire on the part of man. To fulfill his role as a man, a person must be free in order to obey the Lord's command to "Be fruitful and multiply and replenish the earth and subdue it." If a situation is created in which everything is controlled from the outside so that the outcome is sure and fixed—and there is nothing a person can do that would change any part of it—people lose interest. The sparkle will leave their eyes and the spring will leave their steps. Because they have been deprived of their freedom of choice, their will loses its sensitivity. This is what has happened in many a dictator state. In order to achieve any degree of happiness, man must be free to choose.

It is because man has the power of choice that the Gospel is presented to him, and he is invited to receive the Lord Jesus Christ as his Saviour. When God offers His Son to man, the understanding is that man has the capacity to receive Him. Of course the natural man's will has been rendered insensitive to the Gospel appeal due to sin. God in His sovereign mercy revives the will so that man is enabled to receive for himself the gift of salvation.

MAN IS RESPONSIBLE

Because man has the power of choice, he is held responsible for what he does. When man first sinned, God called to him, "Where art thou?" (Gen. 3:9). When Eve stood before God, He asked her, "What is this that thou hast done?" (Gen. 3:13).

These questions were not for God's information. God knew what Adam and Eve had done, but they needed to answer for what they had done. They needed to acknowledge for themselves that they had been disobedient to God's command. God was saying in effect, "You pass judgment upon yourself. You admit and answer for the misdeed you have committed."

When Cain killed Abel, the Bible tells us that God confronted Cain. His question was, "Where is Abel thy brother?" (Gen. 4:9). It was evident that God knew where Abel was because He told Cain afterwards, "The voice of thy brother's blood crieth unto me from the ground" (Gen. 4:10). Cain is called upon to admit his deed and acknowledge his sin before God. God created man in His own image, gave him the power of choice, and holds him responsible to answer for his actions.

The word *responsible* has in it the word *response*. Man is obligated to make response to God for what he has done, because man is not the lord of creation. He is not even the lord of himself. God is Lord and man is His creature. God created the world in which man lives; and man lives under the eye, or the supervision, of the Lord.

Man is dependent upon God, the Creator, for all things. The body that he has is given to him; the world in which he lives is given to him. The air he breathes, the water he drinks, the life and strength that he has in himself—all are given to him. The circumstances under which he lives, the sun that shines, the rain that falls, the people that are in the world—all are gifts from God. Man could not make them; he could not secure them. The entire situation in which man lives is prepared for him.

Man, living in this total, over-all situation, is responsible to God for what he does with it. A great deal is put within the reach of man. Out of all the things that are around him, he can select those things that are good for himself. He can choose those things he needs. Man is not at liberty, however, to take *all* the things that are put around him and within his reach. God wants man to exercise control over himself. Man can exercise his free will and make certain decisions; and yet God has certain things in mind that He wants man to do. Man is not turned loose to do as he pleases. Rather he is to live in this world, realizing his responsibility to God, for God will call him to account for what he has done.

The Bible tells us that the tree of the knowledge of good and evil was put within reach. Man was told not to eat fruit from that tree. He was warned that in the day he did, he would die. Thus God confronts man with a choice of obedience or disobedience. He puts all things within the reach of man. And then He names one thing—points to it—and says, "Not that one." But he leaves it within reach. Man is challenged to exercise self-control in this matter because he is responsible to God. God would have us answer to Him for everything we do.

As a case in point, consider the Sabbath day. God said, "Remember the sabbath day, to keep it holy" (Ex. 20:8). Man was not to work on the Sabbath day. Because God gave man six days to do his work, he was to abstain from any labor on the seventh day. It was a command to be obeyed. Man was free to choose what he would do on the Sabbath day. But if he would enjoy the favor of God, he would do his work in six days and rest on the seventh. Man is free, and yet he is responsible. As Paul says, "Every one of us must give account of himself to God" (Rom. 14:12).

Man in his freedom makes his choices. He may decide to go to church or stay away from church. He may decide to read the Bible or not to read the Bible. He may decide to pray to God or not to pray to God. He may decide to trust in God or not to trust in God. Man will exercise his power of choice as he sees fit, and will do the thing that he chooses to do. Man is never to lose sight of the fact that God continues to ask the same question He asked our first parents, "What is this that thou hast done?"

God is the Judge of all the earth, and He is the Judge of all mankind. He is the One that judges the conduct of man and fixes the penalties. More than that, He is the One who is going to have man be conscious of what he has done. He wants man to become aware of what he is doing; therefore, He puts upon man the responsibility of answering for what he does. Man in freedom makes his choice; then God in justice appraises his action. God calls on man to estimate and judge his deeds. If he has been disobedient to the will of God, it is important that he acknowledge his sin and repent of it.

Throughout the Bible this truth is repeated over and over again; and we find it applies to ourselves. We are not able to escape responsibility for the action that we take, because we have exercised a certain choice. We did what we did because we wanted to do it. God is going to ask, "What is this that thou hast done?" and man must pass judgment on himself in order to answer.

Through *confession,* God brings us to feel our responsibility before Him. God's calling upon man to account for what he has done will bring to man's heart and mind the consciousness of his wrongdoing, because man will then feel it before God. At this spot, there is a tendency on the part of man to lie about what he has done.

We sympathize with little children who are two or three years of age—old enough to give an answer for what they have done—when parents ask them point-blank, "Did you do this? Did you do that?" The little youngsters are tempted to try to get out of it. Their quick imaginative minds are prone to get the best of them, if they feel they have a chance of getting "off the hook." Suppose a little girl comes into a room and her father asks, "Did your mother say you could have that?" The child has a terrific temptation to say, "Yes." If she does, her father will probably let her have it. If, however, this is an outright lie, she is leaving herself open for the consequences when and if the truth becomes known.

Parents might as well make up their minds to it—babies are all going to have to experiment some with lying. They are going to have to try to find out if it is as good as it seems. In many instances it will look like the easy way out. A boy in a Sunday school class was asked what a lie was. After thinking for some time he said, "A lie is an abomination unto the Lord, but a very present refuge in time of storm." We can all appreciate this story because we have all been tempted to head for this port at one time or another.

God is going to ask, "What is this that thou hast done?" Basically man is to be obedient to God. He is so constituted that he is to respond to the natural world around him. He learns to admit the hard facts of life. He does not try to butt his head into a stone wall or try to walk through fire. He admits things the way they are.

Man is to be realistic in his responsibilities to God. He is to obey God's will and carry out His purposes. Only as he does this is he able to fill his role as one created in the image of God.

MAN CAN BE LOST

When is a man lost, and when is a man saved? The Bible says, "For the Son of man is come to seek and to save that which was lost" (Luke 19:10). A great many people have thought that when a man is referred to as being lost, he is somehow wiped out. For them, *lost* means that there is no hope for man, that he will forever remain lost.

What the Bible means can better be seen in an illustration. A mother and her little boy go downtown shopping. The child gets separated from his mother. Has anything happened to the child? Are his bodily organs not functioning? Can he see? Can he hear? Can he walk? Can he think? Yes, but not too well. He is probably scared to death for he is *lost*. But, the *lost* child can be found. His trouble can be overcome in a very simple way—merely get the child back to his mother; restore him to where he was.

So we say a person is lost when he does not know where he is. He is some place, but he does not know where. Can you think back to the last time you were lost? Were you ever lost? Were you ever in a place without any notion of where you were? Perhaps there were trees and there was sky and sun, but you did not recognize any landmark to which you could refer. If you have never had such an experience, you will hardly know what I am talking about. If you have, you will remember quite readily the empty feeling you had in your stomach.

I remember the first time I was lost. I was a boy of about 10 or 11—big enough to do a piece of work by myself on the farm. I had been sent to bring a certain cow home. I had to bring her about three miles. I knew the country well and I knew my directions—north, south, east, and west. I could even tell directions from the sun. However, I went for the cow through a wooded area. I came up to the farmer's house, where I was to get her, from one direction and then started home another way.

Man

When I had walked with the cow about half a mile, I was suddenly lost. I didn't have any idea in the world where I was. I looked ahead on the road and to the hills that were in a certain area. Somehow those hills didn't look right. I was in a bit different position from what I had been several miles over; and nothing looked exactly the same. How puzzled I was over the fact that only three miles from home—in broad daylight—I could be lost. I was out of touch with things.

When the Bible speaks of man's being lost, he is lost not geographically but *spiritually*. Spiritually, in his consciousness, he is out of touch with any point of reference that he can recognize. A good way to determine whether a person is lost is to ask him, "Where are you?" He replies, "I don't know." "Where are you going?" "I don't know." He is lost.

Spiritually speaking, you can discover whether or not a person is lost if you ask him this question: "What is your relationship with God?" The answer may be, "I don't know, except that I believe God made me." "What about your relationship with Him now?" "Well, I don't know." "Where are you going? Are you going to heaven?" Under certain circumstances he will say, "Well, I hope so. I wish I could; if there is a heaven and any way to get there, I'd like to." If you were to get in close touch with that person, you would find that he is spiritually lost. He has no consciousness of his relation to God. He is a lost soul.

Some people think that the word *lost* ought to mean more than that. They believe that a person who is lost should feel bad. When I was lost with the cow, I felt bad. I almost walked back to the farm where I had been to make sure I would get home. I couldn't believe the sun and the shadows that I saw, because everything seemed so strange. When a person feels lost in a city, in a building, or in a crowd—and among complete strangers—there is a feeling of fear. Part of this fright is experienced in loneliness. Nobody likes it. A person does not want to be alone; and he wants to know where he is. Not to know is confusing. It is discouraging. It is disheartening. It is demoralizing.

The condition of being spiritually lost is very common. Yet for many people it is so hard to understand, they do not seem to be able to get hold of the idea. It is enough for a person just to admit, "I do not know my relationship with God. I do not know what is going to happen to me. I do not know where I am going." Many, many people who are lost do foolish things in their own personal lives. They allow their values to go by the board and their characters to break up for no other reason than that they do not know *where they are, where they are going,* or *who they are.* It is, psychologically, an unbearable and intolerable condition.

A person lost in the woods may surmise that three miles north from where he is there is a village, and that two miles south is another little town. If he starts walking out of the woods toward one of these places, there is a strong possibility he will walk in a circle and wind up right back where he started. This has happened more than once.

Since so very few people walk in uncharted woods any more, a more appropriate illustration would be that of a night-flying pilot. A person flying a plane in the dark cannot see the ground; therefore, he has no frame of reference. For this reason, pilots are drilled to fly by their instruments. If a pilot refuses to go by his instruments, there is every likelihood that he will become lost. It happened in wartime during night-bombing missions. Some of our early casualties in the war in Europe were due to the fact that men flying on night missions would not believe their instruments.

Their instruments may have told them they were flying in a certain direction or at a certain altitude, but they had a feeling their compass or altimeter was in error. They flew according to the way they felt and either became lost or had a mid-air collision. It was made a matter of major discipline that a man must fly his aircraft according to the instruments. Why? Human nature could *not* be trusted.

In other words, if a man goes out to do what he thinks is right, he will not go straight. It is not human nature. He may start moving in what he feels is the right direction, but it will be only a matter of time before he comes to a state of *lostness*. After expending a great deal of energy, he may find himself right back where he started. The only way a person can go straight is to have his eye on a point of reference outside himself.

This is what the Gospel does by pointing men to the Lord Jesus Christ. "Behold, the Lamb of God which taketh away the sin of the world" (John 1:29). One of the things that the Bible has done is to reveal God as the Invariable Checkpoint. "I have set the Lord

Man

always before me: because he is at my right hand, I shall not be moved" (Ps. 16:8). This is a sound psychological statement as well as a scriptural one.

Man left to his own devices inevitably becomes lost. It is a comfort to know that God does not wish any man to remain in this lost state. Luke 15 presents a beautiful picture of a sheep, a coin, and a son that were lost and then found. This demonstrates in a vivid and dramatic way God seeking the lost. Here we read, "There is joy in the presence of the angels of God over one sinner that repenteth."

MAN HAS A CONSCIENCE

In addition to being responsible, man has a way of feeling his responsibility. He has a conscience. The Bible says men have "the law written in their hearts, their conscience also bearing witness" (Rom. 2:15).

Man not only answers to God; he also answers to his fellow men. Many of the things man does, he does because of other people. He wants other people to think well of him. Therefore, he acts in a way which he thinks will meet with their approval. As long as it doesn't cost him too much, man is likely to act to please others. When it costs him something, then there may be a different story. Nevertheless, man feels responsible to a certain extent to his fellow men.

Man is also answerable to himself. He judges his own actions and deeds. This is conscience at work and shows man's moral responsibility. It reveals that man feels responsible for his actions— whether good or bad.

Have you ever stopped to think how early conscience develops in a child? How soon does a baby become conscious of whether or not it is doing the right thing? Most children will act in certain ways to gain the approval of grown folks. Sometimes children act in ways that will annoy their elders. They find out what will irritate, and they do just that to get a perverse pleasure out of seeing someone upset. Children and adults alike have the capacity within themselves to sense that certain things are right and other things are wrong.

If a person does not know his right hand from his left, we say he is mentally retarded. So if someone has no sense of the rightness or the wrongness of his action, we say he is morally retarded. The normal human being has a sense of the fitness of what he is doing. He knows whether his acts are good or not good in the eyes of other people.

Some people are quick to claim credit for what is good. They want to be seen when they do something good. They want to be noticed when they do right. Thus they prove their ability to judge themselves. The average person has a feeling of well-being when he engages in something that gains the approval of his fellow men.

When a man does something wrong and society frowns upon it, he is inclined to deny that he did it. This can be seen when a child drops something. The child's first reaction is to cover it up, moving as far away from the scene of the act as possible. A child acts in this way because he feels the wrongness of what he has done. He is uncomfortable and wants to get away from it as quickly as he can. This is true as long as he lives. Conscience is an inward gauge that measures our conduct. It is a device that is in us to keep us on the level.

A person's conscience is like an inward balance wheel. He feels within himself whether he is doing right or wrong. The form of a man's conscience is taken from the community in which he grew up and from the people he has known. Each class of people has a different conscience and will feel differently about various things. The customs and the habits of the community have their effect on the feelings of anybody.

Conscience can be informed and changed. A better conscience can be had as the days go by. And when one becomes a Christian, a Christian conscience is developed. This is the best. A Christian, however, is not limited to his conscience for his sense of right and wrong. He has direct guidance from God through the Scriptures. God gives the Holy Spirit to the Christian to guide him in God's Word. The indwelling presence of the Holy Spirit is an invaluable guide to the happy Christian life.

It has already been said that as soon as children are old enough to feel disapproval, they start acting in certain ways because they want to be liked. However, they do certain other things because they want to irritate their parents. The feeling of conscience is operating in them. The desire for approval is a great incentive, and it can be used. If man once is happy in the feeling that what he has done is pleasing to people and he enjoys their pleasure, he will do more and more to please them. The Apostle Paul, in speaking of his own Christian experience, says that he was ambitious to be well-pleasing in the sight of God. The Lord Jesus said, "I do always those things that please him (the Father)" (John 8:29).

It is characteristic of all people that they are aware of what they are doing. They may not have complete understanding of their actions, but they know whether their behavior is agreeable or disagreeable to the *powers that be*. This is part of a man's guidance system. Approval is a great incentive in doing the right thing; and disapproval is a real deterrent in keeping man from doing the wrong thing. Many a time we would like to do certain things; but we hold back, for we know that someone would not like it. On other occasions, we don't want to do a certain thing; but we do it, because someone would like it and approve it.

The Christian is aware that he is responsible for his thoughts, words, actions, and deeds before God. If he has the feeling of assurance in himself that he has done that which is well-pleasing in God's sight, he can have a free mind. However, if he has a feeling within that he has not done what he should have done, then the feeling of distress will overcome him. Christian people with an understanding of the Gospel will know that what God primarily wants them to do is to turn to Him. A person who from the bottom of his heart knows that he has put his trust in the Lord will have the assurance that he is doing what God wants him to do.

The non-Christian is not nearly so sensitive to the will of God because his experience is not God-related. He takes notice of things he should not have and should not take; but he wants them for himself, and he winds up taking them. Although he can act against his conscience so often that it does not disturb him much after a while, he is still not completely free to act as he pleases. God in His *common grace* continues to work in the life of the non-Christian. This conscience, or law written on his heart, will continue to disturb or guide. In the providence of the Lord, it can prove to be a real factor in the eventual conversion of a sinner.

The conscience will never be a sufficient guide so far as conduct is concerned, because the conscience of man is always limited to his past experience and environment. But it can produce a wholesome dissatisfaction in the heart of man and give him a sense of right and wrong. As surely as a man feels he has not turned to God as he should, then he will know that this is the time to come to God. He will know he is on the wrong road. If a man departs from the will of God and gets into wrong things, his conscience will make him aware of it. Man can be thankful that God has given him a conscience.

MAN SUFFERS IN DISTRESS

We sympathize with anyone who is suffering. The problem of suffering is as old as the human race. It is a well-known fact that man can suffer physically. But to say he can suffer *in distress* implies a deeper kind of suffering. His heart can be heavy and burdened. He can be heartbroken. When he considers his actual condition, looks ahead to consider how things are going to be, or looks back and considers how things have been—a man can hurt; he can have pain. Trouble is distressing. It is not only that trouble is puzzling and disturbing, but it can hurt a man inside.

Man suffers in *failure*. He suffers when he is not able to adjust himself to his environment. Man is in the world. He is to subdue the earth and have dominion over it, and he suffers when he does not get this done. If at any time the earth seems to rise up and slap him down, man gets hurt. If he is able to manage his ordinary living, he can experience a sense of well-being; but if not, he feels bad.

If a person is not able to obtain enough food, he is hungry. If he is not able to secure enough water, he is thirsty. Physical suffering is involved in both hunger and thirst. If a person is not able to achieve what he set out to do—or if what he does results in loss—so far as this world is concerned, he will suffer. The human being is a sensitive creature. In general, a man suffers from the frustration of defeat.

The person who can *suffer* is the person who can rejoice. The person who can be sad is the person who can be glad. Man has feelings—emotions—and they give value and significance to the things that happen in his life. The things that man feels good about and enjoys, he wants to have as much as possible. But the things that he feels bad about and that hurt him, he wants to avoid in every way possible. Toward anything that can hurt, man experiences fear, depression, and frustration.

The newborn baby suffers only because it is hungry or because it has physical discomfort. Very early—long before it can talk—it becomes conscious of human companionship and begins to suffer from *separation*. How terrible it is for a baby to be truly separated from the person it has learned to love and trust. Many fathers go through the experience that at a certain stage in a child's life, the child doesn't like to see Daddy go away. It hurts the child. Usually, if Mother is there, it is still all right. But if both Mother and Daddy walk out, it can be a most distressing experience for the child. It can't seem to bear the feeling of being *separated* from those whom it loves.

Man also suffers in *bondage*. If he is not able to do what he wants to do, he is distressed. People who have habits that bind them are suffering in distress. We meet people every day who are experiencing sorrow, regret, hurt, and pain. We may ask such persons about their health and get this response: "I feel fine." We may ask them if they have financial need, only to hear, "All my debts are paid." It is then that we realize that we are seeing evidence "Man shall not live by bread alone" (Matt. 4:4). The need of such persons is not physical or material, it is *spiritual*. A man can be in the bondage of sinful habit to such a degree that he becomes greatly distressed.

Physical pain is relatively small when weighed among the various experiences of distress. People can have hurt and sickness, aches and pains in their body, but those are not the longest nor the deepest kinds of suffering. Consider the suffering that is in *loneliness*. Reflect on the suffering that comes to one who is lost. He wishes he knew where to go, but because he does not know which way to turn, he is filled with a sense of frustration and fear. When man has dropped out of touch with God so that he is not receiving His guidance, he is alone in the world.

When man does not know where he is going—nor what is going to happen to him—he is filled with fear. He has a sense of frustration. He is lonely. All these are troubles. We read in the Bible, "Yet man is born unto trouble, as the sparks fly upward" (Job 5:7). Due to trouble, man suffers. And it is the suffering of mankind that makes the Gospel so important and so appealing. "For the Son of man is come to seek and to save that which was lost" (Luke 19:10). Christ came to the suffering that He might ease and take away their suffering. God is spoken of as "The God of all comfort; who comforteth us in all our tribulation" (2 Cor. 1:3-4).

Often our suffering is relieved—in some degree—if someone shares it with us. One of the good things about having a friend is that when you tell your joys to him, you double them. If you tell your troubles to a friend, you cut those troubles in half. God wants to be a great Friend to mankind, "a friend that sticketh closer than a brother" (Prov. 18:24).

It is the suffering of man that attracts the compassion and mercy of God. Matthew 9:36 explains, "But when he saw the multitudes, he was moved with compassion on them, because they fainted, and were scattered abroad, as sheep having no shepherd." For a sheep, it is a suffering experience to be separated from the shepherd. Christ could use no better illustration to describe the frightening feeling of aloneness in man.

Christ, speaking to His disciples, said, "The harvest truly is plenteous, but the labourers are few; Pray ye therefore the Lord of the harvest, that he will send forth labourers into his harvest" (Matt. 9:37-38). Christ sent His disciples among human beings to tell them that God is willing to share their sorrows and their griefs. They can come to Him with their burdens, and He will give them rest. Christ probably spoke no word that has a greater appeal to men than, "Come unto me, all ye that labour and are heavy laden, and I will give you rest" (Matt. 11:28).

Being *weary* from labor and *heavy laden* is a form of suffering. The weariness which comes from the exhaustion of hard work and being weighed down with a burden is enough to give man an oppressing sense of distress. "Take my yoke upon you, and learn of me; for I am meek and lowly in heart; and ye shall find rest unto your souls. For my yoke is easy, and my burden is light" (Matt. 11:29, 30).

The great promise of the Gospel to the whole world is that it meets man in his suffering. Suffering is a result of sin. The Bible makes it emphatic that the soul that sins, shall die. "The wages of sin is death" (Rom. 6:23). The fact that man experiences suffering suggests his need for help. He needs help from God. God matches the distress of mankind with His own grace and mercy coming to man in his suffering.

"But the gift of God is eternal life through Jesus Christ our Lord" (Rom. 6:23). We can encourage people in suffering and distress to "learn of him," that they may know that the Lord has them in mind, and He is looking upon them with thoughts of pleasantness and peace. God would like to help us; He can help us if we will come to Him. In the providence of God, suffering can be used to help us realize the wrongness of what we are doing.

Man suffers in distress, but God can truly comfort him.

CHAPTER THREE

Sin

THE trouble with man is *sin*. All his suffering and misery is due to *sin*. Pain, loss, heartache, frustration are basically caused by *sin*. This is something man does, but he never needs to learn it. It is as natural for a man to sin as it is to breathe. The Bible tells us God did not create man with sin, but when the first man Adam sinned, all his descendants were involved so that sin appears in them. "There is no man that sinneth not." "All have sinned and come short of the glory of God."

The wonderful truth in the Gospel is that man can be saved from *sin*. Jesus Christ is the Saviour who redeems, delivers, cleanses a man from all *sin*. God is holy and cannot tolerate *sin,* but Christ Jesus is able to reconcile the sinner to God by His own grace. "As in Adam all die, so in Christ shall all be made alive." "Where sin abounded, grace did much more abound."

THE LAW OF GOD

"The law of God" is an expression used many times and in various ways in Scripture. The word *law* usually means something that has been made a rule. So we speak of the *laws* of the land. Such are certain rules put down by the government to show right and wrong. Another use of the word would be to say that the *law* of anything is the nature of it. The *law* of falling bodies would be the rate of speed at which they fall. The *law* of steam would be the way in which it exerts pressure. Thus the *law* of anything would be its characteristic way of acting.

And so we may speak of things happening according to *the law of God*. *The law of God,* in this instance, would be God's way of doing things. It would refer to something that is in His nature. Anything concerning us that would be agreeable to the nature of God would be the "law of God" for us.

Sin

From one point of view the "law of God" is set forth in the Ten Commandments. These are properly called "the Ten Words of Moses" and were given to instruct the people of God as to what is right and wrong. They show something of what God expects man to do and not to do.

What they mean can be seen by looking at traffic laws. For example, if the law of a community says the speed limit is thirty-five miles an hour, this means that there are so many people living in that small area, and the situation is so congested, that thirty-five miles an hour is the safe speed at which to travel. After the establishment of the thirty-five-mile-an-hour zone, the sign is set up, and then the law is fixed. Driving faster than that means the law has been broken, but it also means such driving is unsafe in the area.

God's actions show holiness, goodness, and justice. The Ten Commandments are in line with His way of doing things. It is because God is honest that "thou shalt not steal." It is because God created man in His own image that "thou shalt not kill." It is because God gives children parents to watch over them and to guide them that "thou shalt honor thy father and thy mother." It is because God tells the truth and would have men tell the truth that He makes it a law that "thou shalt not bear false witness." So the Ten Commandments are like God. They show how God expects a man to act because God is the kind of Person that He is.

What the Ten Commandments show is reflected in man's own conscience. People who do not have the Ten Commandments in their literature may still feel in their own hearts the rightness and wrongness of their actions. The sixth commandment says "thou shalt not kill," but killing was wrong for anybody all the time. The commandment simply says in so many words that killing is wrong. No man anywhere thinks killing is right. We can be angry with a man and feel like killing him, but our conscience will tell us it is wrong to kill a man just because we feel like doing it.

If any man has never heard the commandment "thou shalt not steal," but is old enough to know his right hand from his left, he knows that stealing is wrong. Pagan people who have never heard the Ten Commandments know that stealing is not right. This is seen in that they do it in the dark of night. Any time someone has to hide to do something, he shows that he knows it is wrong. The Ten Commandments say that man is not to steal; but if the Ten

Commandments had never said it, man would yet know it was wrong.

The Ten Commandments are like a fence on a mountain highway. Any man driving on a narrow mountain road can look over the side and see the deep canyon going straight down. He certainly does not want to slip down there. He wants to stay on the road. Beside the road are little white posts, sometimes with a chain running from one to another. That fence would not hold the motorist if his car ran into it. Seldom are such fences strong enough to keep a car from falling down the embankment. Actually that fence does not make it dangerous to go off the road. It was always dangerous to go off the road; and if those posts were not there at all, it would still be dangerous to go off that road. The fence simply shows where the danger is, and so it is a real help. Those posts cannot make the driver stay on the road, but they show him where it would be wrong to drive. In the same way the Ten Commandments do not make anything wrong. Whatever is wrong is wrong, but the Commandments say it in so many words that man can see it clearly. They are like a fence along the highway of life, and so are a real help in guiding conduct.

Sometimes we use the term *the law of God* when referring to the Bible. The New Testament uses the term *law* to refer to the writings of Moses. When speaking about *the law of God,* we usually mean something written. In this way we refer to the Ten Commandments that were written on tablets of stone. Whether *the law of God* is understood to be the Ten Commandments, the writings of Moses, the whole of Scripture, or the very nature of God, the main thing is this: there are some ways of living which God approves and other ways which He disapproves. God wants man to live in a way that would be pleasing in His sight. When a man does this, we may say he is living "according to the law of God." When any man acts in any way that is contrary to what is shown in the Bible to be the will of God, he will know that he has sinned. If any man acts in line with the nature of God, he is doing God's will, keeping God's law, and that is what makes a man well-pleasing to God. If we want to know what will please the Lord, we only need to find out what the law of God is. This is one of the real reasons for Bible study. The Almighty God is our Maker. He has His will for us and has revealed it in the Scriptures. He wants us to obey

Him. Any time we go against His will, breaking *the law of God,* we sin. Because we might blunder foolishly into breaking *the law of God* even when we don't want to, we read and study the Bible so we may know what He wants us to do.

> "Thy Word have I hid in my heart, that I might not sin against thee" (Ps. 119:11).

THE NATURE OF SIN

The word *sin* is a *God-word*. I mean if you do not have any idea of God you will not have any idea of *sin*. *Sin* is anything in a human being, in his attitude or in his actions, which is not like God.

The Shorter Catechism says "Sin is any want of conformity unto, or any transgression of, the law of God" (Question 14—The Westminster Shorter Catechism). "Any want of conformity unto" means that anything that falls short of or does not comply with the law of God is *sin*. "Any transgression of" means anything that goes contrary to the law of God is *sin*. Sin then is anything different from the nature of God. Inasmuch as God is a certain kind of Person, anybody not like that is sinful. Since God will always act in a certain way, anything not done that way is *sin*.

The word *sin* is used in at least three different ways. First, it is used about a man's actions. If we act in a way which is not agreeable to the will of God, a way that is not in line with the law of God, that *act* is *sin*. Second, it is used to refer to a man's *nature*. We say that man is born sinful. We do not mean so much that when he is born he is full of wrong actions, full of sins, as we mean that his nature is to do wrong. He is sinful in the sense that his nature is full of the disposition to go in his own way and not in God's way. Third, the word *sin* is used to refer to the *status or standing* of a man before God. How does any man stand in relation to God? Man is a sinner. He stands before a holy God guilty of having done wrong and cannot have any dealings with God as long as he remains in this state.

No matter how the word is used or defined, every time the word *sin* is used, we have *God* in mind; and we mean to say "This is not like God." Any action, any attitude, any condition, any state, any way of doing things not like God we call *sin*. When it is like God, we call it "godly." If an act is right and is in line with God's will, it is "righteous." Sometimes sin is crude and vulgar, and at other times it is refined and cultured. Sin may not always look bad to human beings, but it is never pleasing in the sight of God. In fact, we may say that anything that is not pleasing in the sight of God is not like God and therefore is *sin*.

Sin has an effect upon people. The Bible says that the soul that sinneth shall die. This means when any soul acts in a way that God would not approve, it shall die. This dying process has several effects upon a person. The soul that sins is *separated* from God. Sin makes a man a stranger to God. Think of friends who become separated. If they remain apart very long, the friendship begins to cool off. In order to keep friendship, friends must have dealings with each other. What is true of human friendships is also true with God. If I sin in the sight of God and my sin has not been forgiven, I have a feeling of being away from God. I am separated from Him; and if I stay that way, I begin to feel that I am a stranger to God. From separation I move on into *isolation*. I feel I am alone, and God has nothing to do with me at all. I can hear about God with my ears as people talk about Him; but deep down in my heart I do not think about Him. I do not have any feeling about Him. I think He is a long distance away. And then things get worse.

Sin has the effect of *deteriorating*. A man will become worse after he has sinned. When God is with a man, He has the same effect that sunlight has upon a plant. If a man is dwelling in fellowship with God, he is drawn closer to Him. When a man is separated, alienated, and isolated from God, he does not have this blessing. He has in effect cut himself off from the source of help and his condition becomes worse and worse.

Sin is used as a word in different ways. It can be used in connection with the breaking of a law. For example, the law of God says, "Thou shalt not steal," so when I steal, I sin. The law of God says, "Thou shalt not bear false witness," so when I lie, I sin. Any time I disobey the law of God, I am sinning. If I act in a way that God would not act, I am sinning. These are spoken of as the sins of *commission*.

The Bible also points out that there are sins of *omission*. In the New Testament, we read, "Therefore to him that knoweth to do good, and doeth it not, to him it is sin" (Jas. 4:17). That is, the failure to do good when I know what would be good, is sin. If I know what ought to be done, and I do not do it, then I am not like God. That is sin. If I fail to do something good because of ignorance, I am not as responsible as I would be if I had known what to do. This is the state of the man who does not know Christ Jesus. As the Lord said, "And that servant, which knew his Lord's will and prepared not, neither did according to his will, shall be beaten with many stripes. But he that knew not, and did commit things worthy of stripes, shall be beaten with few stripes" (Luke 12:47, 48). This does not altogether excuse the sins of ignorance. Sin is still sin whether we are informed or not.

The meaning of *sin* is made even more clear when we read, "... for whatsoever is not of faith is sin" (Rom. 14:23). Here we need to understand what is meant by *faith*. Faith is responding in obedience to the revealed will of God. God reveals His will, and when man responds to it and accepts it, this is believing God. Any action on his part which is *not* in response to the revealed will of God is *sin*. If a Christian person does not know the will of God, he can seek God's face in order to learn His will. If a Christian is facing a problem and proceeds without seeking God's will, then he is sinning. The Lord Jesus always looked to His Heavenly Father for guidance. The man who has faith in Christ as Saviour and Lord must always look to God for this same guidance. He must respond to the revealed will of God or else he is guilty of sin.

Several times I have made such statements as "it is not like God" and "it is not like the Lord Jesus Christ." Now we will naturally ask, how can a man know God? We would say with the Apostle Philip, "Lord, show us the Father, and it sufficeth us" (John 14:8). You will remember Jesus answered him saying, "Have I been so long time with you, and yet hast thou not known me, Philip? He that hath seen me hath seen the Father" (John 14:9). This means that so far as you and I are concerned, if we should question in any given situation what the will of God would be, we would only need to look to the life of Christ as recorded in the Bible. He was the true Son of God and lived without sin. In the Scriptures we can read how He lived, and we can be sure when we live that way we will be living in the will of God.

Suppose I am face to face with a situation and I do not know for sure what is right or wrong, but I go ahead and act. This is not as the Lord Jesus would do. When He was faced with a problem, He prayed. In Gethsemane, Christ prayed, "O my Father, if it be possible, let this cup pass from me: nevertheless not as I will, but as thou wilt" (Matt. 26:39). I would say that any action on our part in which we do not follow the example of the Lord Jesus Christ is out of conformity with the will of God and therefore is *sin*.

THE COURSE OF SIN

After seeing that sin is any action on our part which is not according to God's will, we can understand now how sin happens. We can ask, how does sin actually take place? And we can get the answer by looking at Genesis 3 to see what happened in the Garden of Eden.

Sin always happens while people are living their lives in this world. This is how it happened with Adam and Eve. The first thing that happened was *temptation*. Temptation in itself is not sin. It happens when we are in a situation that makes us want to act in some way to please ourselves. It leads us to sin if the way we act is not God's way.

The New Testament says, "For all that is in the world, the *lust of the flesh,* and the *lust of the eyes,* and the *pride of life,* is not of the Father, but is of the world" (1 John 2:16). Those three expressions show the three ways temptation comes to a human being. The first way is the *lust of the flesh.* The common word for this is *appetite.* Lust means strong desire. The flesh means everything that man has in him naturally, centered in his physical body. The lust of the flesh as it arouses a man's appetite becomes a craving or a longing. This appetite can lead a man to doing wrong when he lusts after or has an intense craving for that which is not lawful for him to have. In this way his appetite becomes a way of temptation to a man.

The second way in which temptation comes is the *lust of the eyes.* This strong desire involves *imagination.* As a man's eyes begin to wander there are certain things that attract his attention. Some of these things are carnal and fleshly, and yet they look good through the eyes of the man. He begins to imagine what he would like to have or what he would like to do and forgets it might be displeasing to God.

The third way is the *pride of life*. This can be called *vanity*. Vanity gives a man a high opinion of himself. When a man is vain, he gets to be puffed up with a sense of his own importance. He feels almost as if the whole world exists just for him and for his selfish interests.

We are always in a situation that presents temptation to us when we are influenced by our appetite, what we would like; or by our imagination, what looks good; or by our vanity, what would make us feel big. These three lines of appeal are allowed to come to us one way or another to test us or tempt us to act in ways that are displeasing to God. However, this is not yet sin. The Bible tells us that the Lord Jesus, when He was here upon earth, "Was in all points tempted like as we are, yet without sin." Although Jesus was tempted, He never sinned. Being tempted is not sin: sin follows temptation.

Adam and Eve committed *sin* when they took of the fruit, when they *acted* in disobedience to the revealed will of God. God had said to them, "For in the day that thou eatest thereof thou shalt surely die" (Gen. 2:17). He commanded, "Don't eat," and gave them a reason, "because thou shalt surely die." However, they did eat, and they did begin to die. Their sin was not in the temptation but in this act of disobedience. Temptation does not become sin to us until we act on it. Such action does not need to be outward action. Man can act in his heart. He can be attracted to the sinful; he can turn to it. As a man follows his appetite, imagination, and vanity within his heart, his inward attitude can be *sin*. Jesus calls attention to this form of sin in the Sermon on the Mount. Take the matter of adultery. Jesus said, "Whosoever looketh on a woman to lust after her hath committed adultery with her already in his heart" (Matt. 5:28).

In thinking about what happens when we sin, we must also consider that a feeling that he will be judged can grip the heart of a person who has sinned. Just as Adam was called upon to answer for what he had done, so must we all answer when we have sinned. Adam and Eve, after they had sinned, saw that they were naked, and they sewed fig leaves together to make themselves aprons. After they covered their nakedness, they hid themselves. Why? They were afraid. What were they afraid of? They were afraid of what God would do to them because of their disobedience. The fig leaves they sewed together were not good enough to cover them. They were ashamed of themselves and felt guilty; therefore, they tried to hide in the Garden of Eden from God. When Adam and Eve had hidden themselves, God called, "Adam, where art thou?" He made Adam come out into the open to Him. When Adam was asked why he hid himself, he admitted he was now afraid of God. *Guilt* is a feeling that comes over us after we have done wrong. A man flees from God because he is afraid that God is going to deal in judgment with him. The word *judgment,* with reference to sin, is simply God saying we have done wrong and that He will punish us for the wrong we have done.

When God asked Adam, "What is this that thou hast done?" God called him to account. God spoke to Adam and Eve and told them that because they had sinned certain results would follow. Sometimes the judgment of God leads on to an immediate penalty; but this is not always so. God can judge a deed to be sinful, and then under certain conditions He may see fit to delay or even to omit the punishment. He can wait for a long time to deal with the sinner.

Associated with judgment is the word *curse.* In God's judgment He said that the man, the woman, and the land were going to suffer. He said to Adam, "Thou shalt die," which means, of course, he would begin to suffer and at the end of it all he would be dead. When God pronounced His curse upon the man, the woman, the serpent, and the soil, He was stating outwardly, openly, publicly what was going to happen because of the wrong which Adam had done.

When we put all these things together, we have the course of sin. We see that sin begins with temptation. It moves on into action, which is the sin itself: the transgression of the law of God. Then comes guilt, which is the way the person feels about his sin, and that is followed by judgment, whic s the way God deals with the sinner. The curse, which is the penalty on the person because of the sin that he has done, is then spelled out; but the story is not complete until we refer to *grace. Grace* is that action of God in which He saves us from our sins. Grace is God acting for us in ways we do not deserve and which we have not earned. If a person could pay for the blessing of God, it would not be grace any more; but when he is dependent upon God and has nothing with which to pay and receives from God as free the things that really matter, that is the grace of God. Although we have sinned and become alienated from God, we can be reconciled and forgiven of our sin because of the grace of God. How marvelous is His grace! "Where sin abounded, grace did much more abound: that as sin hath reigned unto death, even so might grace reign through righteousness unto eternal life by Jesus Christ our Lord" (Rom. 5:20-21).

FORGIVENESS OF SINS

The great truth about sin for Christians is that God *forgives* sin. Sin is as human as human nature. Man naturally sins. He acts in ways which are not like God. Sin has an effect upon man in that it changes him, it spoils him, it turns him away from God. The most wonderful truth in the Bible is that God forgives sin. This forgiveness is possible not because we deserve it or that we have earned it, but because of God's mercy and grace.

The word *forgive* is a common word in our language, but I wonder how many of us have ever stopped to think what it really means. Have we ever tried to think about what actually happens when we *forgive?* The essence of forgiving is *giving*. The main part of the word is *give*. When we forgive anyone, we are giving that person release from the wrong he has done to us. We give up any right or intention on our part to get even with him. We give away the right and the privilege to retaliate against him. If we forgive someone, we are giving that person liberty and freedom from what we might have done.

Let us say that a man has cheated me out of forty dollars. In my dealings with him, I trusted him, and so he got away with forty dollars of my money. He owes me forty dollars; and I have the right to collect it. If I forgive him, I give him release from what he owes me and that is as if I gave him the forty dollars.

Forgiveness does not mean that I tell the man that what he did was all right. If it was all right, there was nothing to forgive. When I was cheated out of forty dollars, that was forty dollars wrong. and let's keep it straight. Righteousness, according to the law, would mean he should pay me the forty dollars.

In the Old Testament the idea of righteousness is brought out as an "Eye for eye and tooth for tooth" (Ex. 21:24). Some people would say this is terrible, but actually it is the fair and just thing to do. Suppose I become involved in an argument with a man, and he gets rough with me. We begin to scuffle, and in the course of the fight he knocks my eye out. He should not have done it, but he did. The law of Moses says I would be justified in knocking out his eye. Someone will say, "Isn't that terrible?" Surely, but it was terrible to have my eye knocked out, and it is no worse for him to have his eye knocked out. It is fair and square.

Another will say, "That is just the law of the jungle." Oh, no, that is not the way it would happen if human nature were not held back. If somebody knocked out my eye, what would I feel like doing to him? I would want to "knock his block off." I would want to completely annihilate him for what he did.

To illustrate further, suppose someone picks a fight with me and knocks out a tooth. Then I have the right, according to the law of Moses, to retaliate in kind. Moses would say, "How many teeth did he knock out?" "One." "Well, then you can knock out one." "Two." "Then you can knock out two." Someone may say, "How awful!" Remember! It is no more awful for him than it was for me. Again, someone will say, "That is the law of the jungle." Again I say, no. The law of my human nature would be that if he knocks one tooth out of my head, I'd not stop with one tooth from him. I would knock every tooth out of his head. But Moses in the law would say, "No, you harm him only as much as he has harmed you." This is justice, but of course it is not forgiveness. If I forgive him, I give him release from what he did to me, and do not hit him at all.

Think back to the illustration I used earlier. The man cheated me out of forty dollars. If I forgive him, I say "Cancel it." There is to be no collection. I let it go. That may sound pretty simple, but it is not. If someone does you an injustice, your first impulse is to hurt him. Somebody slams the door in your face. What does it make you feel like doing? Just wait 'til he comes through that door and you get a chance to slam it! Then you would be even.

Getting even with people is a real delight for some. To have been done an injustice, and to be able to pay it back really appeals to the human heart. We may not want to admit it, but this is the truth. Some people are truly stimulated by the chance to get even. When somebody does them wrong and they get mad, they walk around with more life than they have had for weeks. There is a new spring in their step, their eyes sparkle, and their hair curls, just because they are mad. They are going to get even, and they have a thrill surging through them. Then, too, when they are mad, they don't have to be nice to people. They don't have to pick up anything others drop on the floor; they don't have to wait on them; they don't even have to cook a meal for them; they can just get mad and stay mad. They can get even with people and take out of them everything they owe them and as much more as they can get.

Of course, this is not forgiveness. If you are going to forgive, you give the person release from what he has done wrong. You do not do anything to get even, and believe me that is not easy. You just have to swallow the injustice and that is bitter. You might want to get even, but if you have grace in your heart, you will feel led to forgive. God has grace in His heart; He wants to forgive our sin. When God forgives, He actually releases us from the wrong we have done against Him and never collects for it. He will never retaliate against us.

The forgiveness of sin presents a real problem to God, but He *can* forgive because of what Christ Jesus has done. When the penalty for sin has been paid, God has to be fair; He has to be just, and that means I can go free. However, God cannot *overlook* my wrongdoing. If He did, He would have to overlook all wrong, and the devil could laugh at Him. God cannot play favorites. The great question is then, how is God going to forgive me my sin? How is He going to give me release from what I did wrong? Simply put, He can do it because Christ Jesus died for my sins. Christ paid the penalty so that I could go free.

Years ago, a friend of mine, a fellow student, was caught driving too fast in the city of Los Angeles, California. He received a ticket for speeding. When he was called to appear, he asked me to go down to the police court with him. I had never been in a police court in my life, but I went with him and had my eyes opened on how these things are done. When my friend stepped up before the court, he was asked, "Did you drive too fast? The reporting officer says you drove more than thirty miles an hour. Did you?" My friend began a story to explain how it was, and the judge interrupted and asked, "Did you?" He replied, "Yes." The judge said, "Thirty dollars or thirty days. Next."

They took my friend over into a little enclosure from which he was not going to be released until he had paid the thirty dollars. He didn't have the money, and so he was in jail for thirty days, unless I put up the thirty dollars. I walked all the way to the Institute where I was staying to get my last thirty dollars out of the bank. In due time I arrived back at the police court. An amazing thing happened when I produced my money. They didn't even ask me my name. I tried to tell them, but to no avail. They were only interested in the name of the man who had committed the crime. They had his name, took my thirty dollars, and gave me a receipt for *him*. I went to the cell where *he* was being kept, and they let *him* out. They never did ask me my name; they just took my thirty dollars. On the basis of my thirty dollars, he walked out as if he had not done anything. He was *forgiven,* and they gave him release on the strength of the fact that I gave thirty dollars.

That is the way it is with me and my sin. When I have done wrong, I am entitled to suffer death. The Lord Jesus Christ suffered death in my place and because of His death I am enabled to go free. I go free, because He died for me, and I am treated as if I had never done wrong. This is the forgiveness of sin that demonstrates the matchless love and mercy of God, because He gave His own Son to die for my sin in order that I could go free.

SACRIFICE FOR SINS

There is a very important element in the forgiveness of sins which is often overlooked. It is that God has a basis for the forgiveness of sin. He does not forgive sin just because He is kind and gracious. Certain conditions must be met. A necessary provision needs to be made for the cancellation of guilt. When sin occurs, when man does something wrong in the sight of God, he frustrates the will of God and disobeys and breaks the plan of God. To that extent he is in debt and unfit. It is therefore needful that something be done in order that the sinner might be able to stand before God free of guilt and worthy of God's favor.

If a child puts its hand into boiling water, something is going to happen. There is no use for the mother to say, "Oh, my poor child, I am sorry that that happened to you. We'll just act as if it hadn't happened"; because the child *was* scalded. When sin occurs, something actually happens. When a man does wrong, it is as if he cut off a finger. We may feel sorry for him, but this does not put the finger back. In other words, sin against God, the breaking of one of the laws of God, is something really done; and it is not possible for God to say He will just forget about it. A debt has been incurred, and it must be paid. The New Testament reveals that God is willing and ready and able to forgive, because the debt has been paid. And it is this payment of the debt we now want to consider.

God's reaction to sin is judgment. If a human being breaks a law of God, a certain penalty must follow. If I violate a law of nature, certain consequences follow. If I say I don't believe in the law of gravity and then step out of a second-story window, I will wind up with broken bones in spite of what I may have said. Spiritual laws are not less real than the physical. One of the spiritual laws is that God is angry with sin, and so "The wages of sin is death..." (Rom. 6:23). The wonderful thing about the Gospel is that the penalty that the sinner deserves is taken by Christ. He intervenes on behalf of the one who has violated the spiritual law. Christ steps in and takes the burden upon Himself. As John states it, "If any man sin, we have an advocate with the Father, Jesus Christ the righteous: And he is the propitiation for our sins: and not for ours only, but also for the sins of the whole world" (1 John 2:1-2).

Propitiation is a big word, and the reason it is in the Bible is because there is no little word to use for it. It has to do with turning away wrath by use of an offering. It refers to something that makes a person inclined to be gentle with you and gracious to you when you have acted in a way that deserves judgment. The Bible sets forth the view that the sin of man brings on the wrath of God. The death of Christ on the cross turns away the wrath of God so that He can be gracious and kind to us in regard to our sin. This effect of Christ's death is what we call *propitiation*. We say He propitiated God. Paul writes, "Being justified freely by his grace through the redemption that is in Christ Jesus: Whom God has set forth to be a propitiation through faith in his blood..." (Rom. 3:24-25). It is because Christ has borne our sins in His body on Calvary's cross that we can be forgiven. Because He has paid the penalty, we can walk out free. Christ died for us, and God can deal with us as if we had not sinned.

In 1 John we read these familiar words, "If we confess our sins, he (God) is faithful and just to forgive us our sins, and to cleanse us from all unrighteousness" (1 John 1:9). Why does it say that He is "faithful and just" to forgive us our sins? God does not forgive us our sins because of our confession but because of Christ's death for us on the cross. However, it is not until we confess our sins that we receive the benefit of the death of the Lord Jesus Christ. When we come to God and admit that we have sinned, we can claim from God what Christ has provided for us. God is then faithful and just to forgive.

Christ's having paid the penalty is the basis for our use of the phrase "for Christ's sake." God the Father thinks about the Lord Jesus Christ, sees how He has paid the penalty, and lets me go free. He does not let me go free for my sake or because I have confessed my sins. There is not anything I can do to justify myself in the sight of God. It is only because Christ died for me and God is willing to look on me through Christ's sacrificial death that I can receive the forgiveness of my sins. Christ offered Himself as a sacrifice for sin. The Bible says, "Cursed is every one that hangeth on a tree" (Gal. 3:13). Christ actually took the curse that belonged to me in His own body in order that I might be set free of the consequences of sin.

Very early in Scripture (Gen. 3:15) we are told that God's plan calls for an innocent substitute to be offered up as a sacrifice to Him for the sins of His people. This does not mean that God is cruel and unfair. It just means that sin is that awful. It is the sin that is cruel and unfair. God so loves us that He gave His own Son to be our sacrifice. The Lord Jesus Christ was the innocent substitute who went to the cross and suffered for our sins. Today the sinner can come to God, openly turn to God, call upon Him; and God is able to forgive him. For this Christ died, and so we speak of His being the "sacrifice for sins" on our behalf.

THE SIN OFFERING

Man is separated from God because of the presence of sin in his life. How can he then possibly draw nigh to God that he may be helped? The Bible deals plainly with this problem.

God spoke to Moses on Mt. Sinai and made plain how a sinner could come to Him. In the Old Testament there was a definite procedure which a sinner had to follow in coming to God.

The worshipper who was conscious of sin in his life was required to bring a living animal as a sacrifice to be offered by the priest. God wanted man's perfect obedience, but when man failed in that, God provided a way for a sinner to approach Him through sacrifice. Man was to bring a clean, unblemished animal which had nothing to do with his sin, and put it to death. The life and blood of the innocent animal was to take the place of the sin in the life of the worshipper.

The sacrifice was commonly a lamb; but sometimes an ox, a goat, or a dove was brought. The live creature was brought to the altar, which was the place of worship. Here the individual laid his hand upon the head of the living animal and confessed his sin. The understanding was that his sins were put on this living creature so that it would be counted as if it were guilty, and would be dealt with as if it were the sinner. Of course, the worshipper knew perfectly well that the lamb was not responsible for what the man had done. God also knew it, but this was a way of picturing something that would take place some day in reality. It was pointing forward to the day when Jesus Christ would appear as the Lamb of God and the sinner would put his sins on Him.

After the sinner had made confession upon the animal as the innocent living substitute, the priest would put the creature to death, and take the blood and sprinkle it on the altar of the tabernacle as proof that a death had occurred for sin. Thus the sinner could come into the presence of God at the altar on the basis of the death of an innocent substitute.

Anyone hearing this for the first time may wonder why the sacrifice is necessary. The practical answer is that this is the way that God arranged for men to follow in coming to Him. This is the way He has sanctioned and endorsed. He says, "For the life of the flesh is in the blood: and I have given it to you upon the altar to make an atonement for your souls" (Lev. 17:11). Maybe you and I wouldn't do it that way, but let us keep in mind that you and I are not like God. I can imagine someone saying, "I personally don't see why God wouldn't just overlook sin. Why wouldn't He just forget about it?" The reason is plainly indicated in the Bible. God is not only loving, merciful, and just; but He is also holy. Because God is holy, He cannot overlook sin. A reliable surgeon cannot ignore unclean instruments. He must sterilize whatever he intends to use. It is necessary that some cleansing provision be made for the sinful and unrighteous person to enable such a one to come into the presence of the One who is altogether holy.

It is a law of life that disobedience bring suffering. If a child does wrong, someone will suffer. If parents neglect disciplining or punishing their child, then they themselves will probably suffer. If parents want to take this on themselves, that is their privilege, but someone must suffer for disobedience. No one ever breaks a law without someone's suffering. Some parents are willing to endure the consequence of their child's wrongdoing. It is this way with God. He is willing to suffer for our disobedience, and it cost Him the death of His Son.

The Bible helps us to understand how this is. The ritual in the time of Moses was set up so that the worshipper would bring the sin offering to the tabernacle and confess his sins upon that offering. Then the sin offering would be slain, and the blood would be sprinkled in the place of worship by the priest. This was the way to come to God. The worshipper would know that the forgiveness he was going to receive was not free. It was free to him, but it cost the death of the sin offering. The New Testament tells us that "Ye were not redeemed with corruptible things, as silver and gold . . . but with the precious blood of Christ, as of a lamb without blemish and without spot" (1 Pet. 1:18-19).

This whole idea of the shedding of blood and of another creature's dying in my place is summed up in the words *expiation for sin*. To express it simply, another person bears the burden of my sin and guilt by dying in my place, and his blood is brought into God's presence and presented before Him to show that my debt is paid. God in Himself is such a Person that He must be righteous and fair and just. And so whereas the soul that sinned should die, God is able to release that soul from that obligation to die and forgive the guilt of his sin because one has already died for him.

In the Old Testament ritual, on the Day of Atonement the priest took the blood of the slain lamb and carried it into the very presence of God, into the Holy of Holies. After a time the priest came out to the people and pronounced upon them forgiveness of sins. This meant that God had accepted the death of the sacrifice on their behalf. When the priest declared that sins were forgiven, he pronounced pardon and the worshipper walked away free. He was now free to have communion with God without fear. The requirements of the law had been met. The sin had been cleared away. Atonement had been made.

The word *atonement* which comes from the verb *atone* interestingly enough does not have any Latin or Greek root. It comes from an English phrase meaning *at one*. *Atonement* means that the sinner and God are made *at one;* they are reunited. The great Day of Atonement for Israel was the day when all the people came before God and confessed their sins as a nation. The blood of the sin offering was shed and then was taken into the presence of God. God and His people were reconciled and reunited, not because of any magic in the blood itself, but because the people *believed* God.

As a parallel to the Old Testament ritual, the New Testament presents the sacrifice of Jesus Christ. Through the sacrifice which Jesus made in order to bring the sinner and God together—*at one* —He effects the reconciliation. He is the "sin offering" for every believer who comes into the presence of God honestly and sincerely admitting his sins and putting his faith and trust in the death of the Lord Jesus Christ to forgive his sins. God will receive Christ's death on behalf of the believer and set him free. The significance of the sin offering of the Lord Jesus Christ is that man can now come into the presence of God as His own child, at one with God. In this way God can be "the justifier of him which believeth in Jesus" (Rom. 3:26).

THE LAMB OF GOD

The term *the Lamb of God* means something special to anyone who knows the Bible. In the Old Testament, worship was based upon the sin offering, a sacrifice which was usually a lamb.

The Old Testament relates the story of Abraham's offering up his son, Isaac, on the altar. As they were coming to the place where the altar was, Isaac asked his father where the sacrifice was. Abraham answered him saying, "My son, God will provide himself a lamb for a burnt offering" (Gen. 22:8). At that time Abraham had reason to believe that the sacrifice God would require would be his own son, Isaac. But the story points out that God provided a ram. With this in mind, when we use the phrase *the Lamb of God,* we are thinking of a sacrifice which God has provided that is going to be offered up for the sins of the people. It brings immediately to the mind of Christian people the sacrifice of the Lord Jesus Christ at Calvary.

The Passover (Ex. 11 and 12) was one of the most significant events ever to occur in the history of Israel. At that time the children of Israel were called Hebrews and they were being held in captivity in Egypt. Pharaoh was unwilling for them to return to their own country; and through Moses, God dealt with Pharaoh by bringing one plague after another upon the land of Egypt. The last of the plagues was the plague of death which was to come upon the first-born in each household. When the word was passed through Moses to Pharaoh that the first-born would die, everyone was included. The Hebrews were included as well as the Egyptians, but God provided a way of escape for them. He told Moses that the head of each household should take a lamb and, after checking to be sure that it was without blemish, should slay it and put its blood upon the doorpost. "And when I see the blood, I will pass over you, and the plague shall not be upon you to destroy you" (Ex. 12:13). The word *Passover* is derived from the language used here. The death angel *passed over* the houses where the doorposts were sprinkled with blood.

The question is often raised as to whether or not it made any difference whether the people in the house were good or bad, devoted or careless. The Bible narrative does not say that the angel of death looked to see about the character of the people in the house; he looked to see the blood on the doorpost. If he saw the blood, he would pass over. The truth to be seen here is that as any sinner comes before God under the blood of the Lord Jesus Christ, it is the blood of Christ between man and the Father which God sees, and for the sake of the blood He passes over man's sin. When God looks down on any sinner who is trusting in the blood, He is reminded of the death of Christ; and because Christ died for the man, the man goes free for Christ's sake. Paul in writing to the Corinthians said, "For even Christ our passover is sacrificed for us" (1 Cor. 5:7).

When John said, "Behold the Lamb of God, which taketh away the sin of the world" (John 1:29), he was referring to the fact that Christ Jesus would die as the sin offering. And thus it would be true that Jesus' death on Calvary's cross for sin makes Him "the Lamb of God" for any individual person. In that respect He fulfills Isaiah 53, which sets forth the whole idea of Christ's suffering in our place and being the Lamb of God, which dies, taking away the sin of the world. "But he was wounded for our transgressions, he was bruised for our iniquities; the chastisement of our peace was upon him; and with his stripes we are healed" (Isa. 53:5).

The word *reconciliation* is used to refer to the fact that the sinner is brought back into the presence of God. Reconciliation would not mean anything unless first there had been alienation and separation. The picture drawn for us in the Bible is that God made man in His own image so that man could have fellowship with Him. But when man sinned, he became a stranger to God. Man was ashamed of his sin and felt a sense of guilt. He knew he deserved the wrath and punishment of God. As long as this was the case, man could never have close, personal, living fellowship with God. However, the Lord provided a way for sinful man to have his sin and guilt taken away. Christ suffered as the Lamb of God fulfilling the requirements of the law. Death came to Him and because He died, death does not have to come to the man who believes in Him. Such a man goes free. With man's guilt pardoned and his sins forgiven and carried away, he is now reconciled to God. He can come into the presence of God, where there is no longer any fear of punishment.

This does not mean that God has decided that sin does not matter. We should never feel that coming into the presence of God, free from sin, is a light thing. Coming into the presence of God without guilt is a free, gracious privilege extended to the penitent sinner because Christ died for him. We have been delivered from guilt, but the price was the precious blood of the Lord Jesus Christ. We are free from punishment, but that is only because He bore our punishment in His own body on the cross.

The Old Testament *sin offering*—confession of sin on a spotless lamb, the offering slain, and sin carried away—helps us to understand the death of Christ when the Apostle John writes, "Behold the Lamb of God which taketh (beareth) away the sin of the world."

THE HIGH PRIEST

Throughout the Bible the idea of the *high priest* is brought out to show how one particular man is provided to help in guiding the sinner who wants to worship God. The high priest acts on behalf of sinning people. In the Old Testament there is shown to be a big gap between the Holy God in heaven and sinful man on earth. Man knows he needs the help of God but is unable to figure out how to come to God for such help.

We may remember there was a certain prescribed ritual to be performed in worship in the tabernacle. The sacrifice was to be slain at the altar; the high priest, representing the sinful people, was to wash at the laver; the light was to be burning on the golden candlestick; the shewbread was to be on the table; the incense was to be burned on the altar of incense. On the Day of Atonement, the high priest would then enter the Holy of Holies. As he came into the presence of God at the mercy seat, he would sprinkle blood on all the articles of furniture. All this any ordinary man would not know how to do. God, therefore, in mercy provided priests to go in for man.

In mercy and grace, God arranged that man does not have to grope his way into His presence in blind uncertainty. We may well be ignorant or unsure in ourselves, but God supplies us with a Guide, a High Priest who knows how to approach the Holy One and bring our case before Him.

The New Testament uses the word *advocate*. "We have an advocate with the Father, Jesus Christ the righteous" (1 John 2:1). Jesus Christ became incarnate so that He could be our High Priest. Christ is the One who goes into the presence of God to plead for the sinner. Because the Lord Jesus came in the form of a man, He knows what we as men are facing. He can sympathetically deal with us and act for us in the presence of God. He knows what the holiness of God requires, and He can meet it. He takes over our case, goes into the presence of God, and intercedes on our behalf. Christ Jesus is our High Priest.

The office of high priest over all the other priests was very much like the office of general manager or executive editor. He was in charge of all the others. He personally performed the highest office. An example can be drawn from our church today. There are ministers, elders, and deacons. All are church officers, but there are different levels among them. In the time of our Lord, more than one chief priest lived in Jerusalem, but there was only one high priest.

Christ Jesus is our High Priest who has gone up into heaven on our behalf and in the presence of God intercedes for us so that we might be kept by Him. "Wherefore he is able also to save them to the uttermost that come unto God by him, seeing he ever liveth to make intercession for them." This means we have One in heaven who lives always making intercession for us. Jesus Christ is our High Priest in the presence of God.

If a man turns to God, he may be confused as to how to approach Him. What should he do and say? It is a comfort to know that by turning to Christ Jesus as He is set forth in the Bible an all-sufficient Advocate is presented who knows what to do and say before God. The Lord Jesus as our High Priest before God is One who can be trusted completely. No man need be hindered in coming to God because he does not know what to do.

There will be times when we have burdens that will be so intricate and difficult we hardly know how to pray. We don't know whether to ask that a loved one should live, because if he lives he may be crippled, infirm, or an invalid for the rest of his days. We don't know for sure whether to ask that some loved one should prosper in business. If he does prosper, he may become vain, proud, and worldly. We don't know for sure whether to ask that someone in our own family should be delivered from trouble. It may be that trouble is what that person needs, and God will know that. "We know not what to pray for as we ought, but the Spirit itself maketh intercession for us" (Rom. 8:26). For our guidance in prayer we have a High Priest in the presence of God praying for us; and when we go to prayer, we should yield ourselves to the ministry of the Holy Spirit, who will take the things of the Lord Jesus Christ and show them to us. One of the things that the Holy Spirit will show us about Christ is His present ministry as our High Priest, and we will find ourselves praying with liberty to ask for certain things because Christ is interceding in our behalf about those very things. He is praying about our need at the moment we pray because He is our High Priest, "Who has compassion on the ignorant and on them that are out of the way" (Heb. 5:2).

CHAPTER FOUR

The Priesthood

ONE of the most important things the Bible tells us about God's great work in saving sinful man is that God arranges to help the sinner come to God. It is like a free medical service where there is not only a fully equipped hospital with a competent staff of skilled doctors to which the poor can come at no cost, but an ambulance service with capable attendants is provided to bring any to the hospital who might not otherwise come. This ambulance service is called the *priesthood*. God has planned that persons who know what to do should be on hand to help the poor, needy soul who might stay away because of ignorance or weakness. Let us examine the whole operation of bringing sinners to God that they may be saved.

THE TABERNACLE

In the Old Testament just after Israel came out of Egypt and while they were traveling across the desert, the place of worship was called the *tabernacle*. There the people could meet God face to face as a man talks with his friend. Later in Israel's history the place of worship was named the *temple*. The *tabernacle* and the *temple* were very real factors in the spiritual life of the people.

The word *tabernacle* is still in use today. With us it generally suggests a temporary structure open on the sides, without walls—a pavilion. The tabernacle in Israel's history was a temporary structure. It looked like a tent, but it was built carefully according to a given plan. Every detail in it had much significance because it showed the people of Israel how they should approach God in worship.

Israel was organized into twelve tribes. The tabernacle was placed in the very center of the camp with the tribes surrounding

The Priesthood

it, three tribes to the north, three tribes to the east, three tribes to the south, and three tribes to the west. It was placed in the center of the camp to impress the people with the fact that God was in their midst. They were to realize they could meet God in the tabernacle.

During the forty days which Moses spent on Mt. Sinai, he received the Ten Commandments from God. God also revealed to him the blueprint for the tabernacle and its furnishings. Every aspect of the tabernacle's construction was specifically described, and every detail of the furniture's construction and arrangement was precisely stated. Everything had special meaning; even the arrangement of the various furnishings was significant.

The tent building itself was rectangular. It was closed on three sides and open at one end. The interior of the tabernacle was divided into two parts. The part that was by the open wall and which would be entered first was called "the Holy place." A dividing curtain, commonly called the veil, separated this front part from the closed room at the rear. The room farthest away from the door was called "the Holy of Holies." Sometimes it was called "the Holiest of All." The Ark of the Covenant was kept in the Holy of Holies. This Ark was a rectangular box which looked like a chest, on which were the golden Cherubim. This was called the mercy seat, where the presence of God would be.

Outside the tabernacle, in the yard, was an altar—the place where the animal sacrifices were slain. The worshipper would bring his sacrifice to the altar. He would put his hands on the lamb and confess his sins to signify that his sins were being put on this innocent substitute. The priest would then take the lamb and slay it. At that point the worshipper experienced forgiveness, because when the lamb died in his place, he would not have to die and God would forgive him his sins. That was the first step toward God. In our day and time, the first step toward God is to confess our sins and to believe in the Lord Jesus Christ, who died for our sins. That the blood of Christ is shed on behalf of sin is the first thing a person must realize as he comes to God.

Moving from the altar, the priest, representing the penitent worshipper, came to a rather strange object. It looked like a big tub filled with water and set on a stand. This was the *laver*. Here the priest was washed. He was being ceremonially cleansed.

All this shows how the sinner, represented by the priest, was forgiven and cleansed. From this point the priest entered the Holy place. Immediately through the entrance on the left and on the right, there were two articles of furniture. The one on the left was a seven-branched *candlestick* with light shining forth. This symbolizes *understanding*. This would signify that when man comes into the presence of God, forgiven and cleansed, he receives knowledge of the grace of God.

On the right side of the Holy place was a table called the table of *shewbread*. During the days when the children of Israel were in the desert, a pot of manna was placed on the table. The manna was later replaced by bread. The manna was a symbol of nourishment and strength. It signified that God would feed His people. Today it is the man who feeds on the manna of the Word of God who is nourished and is strong in faith.

Proceeding on in the Holy place, the priest came to a small *altar of incense*. It was located in front of the *veil,* the curtain that separated the interior of the tabernacle into its two rooms. On this altar was an incense burner with perfume burning all the time. It pictured, in Israel's experience, "a sacrifice of sweet smelling savour" to God, the prayers of the saints offering praise and thanksgiving to God. This plan of the tabernacle shows that man does not praise and thank God until he has been forgiven, cleansed, understands the ways of God, and is strong in faith.

Behind the altar of incense was the veil, and beyond this the priest generally was not permitted to go. Only once a year did the high priest go through the veil into the presence of God. This was the innermost part of the tabernacle, the place called the *Holy of Holies*. The Ark of the Covenant was located here. There were three things in the Ark. There were the tablets of stone which Moses brought down from Mt. Sinai, Aaron's rod that budded, and some manna from the wilderness. The most important thing it contained was the law. The top of the Ark, between the Cherubim, was the mercy seat. It was there that God would meet with His people face to face on the Day of Atonement.

After Israel settled in the land of Canaan, they no longer traveled about from place to place or lived in tents. They began to build their houses of stone. It was at this time that their place of worship was changed from *tabernacle* to *temple*. The only difference between the temple and the tabernacle was that the temple was a permanent structure. Solomon built the temple of stone and of cedar, a glorious permanent building but built exactly after the pattern of the tabernacle. It had the same purpose, to show the people that God was in their midst and to guide them in their worship of Him. The sinner confessed his sin; he experienced forgiveness; he received light of the knowledge of the glory of God; he was made strong in faith; he gave thanks to God; he came into His presence and God talked with him face to face, as a man speaks with his friend. That was the route mapped out by God and traveled by the children of Israel. This map has not changed. It is the route to be traveled by men today.

CLEANSED BY THE BLOOD

We read in the Bible that sin is taken away by the shedding of blood. What is meant by the phrase *cleansed by the blood?*

Sin not only separates, alienates, and isolates a person from God; it also defiles the soul. When I sin, something happens that corrupts my mind and ruins me. A much simpler way to describe it would be to say that sin is the dry rot of the soul. Guilt affects the soul as rust affects metal. If a man's sins remain with him, they will eat his heart out.

God arranges to cleanse the soul from sin. When a penitent soul confesses his sin, God cancels the sin, forgives the sinner and washes him clean. This is a remarkable truth. *Cleansed by the blood* means washed clean because Jesus Christ died for sinful man on Calvary's cross. Every time the term *the blood* is spoken, it brings to the Christian's mind the death of Christ on the cross. To say that I am *cleansed by the blood* means that the defiling effects of sin are removed from my heart when I accept Christ's death for myself. This brings to mind the wonderful kindness of God in the old saying, "The light that reveals is the light that heals." Just as surely as I become aware of my sin and confess my sin, God begins to heal and take my sin away.

Unconfessed sin somehow sticks to a man. If a man is not conscious that God has forgiven his sins, if he does not understand and believe that Christ, in dying on Calvary's cross, bore his sins in His own body so that his sin is now on Him, that man's sin sticks to him. It is like soot. The more it is rubbed, the more it spreads.

It cannot be gotten rid of. To be completely removed, sin must be confessed, and man must believe that God has accepted Jesus Christ's death on his behalf. In the death of Christ, through God's remarkable spiritual chemistry, sin is dissolved. It is gone. The blood of the Lord Jesus Christ not only takes away the sin but also the memory of it. We read of the Lord Jesus Christ: "Unto him that loved us, and washed us from our sins in his own blood" (Rev. 1:5). In the words of the old gospel hymn:

> There is pow'r, pow'r,
> Wonder-working pow'r
> In the blood of the Lamb;
> There is pow'r, pow'r,
> Wonder-working pow'r
> In the precious blood of the Lamb.

It is difficult to describe the process, but the results are real. After confession has been made and forgiveness is received, cleansing follows. The death of Christ accomplishes these wonderful results.

Hebrews 9:14 states, "How much more shall the blood of Christ, . . . purge your conscience from dead works to serve the living God?" It seems that when a man has done something he should not have done and knows that he has sinned, the consciousness of his wrongdoing lingers with him. As long as he is careless and indifferent about spiritual matters, this does not seem to bother him; but when he has become sensitive to spiritual things and thinks in terms of God in heaven, the memory of his sin besets him and haunts him. As long as such things are on his conscience, they defile and hold the man back, hindering him from serving God.

The world cannot understand why Christian people are not always depressed about their sin. Worldly people do not care one way or the other about sin; and so they have no reason to become depressed. Christians, however, care about their sin, because they know they have displeased God. If this is true, why are not Christians in a constant state of depression? The thing that the worldly person does not seem to grasp is the fact that God forgives and cleanses sin that has been confessed.

There are some Christians who, for one reason or another, actually think there is a virtue in thinking about and dwelling upon their sin. This type of introspection is not wholesome and has no

The Priesthood

basis in Biblical teaching. There are some professing Christians who spend a great deal of time lamenting the fact that they are not as good as they should be. Under the cloak of humility they speak of all of the things they have done wrong. This kind of confession not only detracts from the person's testimony but is dishonoring to God. God says, "I will remember their sin no more" (Jer. 31:34). If God has forgiven and forgotten our sins, why should we continue to be exercised over them? Why not believe that Jesus Christ died for them and that Almighty God has forgiven them, and give Christ the glory? This is truly humbling, but it gives release. The person who knows there is nothing against him is the person who can spend his time in thinking about what he can do to please God.

Let me use a personal illustration. When I first became a Christian, an old farmer who was a neighbor heard that I had been converted. In the community in which I grew up, this was a rather unusual event. This neighbor asked me, "Do you think you are going to go to heaven?" I replied, "Yes." "Are you sure you are going to go to heaven?" Again I said, "Yes." He said, "You must think you are pretty good." That had never entered my mind, but it came to me to tell him, "No, I am not good, but my Lord is good, and He is the One who is going to take me to heaven." The old man began to think. He said, "You mean to tell me that you think that when you get to heaven you are not going to have to pay for the things you have done wrong?" To this I replied, "That is exactly what I mean to tell you. I am not going to pay for what I have done wrong." He thought about it a bit further and asked, "You think you are going to get off free?" "Yes, I think I am going to get off free." He could not understand how I could be so sure of myself. It was simply a matter of taking God at His word. He had the idea that I should wear crepe on my sleeve because of all the wrong I had done. Actually if I should wear crepe all my days, I would never be able to feel sorry enough for the wrong I have done. But this is not the way it is done. Salvation is a matter of accepting what God has done for me through Christ. He has taken my sins away, and I am completely and absolutely free.

Children would understand the term "I am home-free," and some people would understand "I am scot-free." This point bears emphasizing, for when man is conscious of being free, his spirit is filled with gratitude; and he wants to do right in the sight of God.

The person who is really forgiven wants to do right. He hates the sins that once hurt the Lord Jesus Christ. He has been forgiven and his sins no longer defile his memory. He has been *cleansed by the blood.*

CONSECRATION

The words *consecrate* and *consecration* are used over and over in the Old Testament. The definition of *consecrate* is "to set apart for a sacred purpose." *Consecration,* being the noun, means *dedication* and *devotion to God.*

Consecration is used in referring to a Christian's service to God. How can a man serve God? I cannot make God rich with my money. I cannot do His work with my hands. The one thing my human heart can do toward God is to honor and reverence Him. To honor God is to esteem Him and lift Him up above everything else in life. The attitude of my heart and mind should be that there is nothing to compare with God.

A common way to honor a person is to set things aside especially for him. When a guest is visiting us, we make a room ready for him, and the children are told to stay out of that room. It is set aside for that person. The same thing is done when a family wants to honor the father in the home. He is given a special chair in which to sit, and the children are not supposed to sit in that chair. That one chair is for the father and no one else.

With reference to God, certain things may be said to be *sacred* and certain things said to be *common.* Things are not sacred in themselves. They are *made* sacred by setting them aside for a special use. In this way a room can be made a sacred room. All the other rooms in the building can be used for various things, but this one room in saved for a particular purpose. A book can be made a sacred book and as a sacred book it is not used like an ordinary book. It is kept for a special purpose. For many people, the Bible is a sacred book. The church sanctuary is a sacred room. The pulpit is a sacred place. All these have been set aside specially for a particular purpose. When anything has been designated to be used for a specific, holy purpose, it is then a sacred thing. The process of making anything sacred is *consecration.*

In the Old Testament there was a certain procedure to be followed in consecrating the priest. This can be of significance to us.

The Priesthood

It is described in Exodus 29. Certain persons were chosen out of the tribe of Levi and were then consecrated to the office of priest. From that time on, they were to devote themselves entirely to this office and were to be considered as sacred to God. They were not to be available for anything else.

The consecration of the priests followed a very definite order. First there was the act of *washing* their sin away. They were to be clean. This remains true today. If any man is going to come into the presence of God as a servant to be consecrated to Him, then those things that are not acceptable to God must be washed away.

Secondly, attention was given to the way the priests were dressed. They were to wear *prepared garments* in the service to which they were called. A prescribed uniform, with every part especially set aside for this one service, was given to them. The idea was that God outfits His servants to come into His presence. This is still the way God does today.

The third step was the *anointing*. Anointing with oil in the Old Testament meant that the grace of God was being given. God gives His grace to help His servants in their work. In the New Testament this *anointing* is done in the giving of the Holy Spirit. Throughout the Bible we learn that God gives His people special grace to do what He wants them to do. So if God calls a man to be king, this man is anointed, given special grace for this task. If God calls a man to be the commander of an army, He will give to that man the special understanding and skill he needs to be a successful commander of an army.

Thus the priests were washed and clothed and anointed with power from on high in order that they might serve the Lord. But as we read on we see it was arranged that there should be a *sin offering* made for them. This means that even though they were consecrated they were still imperfect. Although they were fully committed to serve the Lord there was still something lacking. There would still be sin in their lives, and they needed to be forgiven even as they served God.

A second offering was also described. This was a *burnt offering*. The difference between the sin offering and the burnt offering was that in the sin offering the blood was taken in and sprinkled before God, showing that an innocent creature had died on behalf of sin, but in the burnt offering the whole body of the slain animal was brought into the presence of God and there was totally consumed by fire. This was to show complete, total yieldedness to God and utter obedience to Him. This ceremony showed that the priest was to be sincerely obedient to God.

The final step in the procedure was that they were *marked with blood* on the tip of the right ear, on the thumb of the right hand, and on the great toe of the right foot. This shows a very important truth about anybody who serves God even today. Marked with blood on the ear, a man would listen to God because Christ died for him. Marked with blood on the hand, he would work for God because Christ died for him. Marked with blood on the toe of the right foot, he would walk with God because Christ died for him. Listening with the ear, doing with the hand, going with the feet— everything done because Christ died for him. This was the ceremony of consecration of the priests showing that they were to be used in a very special way in serving the Lord.

BEING SANCTIFIED

To fully understand what the Bible means by being *saved,* it is important to know what is the meaning of being *sanctified.* But to know what being *sanctified* means, it is necessary to consider several other things.

One thing the Bible makes clear is that there is *a difference between God and the world* He created. The Bible emphasizes that man should pay more attention to God than to the things He has created. Man should be more concerned about the needs of his soul than the needs of his body. "Man shall not live by bread alone, but by every word that proceedeth out of the mouth of God" (Matt. 4:4). Man does live by bread, it is true, but not by bread only, because there is more to man than his body. "Every word that proceedeth out of the mouth of God" speaks for the soul. Jesus, on another occasion, stressing the difference between the soul and the body, said, "For what is a man profited, if he shall gain the whole world, and lose his own soul?" (Matt. 16:26). The world is one thing, but the soul and its relationship with God is something else and much more important.

Jesus gave further emphasis to this thought when He taught, "No man can serve two masters: for either he will hate the one, and love the other; or else he will hold to the one, and de-

The Priesthood

spise the other. Ye cannot serve God and mammon" (Matt. 6:24).

Another Biblical idea which helps us understand sanctification is that *love demands exclusive affection*. When a man is said to be in love, it is taken to mean that he gives his full affection to the loved one. This is what is cherished in the Christian concept of marriage. This love and affection involves complete commitment. God calls upon man to love Him with whole-hearted devotion. He will accept nothing less than this.

When God tells His people that He wants them to be sanctified, he means for them to make a distinction between Himself and the rest of the world. He also wants them to commit themselves to Him in exclusiveness. They are to worship Him and Him alone. They are to serve Him with a devotion that is full and complete.

Many readers of the Bible have been disturbed by the description of God as One who is jealous. "For the Lord thy God is a jealous God" (Deut. 6:15). They have a concept that jealousy is an evil and selfish thing. Jealousy can have the meaning of suspicion, but it can also have the meaning of watchfulness. The Bible uses jealousy as it relates to God in the sense that He watches over us carefully. As the Maker and Keeper of the world, God wants men to worship and love Him rather than any thing and He will be satisfied with nothing less.

This demand for exclusive affection can be seen in many places. Husband and wife are to belong to each other and no one else. Children and parents belong only to each other. God wants His people to realize they belong to Him in a way that they do not belong to anyone else on the face of the earth. They are to esteem and love Him above all others. They are to be set apart in a special way as wholly committed to Him. This is what being *sanctified* means.

A common notion is to think being *sanctified* has something to do with morality or ethics, that a person who is sanctified is a person with a very superior morality or a person of unusual spiritual attainment. Unusual spiritual attainment and superior morality are good, but this is not the meaning of being *sanctified*. The concept of sanctification cannot be understood apart from the idea that the person or thing sanctified has been especially set apart by God. The tabernacle was a sanctified place. Vessels and furniture were sanctified. The Sabbath was sanctified. The basic idea in the Bible is that things set aside for a particular purpose are "sanctified." When a person is set aside for God, his morality will improve, his ethics will be good, and he will grow in spiritual attainment. This is the result of being sanctified, but it is not what being sanctified means.

All this is illustrated for me in something that I noticed as a boy at home. I grew up in a small country town and an important place in that town was the railway station. Passenger trains went through twice a day. One went east and the other went west. This was an event in a small town, and it was an exciting thing to be at the railway station when the train went through. The long platform on the railroad station was made of wood and the railroad station was also made of wood. The town was too small to have a fire department, and its only water supply was the town well. If there ever was a fire, it was a matter of carrying the water from the well to the fire or at best stretching a long fire hose from the well to whatever place in the town was burning. Usually, the water reached the place a long time after the fire was over, but that was the fire protection we had. The railway station did not want to be dependent upon the Volunteer Fire Department; therefore, they had their own arrangement. On the station wall was a glass case filled with tools and underneath were the words *for fire only*. Those tools were not to be used for anything else. The expression *for fire only* actually meant *sanctified for fire*. They were set apart for that use. Big barrels of water were placed on the platform and beside each barrel was a pail painted red with white letters, F I R E, on it. The pails were not tied down; they were just sitting there. They were the kind of pail every farmer used in connection with his daily work, but no one ever took those pails. Everyone understood that they were *for fire only*. They were "sanctified" pails, set aside for a particular purpose.

When the Lord said, "Sanctify yourselves" (Lev. 20:7), He meant "Put away other things, leave off everything else, and commit yourself only to God." When persons are set apart for God, the basic principle involved is love. They are committed entirely, permanently, to God in love. They are sanctified unto Him, and they are the people the Bible calls *saints*. The root of the word *saint* and the root of the word *sanctify* is the same root. The *sanctified ones* are the *saints*. The word *saint* does not refer to spiritual achievement as many suppose. It does not refer to people who have lived a lifetime of unusually good behavior. This may be the case, but it is not why they are called saints. They are saints because they are set apart to God in a special way. The marvelous thing about the Gospel is that everyday, workaday people can become "saints" of God.

When God says to people, "Sanctify yourselves," and demands that they be sanctified to Him, the way this is done is for each individual to commit himself to God. The person who commits himself to the Lord will undoubtedly grow in spiritual things. Certainly moral virtue and spiritual piety will grow when a man faces God again and again as the Supreme One in his heart. Remember, these are the results of being sanctified and not the way in which a man becomes sanctified. A man can be described as sanctified when he has chosen God rather than His creation, and has given his heart in loving devotion to Him. A work of grace has taken place and the man has come to the realization that there are all kinds of things in the world, but none of them are equal to God. This is the person to whom God will commit Himself and with whom He will be pleased.

BEING HOLY

The English word *holy* can best be understood if the spelling is changed to *wholly*. *Holy* means *"wholly* given over to God." We have just seen that *sanctification* is the process by which one becomes *holy*. A man must be genuinely and sincerely committed to God with all his being if he would become holy.

People are likely to think that the word *holy* refers only to persons who are very good. Upon seeing someone whose spiritual faithfulness to God is steadfast, people are inclined to say, "Oh, my, but that is a holy person." This may be true, but the fact that such a man is good is not the cause of his holiness. Holiness in any man is to be seen in the completeness of his committal to God and the singleness of mind with which he is devoted to God. "Be ye holy" is best understood as a call to being altogether committed to God. One becomes holy when his greatest aim and purpose in life is to worship and serve God.

When the Bible says, "Be ye holy," it does not mean a long-drawn-out process that takes years to do. When the Lord says, "Ye shall be holy for I . . . am holy," this is something that a man can do at once. Those words were first spoken to the children of Israel while they were in the desert. It was as if they had been told, "Be holy right now, because it can be done."

If becoming holy meant I had to live a good life for thirty years so that I could be holy, I could take my time. But the Biblical concept of holiness does not permit delay. You can become holy now. "Today is the day if you will hear His voice."

If one must live an earnest, serious-minded spiritual life for a long period of time before he could be blessed, only the person who lives to a ripe old age could be assured of blessing or of holiness. If this were true, man would be saved by works and not by the grace of God. But holiness is available to any man, even a man with a sin-stained life, when that person turns in penitent faith to the Lord and becomes *wholly* committed to Him.

Many a person has thought that it would be necessary to get himself cleaned up and have everything right before he could begin to live a holy life. If I were to wait until then, I would never get it done. I must come to God first, and let Him take an active part in the cleaning-up process, and He will do it right after my commitment has been made.

When the Bible says, "Follow peace with all men, and holiness, without which no man shall see the Lord" (Heb. 12:14), it is not condemning to eternal damnation all people who die before they have obtained spiritual perfection. It is saying that without holiness it is impossible to have the full joy and blessing of the presence of the Lord. If the heart of a man is cool toward Him, God will not reveal Himself in all His fullness. But if the heart is completely yielded to Him, He will come to that man. "A broken and a contrite heart, O God, thou wilt not despise" (Ps. 51:17). "Behold, I stand at the door, and knock; if any man hear my voice, and open the door, I will come in to him, and will sup with him, and he with me" (Rev. 3:20). Biblical holiness is available to all who will receive the pardon offered in Christ Jesus, the sooner the better.

When one dedicates himself to God, it means he gives himself over to do the will of God. This is the basic idea in holiness. A person who has dedicated himself is one that the Bible would speak of as being holy. Holiness is related to sanctification in so far as the person has been "set apart unto the Lord." As he dedicates himself to serving the Lord, his state and condition is that of "being holy unto God."

The Sabbath is spoken of as a holy Sabbath. It is a day on which God alone is to be served. It is proper to speak of the sanctuary of a church as a holy place. The word *sanctuary* comes from the verb *sanctify,* which means "to set apart." When an auditorium is set apart only for the worship of God, it is commonly called a sanctuary. It is a holy place. When a new organ is installed in a church, it is customary to have a ceremony of dedication. The same organ could have been put in a theater, but it is now put in the church. The significance of the ceremony of dedication is to say that this particular instrument will be used exclusively for playing music in the worship of God. In that sense it is a dedicated, sanctified organ, because it is to be used only for the service of God. This could then be called a "holy" organ.

Every Christian should desire to be one who is dedicated and committed to the cause of Christ in such a way that the term *holy* applies to him. Whenever a believer commits himself to serve God with all he is and has, he is properly called *holy.*

THE ATONEMENT

The word *atonement* is very seldom used in everyday speech. It is a Bible word. In Chapter Three as we discussed the "sin offering" we noted that there is no Greek or Latin root for the English verb *atone.* The word *atone* was originally a phrase, the very same letters in two words, *at-one.* The atonement is the *at-onement.* When Christ Jesus atoned, He *at-oned.* The atoning work of Christ is the *at-oneing* work. Christ brought sinful man, estranged and separated from God, back to be *at-one* with God.

The Scriptures teach that sin separates man from God. In fact, because of sin man was alienated from God. The word *alienate* is based on the noun *alien.* An alien is a foreigner, in a sense an enemy, someone to suspect. To take human beings who were the creatures of God, made by His hand in His own image, and to turn them into aliens, strangers, enemies of God was the work of sin. The Bible speaks of the Gentiles as "being aliens from the commonwealth of Israel" (Eph. 2:12), and Paul speaks about those "being alienated from the life of God through the ignorance that is in them, because of the blindness of their heart" (Eph. 4:18). The heart of man's trouble is that he is alienated from God. God and man have become strangers to each other, and bringing them together again is the *at-oneing* work, the atoning work, of the Lord Jesus Christ.

There is a popular notion that to *atone* for something is to pay up for it. When sin came and separated man from God, the doom of impending destruction hung over man's heart like a Damocles sword. He felt cut off and alienated from God. In His work of atonement Christ dealt with man's sin and guilt. He absorbed the penalty; He paid the fine; He suffered in man's place. "The chastisement of our peace was upon him; and by his stripes we are healed" (Isa. 53:5). In that sense, He paid up for man, and it can be considered a vital aspect of atoning, but the strict meaning of *atone* is the bringing of God and man together again at one.

A word that is very closely associated with *atone* is *reconciliation*. Reconciliation conveys practically the same idea but with special emphasis upon the removing of guilt. In reconciling there is an awareness that a disturbing factor has been removed, and two who have been aliens have been brought together because what separated them has been taken out of the way. In the Biblical sense, reconciliation takes place when sin is removed and man and God are brought together. It is bound up with the work of Christ. "All things are of God, who hath reconciled us to himself by Jesus Christ, and hath given to us the ministry of reconciliation . . . God was in Christ, reconciling the world unto himself, not imputing their trespasses unto them . . ." (2 Cor. 5:18-19).

Atonement lays emphasis on the immediate result of being *reconciled*. When the reconciliation takes place and man is brought back into the presence of God so that he can have dealings with Him, he is *at one* with God. In the Bible, reconciliation and atonement are always used with reference to the forgiveness of sin. The Lord Jesus died for man that man might not need to die, because when He died for man, He carried man's sins away, leaving nothing between God and man. In that sense, Christ reconciled us to God. But, He not only reconciled us, He brought us back together with God, which is the atonement.

Once each year there was a special day when the children of Israel met together for the purpose of celebrating the atonement.

The Priesthood

"On the tenth day of this seventh month there shall be a day of atonement" (Lev. 23:27). On that day when they came together to worship God, Aaron was to bring "two kids of the goats for a sin offering" (Lev. 16:5). "And Aaron shall cast lots upon the two goats; one lot for the Lord, and the other lot for the scapegoat" (Lev. 16:8). When the people had confessed their sins on the one goat, it would be taken out into the wilderness and turned loose and with it went all the sins of the people. It was the scapegoat. The other goat was put to death. Its blood was shed. These ceremonies pictured to the people the fact that their sins were carried away and their guilt was removed.

Every Old Testament sacrifice represents an aspect of the work of the Lord Jesus Christ. Christ on Calvary's cross fulfilled every one of these things. In Himself, when He died, He took man's sins away. In Himself, when His blood was shed, He took away man's guilt so that he could be forgiven.

When the sacrifice was offered up on the Day of Atonement, the priest shed the blood at the altar, brought it into the presence of God, and sprinkled it in the Holy Place. This was evidence that a substitute, an innocent creature, had died for the guilty people. God would accept the sacrifice as being agreeable to the demands of righteousness because the guilt had been expiated, the debt had been paid, and the law had been honored. After receiving from God the assurance that the sacrifice was acceptable, the priest would come out to the people, and raising up his hands to heaven, he would pronounce upon them that their sins had been forgiven. There would then be great joy and a time of feasting, because they had been reconciled to God and the atonement had been effected.

It would not be fair to speak of the atonement without mentioning the idea of joy and gladness that is associated with it. From the human point of view, atonement is like making up after a quarrel. All young lovers know about this. A make-up after a lover's quarrel is two people coming back together after having been alienated. To state it very personally, if you have ever had anything come between you and someone you dearly love, it caused you to have uneasy feelings, perhaps even great grief. When the two of you were at one again it meant there had been genuine forgiveness, and this was occasion for great joy.

Paul, writing to the Romans, said, "We also joy in God through our Lord Jesus Christ, by whom we have now received the atonement" (Rom. 5:11).

THE PRIESTS

Priests hold a very prominent place in the Old Testament. Ordinarily a *priest* is considered to be a sacred person who serves as go-between between the people and God. The office of the priest is not found only in the Bible, as heathen and pagan religions too have priests. The office and the function of the priest, as revealed in the Bible, however, is unique and differs in many important respects from the role of the priesthood in non-Christian religions.

Three offices of service are spoken of in the Bible. Each of them has a special meaning for us, and all of them find their fulfillment in Jesus Christ. They are *prophet, priest,* and *king.*

The word *prophet* literally means "before, or for to speak." In the Biblical sense a *prophet* is one who proclaims or speaks for God. The function of the prophet was that of taking the Word of God and communicating it to men. His specific work was called *prophesying.* Today we understand that prophesying is, generally speaking, the interpreting of the Bible. Any man who takes the Scriptures and interprets them to human beings is prophesying. The office of prophet was usually filled by a man, but there are instances related in the Bible where women were used of God as prophetesses. Miriam, the sister of Moses, is referred to as a prophetess (Ex. 15:20). Deborah prophesied during the period of the Judges (Judg. 4:4). The New Testament makes mention of "Anna, a prophetess" (Luke 2:36).

The word *king* is used in the Bible to refer to a sovereign ruler. Although neighboring nations were ruled by kings for many centuries, Israel did not have a king until the period of the Judges (circa 1100 B.C.). At a time when there was much bloodshed, strife and disorder, they demanded that a king be placed over them to avoid the confusion of having every man doing what was right in his own eyes. Samuel anointed Saul as the first king of Israel (1 Sam. 10:1).

The *king* was the director. He could be likened to a policeman who directs traffic. The policeman may not be any more intelligent or clever than the people driving the cars, but he performs a most

The Priesthood

necessary function. Any kind of traffic cop is better than a traffic jam, and a traffic jam is what results when a number of cars converge on one segment of highway without the services of a traffic director. Such a person was the king. He served by directing the activities of the individuals in the kingdom so that a common purpose was served.

The unique function of the *priest* is found in his ability to approach God on behalf of people who had sinned. No Israelite would dare approach the Lord God of hosts without a mediator, someone who would plead his cause. In the first place, the sinner would not know how to approach God. In the second place, he would feel unworthy because of sin in his life. God gave His people the priesthood in order that certain persons could be set apart to make sacrifices for the people's sin and thus gain the forgiveness of God. This representative or mediator was called a *priest*. Priests in the Old Testament had it in their heart and mind to bring weak, bewildered sinners into the presence of God in order that their sin might be forgiven. The manner and way in which they did this was presented in the first section of this chapter when we considered the Tabernacle. Although the priestly office was hereditary, they were considered to be exceptional men. They were sensitive to the needs of the people and had ". . . compassion on the ignorant, and on them that are out of the way" (Heb. 5:2).

In the New Testament, the office of the priest is performed by Christ Jesus. It is also said of the Lord Jesus that He was made "a priest forever after the order of Melchisedec" (Heb. 5:6). The name Melchisedec is mentioned in Genesis 14, and the story told there is reiterated in Hebrews 7, which says that Melchisedec was the man to whom Abraham went after winning the victory over the enemy who had defeated and taken Lot and the King of Sodom captive. In that situation, Abraham worshipped in the presence of Melchisedec. Nothing was known about him except that he was a king and priest; Abraham bowed down before him, and God has made Christ "a priest forever after the order of Melchisedec." That is to say, God made Christ, who was a king, also a priest.

This extends to Christians, also, for the Bible says that the Lord Jesus Christ "hast made us unto our God kings and priests" (Rev. 5:10). Looking into the original language, some feel that that could well be translated "a kingdom of priests." Peter says that we are "a royal priesthood" (1 Pet. 2:9). The Christian has been called by the Lord Jesus Christ to be a king, in that he is to rule, and a priest, in that he is to pray for others.

The most important thing a Christian can be king of is himself. He is to take himself in hand and serve the Lord. The Bible says, "He that is slow to anger is better than the mighty; and he that ruleth his spirit than he that taketh a city" (Prov. 16:32). God has made men to be kings in that they are to control themselves and walk in His ways.

One of the distinctive doctrines of world-wide Protestantism is the priesthood of all believers. Christians are to understand that they are to be interested in other people and seek to help them toward God.

The function of the Old Testament priest was to represent the sinner before God. A word used in the New Testament to describe this priestly function is *advocate*. An advocate is one who pleads the case of another, a lawyer. The lawyer appears in court on behalf of the accused. When the man's name is called in court, he does not have to do anything more than simply identify himself. Everything will be taken care of by his advocate, who will see to it that things are conducted in such a way that his welfare will be safeguarded.

"And if any man sin, we have an advocate with the Father, Jesus Christ the righteous" (1 John 2:1). Christ intercedes in the presence of God for sinful man. He will not claim that the man has done no wrong. As an advocate, He will confess the man's sin before God. He will not stop with this, however; He will also remind God that a sacrifice has been offered, a substitution has been made. Because another has paid the penalty, it is perfectly right for God to forgive the penitent man of his sin.

"... because Christ also suffered for us, leaving us an example, that ye should follow his steps" (1 Peter 2:21). That puts the responsibility upon the Christian to be a priest, an advocate of other people, going into the presence of God and talking to Him for those people who for any reason look to the Christian for help in coming to receive the blessing of God. John says, "If any man see his brother sin a sin which is not unto death, he shall ask, and he shall give him life for them that sin not unto death" (1 John

The Priesthood

5:16). The Book of Hebrews states that the Lord Jesus Christ "is able to save them to the uttermost that come unto God by him, seeing he ever liveth to make intercession for them" (Heb. 7:25). That is why the Christian's salvation is sure, because the living Lord Jesus Christ is now interceding for him. Every Christian has priestly work to do in praying for others.

THE SHEKINAH GLORY

The whole Old Testament's program of worship was directed to bringing a sinner into the presence of God. When the sinner stood before God, his life would be affected and changed. It was therefore absolutely necessary for each person to come into the presence of God.

Someone might say, "Why doesn't the sinner just do that?" The reason a person could not come boldly into the presence of God is because the holiness of God is such that He would have to judge sin. He has to come before God in a way that is acceptable to Him. When a person is really aware of the greatness and the holiness of God and feels his own limitations, such a person has difficulty in coming to God and in feeling that he has satisfied God's requirements. Until he feels he has satisfied God's requirements, he cannot have the peace and joy he so sorely needs. When a man feels that somehow those with whom he is dealing are really holding something against him, he cannot enter into a full fellowship with them. In order to have a full fellowship with a person, I need to have an assurance there is nothing between me and that other person.

When a child has disobeyed his parents, the parents use discipline, sometimes prolonged discipline. The child may not be immediately willing to admit wrong. He may be rebellious or sulky. As long as the child's attitude is one of opposition, the parent cannot fully receive the child back again. This contention and tension can build up and so deeply affect the child that he is not sure he has fulfilled everything the parents required even though he may have done all he can. He has a feeling that perhaps his parents may still hold something against him. There must be some form of acceptance. It is often a case of "kiss and make up." Perhaps the mother takes the child into her arms and soothes the child in some way. If the quarreling is between men, a commonly recognized gesture for showing it is over and done is to "shake hands on it."

In the Bible God made use of this characteristic of mankind, and He had a way of showing man that everything was all right. The children of Israel built the tabernacle according to the exact plans given to Moses by God; each article of furniture was set in its prescribed place to aid the priest in approaching God; the priests further performed their required functions in the offering of the sacrifices; and when everything had been done exactly as it should be done, "Then a cloud covered the tent of the congregation and the glory of the Lord filled the tabernacle" (Ex. 40:34). This glory was so brilliant that no man could bear it. It is referred to as the *Shekinah Glory*—the visible manifestation of the Divine Majesty. *Shekinah* is a Hebrew word. There is no word for it in the English language. As nearly as can be told, this Hebrew word means "the glory of glories"—the most glorious glory of all, the brightest light that could possibly be.

Later when the temple was built, the Bible says, "that the cloud filled the house of the Lord, so that the priests could not stand to minister because of the cloud; for the glory of the Lord had filled the house of the Lord" (1 Ki. 8:10-11). This was again called the *Shekinah Glory*. It was a mark of God's approval upon complete, total obedience.

How would man know for sure that reconciliation between himself and God was complete? In the matter of atonement, how would the sinner know that the atonement for his sin had been satisfying to God? How would the worshipper know that the priest had offered the prayer that was acceptable to God? God arranged to show His approval by manifesting His presence in a bright cloud of glory.

An understanding of the term *Shekinah Glory* gives insight into Pentecost in the New Testament. Christian people understand that the church is the temple of the living God, the church being the Christian people themselves. "Seeing that he is Lord of heaven and earth, dwelleth not in temples made with hands" (Acts 17:24). Paul writes, "Know ye not that ye are the temple of God, and that the Spirit of God dwelleth in you?" (1 Cor. 3:16).

The Lord Jesus Christ had given His disciples certain instructions recorded in Acts 1 and 2. Christ had shown Himself alive to them; He had been with them some forty days, and He had spoken to them concerning the Kingdom of God. He also "commanded them that they should not depart from Jerusalem, but wait for the promise of the Father, which ye have heard of me ... ye shall be baptized with the Holy Ghost not many days hence" (Acts 1:4-5). The disciples had been waiting before God in prayer for ten days, during which time they arranged for someone to take Judas's place so there would again be twelve apostles. Everything was done strictly according as they had been told. They had been faithfully obedient to God. "And suddenly there came a sound from heaven as of a rushing mighty wind and it filled all the house where they were sitting. And there appeared unto them cloven tongues like as of fire, and it sat upon each of them" (Acts 2:2-3). There was a physical, outward manifestation that indicated the indwelling presence of God. "And they were filled with the Holy Ghost, and began to speak with other tongues" (Acts 2:4). "And there were dwelling in Jerusalem Jews ... out of every nation ... and every man heard them speak in his own language" (Acts 2:5-6). Here God is seen showing His approval of man's obedience by manifesting His presence. This was the real *Shekinah Glory*.

When reading the story of Pentecost, do not let the strange events and the unusual descriptions be discouraging and dim the eye from seeing the truth. The truth is that when man comes before God, faithfully, obediently seeking His face and yielding himself to Him, God will manifest His presence with the consciousness of Himself in man's heart. God is, and God can be approached. A sinning person can come to God He must come to God by accepting the sacrifice of the Lord Jesus Christ for his sins. Christ's blood will cause his sins to be removed, and he will come into the presence of God to worship, having met the requirements laid down by Him. God will manifest His presence to him and give him the assurance of His personal acceptance.

The Lord God, although man cannot see Him, knows man. Man's heart is an open book as far as God is concerned. When man obeys Him, comes to Him, yields to Him, commits himself in consecration to do His will, God will manifest Himself to man by giving him a sense of His presence. He will give His word. He will let men know they actually belong to Him.

The experience of being filled with the Holy Spirit of God, being conscious that God is with man, will comfort his heart, inspire him in service, and give assurance. Peter describes such persons as those "Who are kept by the power of God through faith unto salvation ready to be revealed in the last time" (1 Pet. 1:5).

The New Testament states that God will fill man with His Holy Spirit. Being filled with the Holy Spirit of God, in man's experience today, is the *Shekinah Glory* which is pictured in the tabernacle and in the temple of the Old Testament.

CHAPTER FIVE

Jesus Christ

IF I want to understand the Christian Gospel I need to know about Jesus Christ. There is much in matters of faith that is out of this world. God, heaven, eternity are all things that we cannot see with our eyes or handle with our hands. But Jesus of Nazareth lived in this world. It is true He was more than man, but for our sakes He became a man and lived among men. What He did, He did for men to see; what He said, He said for men to hear; and what happened to Him was what men did to Him. We need to know these things if we want to understand the truth of the Gospel.

He came into this world to show us the way to God, the truth about God, and the life that is in God. This was done so that "whosoever will may come." God wants all men to know what He is able and willing to do for anybody that will come to Him. In order that you and I might know enough so that we could come to God for help if we wanted to do so, Jesus Christ was born of a woman, lived and died in this world.

THE SON OF GOD

The basic element in the word *Christian* is *Christ,* which comes from the Greek word *Christos* meaning "to christen" or "to anoint." Anointing was a ceremony in which oil was poured on a person, indicating that that person was set aside for some specific purpose. Therefore, the title *Christ* was given to a person who had been anointed for a certain work which He was to do.

We use the word *Christ* as a title. It means much the same as the word *king* or *emperor.* The Hebrew word for Christ was *Messiah.* The word *Messiah* in the Old Testament means the same as the word *Christ* in the New Testament.

Where the word *Messiah* is used in the Hebrew language and

Christ is used in the Greek, *Caesar* is used in Latin, *Kaiser* in German, *Czar* in Russian, and *Shah* in Persian. These titles are all closely related to each other. They each refer to someone who has been selected for and installed in a certain office.

The Old Testament pointed forward to a time when God would send One Special Person to bring salvation to His people. Israel expected God would send His Anointed One to rule and to govern His people, and to set up His Kingdom on the earth. They called this expected Ruler the *Messiah*. The New Testament claims Jesus of Nazareth is the *Christ,* whom the Old Testament predicted would come. This means that Jesus is the One who is appointed of God to do His great work on earth.

When Christ Jesus is spoken of as "Son of God," reference is being made to His origin. He was "the Son of God" in a sense that He was *not* "the son of Adam." The title "the son of man" is given to Christ to show He had a human body. This does *not* imply that He was a sinner like all men. He was the "God-Man" but He was not a child of Adam. He was the Son of God. Because He *is* the Son of God, He is *God*.

The Bible speaks of Christians as being "the children of God." Does this mean when we become Christians we become "sons of God" in the same sense that Christ is "the Son of God"? The answer is a most emphatic "No!" Christ Jesus alone can be referred to as *the* Son of God, because He is the only one who was "begotten of God." There is *only one* Son of God who is both God and man. The Godhead is made up of the Father, the Son, and the Holy Spirit. The second person in the Godhead is the Son of God, who became Jesus of Nazareth. Christians become "sons of God" when they are *adopted* into the family of God. They are adopted by God when they receive Jesus Christ as their Saviour and Lord.

Whenever the word *son* is used, we naturally have in mind the word *father*. This is because they belong together. The Son of God belongs to the Father, and these two are alike. Jesus Himself said, "I and my Father are one."

When Jesus of Nazareth was baptized by John in the river Jordan, a voice from heaven said, "This is my beloved Son, in whom I am well pleased." In another place we read that a voice from heaven said, "This is my beloved Son: hear him." The Lord Jesus

Himself talked about how things were between His Heavenly Father and Himself. We read that at one time He said, "The Father loveth the Son, and hath given all things into his hands." On one of His last days on earth before His crucifixion, He prayed, "O, Father, glorify thou me with thine own self with the glory which I had with thee before the world was." In such Bible passages we get the idea that the Son of God is God and was always with God. He is eternally the Son of God. When He became flesh, He became flesh as Jesus of Nazareth, but He always was the Son of God. God did not reach out, take just any man, and make that man good enough and strong enough to bring His will to pass upon earth. He sent His own Son into the world to do that. He sent forth into this world His only begotten Son as Jesus of Nazareth, whom we call Christ, the Son of the living God. When we believe in Christ as the Son of God we are actually believing in God.

When Jesus of Nazareth was here on earth, He showed that God was willing to come down in human form to live among men in order that men could come to God. The Lord Jesus is the only begotten Son, but through Him believers have been adopted into the family of God with Him. As God came down into the world in the person of Jesus of Nazareth, so He wants men to come up to Him through faith in the Lord Jesus Christ.

Jesus of Nazareth was the human form in which the Son of God dwelt among men. He was the "Anointed One" of God who in this world was made in the form of man, but never ceased to be the Son of God. He was the "only begotten" Son of God throughout His earthly ministry. He is the second person of the Godhead—God the Father in heaven, God the Son, for a short while here on earth as Jesus of Nazareth, and God the Holy Spirit, who afterwards came that He might be in the hearts of men.

Some people use the expression "The Christ." The word *Christ* may be used that way. "The Christ" is God's "Anointed One" and is the title given to the Lord Jesus. Worded in that way it carries with it the idea that this is the One whom God chose and placed in this world to do His will.

THE INCARNATION

Jesus is a boy's name, just as children are named Tom or Henry or William. In Christian talk whenever the name *Jesus* is used it refers to the human being called Jesus who grew up at a particular time in a little village called Nazareth. In other words, whenever the name *Jesus* is used in the New Testament to refer to our Lord the human form of the Son of God is brought to mind.

The name *Jesus* is a Greek word. The same name in the Hebrew is *Joshua*. The name *Jesus* appears in the New Testament and the name *Joshua* in the Old Testament. The Hebrew name *Joshua* is really a phrase. It means "God is my Saviour" or "Jehovah is my salvation." The word *Jesus* freely translated means "God is my salvation."

What we mean by the *incarnation* is very nearly the same meaning as in *Jesus,* that God became flesh and took upon Himself the form of man. When the Bible says "the Word was made flesh" it means that God Himself took on a human form. This is what is called the *incarnation*.

When Paul tells what actually took place when the Son of God took a human form he brings out the idea that the Son of God was originally with God the Father. He then goes on to say that Christ Jesus "thought it not robbery to be equal with God." This means "He did not think it a thing to be grasped to remain equal with God." The word *robbery* pictures someone grasping or snatching something. And so Paul is saying that the Son of God who was God with God the Father did not think that it was something to be snatched at, something to be grasped, or something to be clutched to Himself to remain equal with God. He did not try to maintain His position, "But made himself of no reputation, and took upon him the form of a servant, and was made in the likeness of men: and being found in fashion as a man, he humbled himself, and became obedient unto death, even the death of the cross." Through this entire passage it is made clear that this Person existed before He was born in Bethlehem. He was with God the Father. Because He had in mind to do the Father's will, He left His heavenly place with the Father and came into this world. The old hymn sums it up:

> Out of the ivory palaces,
> Into a world of woe,
> Only His great eternal love
> Made my Saviour go.

No human being ever came into the world the way Jesus came.

Jesus Christ

No human being is ever thought of as having lived before and himself deciding to come into the world. Yet this is what the Son of God is reported as doing. The important idea here is that *Jesus was the Son of God before He ever became Jesus of Nazareth.* He existed from all eternity.

It was Jesus who in Gethsemane prayed to His Father and accepted His Father's will that He should be shut away from the presence of His Father in order to atone for man's sins. It was Jesus who went through human death and experienced separation from His Father. It was Jesus whom they took from Calvary's cross and laid His body in the grave. But all the time Jesus was the Son of God.

It was the very fact that the Lord Jesus Christ lived before He came into this world that made it so that He could not be born in the ordinary way, and He was not. The Bible teaches that He was "born of a virgin." The birth of Jesus of Nazareth is mentioned only twice in the New Testament. It is recorded in the first chapter of Matthew and in the first chapter of Luke, and each time it plainly says that He was born of a virgin. John simply says He was "born, not of blood, nor of the will of the flesh, nor of the will of man, but of God." We cannot fully understand how Almighty God could become a Babe in Bethlehem, but our difficulty in understanding this action of God does not change it in any way.

The only thing that was missing in the Lord Jesus Christ while He was on earth as Jesus of Nazareth was His glory. On the Mount of Transfiguration His glory was revealed for a few moments. Peter, James, and John were with Him, and they saw that "his face did shine as the sun, and his raiment was white as the light." Moses and Elijah were there talking with Him while these three Apostles were given a glimpse of the true glory of the Son of God which was veiled from their eyes while He was here on earth. What makes the suffering of the Lord Jesus Christ so tremendous? Is it not that He was the Son of God? What makes His yielding to wicked men so amazing? Is it not that He was the Son of God?

When Peter told Jesus that He should not go to the cross, Jesus answered Peter by saying, "Get thee behind me, Satan." Jesus had plainly told his disciples that He was going to die. When the time actually came for Him to be taken by the soldiers and arrested, however, Peter drew his sword and was willing to attack the whole Roman company to defend his Lord. Jesus told him to put up his sword, and added, "Thinkest thou that I cannot now pray to my Father, and he shall presently give me more than twelve legions of angels?" Certainly this plainly shows He was actually the Son of God. It is difficult to understand the humility of the life of the Lord Jesus Christ on earth. We must remember that Jesus of Nazareth was always with God and that He was God. In the human form of Jesus He yielded Himself and became obedient even to death. And this He was willing to do for us that He might show us the love of God and win us to put our trust in Him that we might be saved.

HIS EARTHLY MINISTRY

The life of the Lord Jesus Christ upon earth is commonly referred to as the earthly ministry of Jesus of Nazareth. This is a very general way of speaking. So far as is known, Jesus the Babe in Bethlehem was just like any other normal baby. He sat on His mother's knee. After returning to Galilee from Egypt with His parents, Joseph and Mary, He grew up in the town of Nazareth. Nothing is written to suggest anything extraordinary. The Bible does not describe the life of Jesus as a boy, but gives only a glimpse of what happened by telling about one brief incident which occurred when He was twelve years of age.

At that time He accompanied His parents to Jerusalem. Since He had reached the required age to be received as one of the men in the Jewish community, they put him through a sort of ceremony. This was when He was sitting with the doctors and asking them questions. Actually, the religious leaders were there to ask Jesus questions much the same as any of our young people would be examined for church membership after having completed a course of study in a Communicants' Class. In this case, it turned out that even though He was only a boy, He was asking the questions of the leaders and was astonishing them.

This story goes on to tell how Jesus became engrossed in talking with the doctors. When it was time to leave for Nazareth, Joseph and Mary did not look for Him, for they supposed He was with some of the relatives traveling in the caravan. After having traveled "a day's journey" they looked for Jesus and did not find Him in the family group. They had to go all the way back to Jerusalem, and there they found Him sitting in the Temple listening to the doctors and asking them questions. Mary took Him aside and said, "Son, why hast thou thus dealt with us? behold, thy father and I have sought thee sorrowing." Jesus said to Mary, "How is it that ye sought me? wist ye not that I must be about my Father's business?" However, we read further that Jesus went down with them to Nazareth and was subject to them in all things.

This incident is the only glimpse the Bible gives of the Lord Jesus from the time He was a little child brought back by Joseph from Egypt at the age of four or five or even less, until He was thirty years of age. The Bible does not mention anything about His youth. That is not important. The Lord Jesus was not living His life in this world the way human beings live their lives. He was the Son of God, and He was brought into this world for a purpose, to give His life a ransom for many. He came into this world to seek and to save the lost. To do that he would have to die in His human form.

At the age of thirty, Jesus began His public ministry. We may be sure that in those thirty years He was human in every way as we are, fashioned like us, made like us, and was "in all points tempted like as we are, yet without sin." When the Bible says "yet without sin," it is saying a tremendous thing. Certainly no human being can ever imagine what thoughts guided the mind of Jesus of Nazareth. Since the Lord Jesus Christ was without sin, there is no need for me to try to figure out what He thought.

I personally think that Jesus of Nazareth suffered in the course of His entire life. What would happen to a boy who would always tell the truth? What would happen to a boy among other boys, who would never do anything wrong? What would happen to a boy who would not fight to defend himself? Would such a one not lead a lonely life? The description of the Suffering Servant in Isaiah 53 very likely not only pictures the last three years of Jesus' life in His public ministry, but probably characterizes attitudes and receptions He encountered all the way through His earthly life.

At about thirty years of age, He began to preach; and when He preached, He preached like John the Baptist. He preached like a prophet of the Old Testament. He preached that God, who made a covenant with Abraham and with David, and who gave the law to Moses, was the living and true God and that all men should be genuinely, sincerely obedient to Him at all times. His preaching in itself attracted attention, but what really startled people and caused them to notice Him were His works, the miracles which He performed. The Gospels clearly show that in the days of His public ministry He exercised power and control over nature and over the lives of men. The element of the supernatural in the ministry of the Lord Jesus Christ cannot be denied.

In the first thirty years, Jesus probably lived very much like other people and did the things that other people would have done, but the Bible does not tell about them. When the Bible begins to tell about the work of the Lord Jesus Christ, every single work recorded is a work that could be done only by supernatural power.

One could say, "Well, I suppose He fed the poor." If anyone thinks Jesus fed the poor by taking some of His own food and giving it to them, that will be his own imagination. The Bible does not say that. What it relates is that Jesus took the lunch of a little boy, blessed it and fed five thousand people (Matt. 14:15-21). No human being could do that.

If it is thought that He helped people who were sick, certainly He did. But, if by helping people who were sick it is thought that He did a work such as the Good Samaritan did (Luke 10:30-37), that He stayed with them, took care of them, eased their suffering by pouring in oil and wine, this too would be left to one's imagination. The Bible nowhere states that He ever applied any such treatment to anyone in trouble. When the leper came and said, "Lord, if thou wilt, thou canst make me clean," Jesus touched him and said, "I will; be thou clean." And immediately his leprosy was cleansed. No mere human being could do that.

Jesus showed an amazing power over nature and the things of this world. Even the people who were with Him were astonished. He commanded the storm at sea, "Peace, be still" and it stopped. Those who were around Him said, "What manner of man is this, that even the wind and the sea obey him?"

A woman who had been sick for twelve years with an issue of blood and had spent all of her living on the doctors but was not helped saw Jesus passing and said in her heart, "If I may but touch his clothes, I shall be whole." She went to Him and touched the hem of His garment. Jesus turned around and said, "Who touched my clothes?" His disciples said, "Thou seest the multitude thronging thee, and sayest thou, Who touched me?" (Mark 5:30-31). Ah! but there had been one who had touched Him in a different way, and the woman knowing she had been healed came forward and fell trembling at His feet. She had merely said, "If I could just touch the hem of His garment, I would be well," and He told her to rise up and go her way, that her sins would be forgiven because of her faith.

Consider also His control over demons. Over and over He showed authority over demons and power to deliver human beings from their control. Men are skeptical today about such things but there is no question that this is what the Bible says.

No doubt the most awe-inspiring acts of Jesus were instances when He raised the dead to life. He warned all people that His acts of complete control over natural and spiritual elements showed He was God and was serving His Father in heaven. The earthly ministry of Jesus Christ shows evidence that God was with Him and He was doing the will of His Father.

HIS DEATH

The life of the Lord Jesus Christ upon earth was marked by a strange outlook. He came into the world to die.

Of course death comes to all people, but most persons put it off as long as possible. But the Lord Jesus came for the simple reason that He would die to save souls.

Shortly after Jesus had begun His public ministry, His disciples took Him to show Him the temple that was being built by Herod. Everyone in Jerusalem seemed interested in it; but Jesus made a comment which to His disciples sounded very strange. He said, "Destroy this temple, and in three days I will raise it up." His hearers did not then understand what he meant, but after the crucifixion and His resurrection they understood that He was speaking of the temple of His body. So we see that from the very beginning of His public ministry He knew He would die and that He would rise from the dead. The greatest thing the Lord Jesus Christ did was to lay down His life "a ransom for many." Death was something that Jesus knew was coming. He knew it was in the will of His Father that He should die in order to save those who would believe in Him.

The meaning of the death of the Lord Jesus Christ can be partly felt as we read of the Garden of Gethsemane. His agony there was not because He was afraid of death. Death of the body would not have mattered to Him, but in His death there was to be a separation from His Father. The eternal Son of God who loved the Father, and the Father who loved the Son, were to be separated, while the Lord Jesus took man's place and suffered for him the consequences of his sins. Sin alienates man from God. When the Lord Jesus Christ was made sin on man's behalf, the sin that was placed on Him took Him away from the presence of God the Father.

On the cross, Jesus cried out, "My God, my God, why hast thou forsaken me?" No doubt the idea of the Father's apparent forsaking of His Son raises a question: how could this be? We need to remember that in ways that go beyond human understanding, the Lord Jesus was made sin on our behalf. We know that God is unable to behold evil. So at the time the Lord Jesus Christ died for sinners, He was evidently in the presence of God bearing man's sins in Himself. The Father would have nothing to do with Him because of the sins. The Father apparently turned away and let Him die. In that separation the Lord Jesus Christ experienced the terrible agony and suffering which was so hard for Him to bear as He thought about it in Gethsemane.

The Bible tells us that while praying in Gethsemane Jesus asked the Father to spare Him if that were possible. Jesus was praying that if there was any other way to save sinners, any way other than by His separation from the Father, let it be done that way. But regardless of His own wishes, if it was necessary for Him to die in order to save sinners, He asked God's will to be done. There is a great lesson for Christians to learn from this prayer of the Lord Jesus. The Bible tells us "Let your requests be made known unto God." The request of the Lord Jesus Christ in Gethsemane was "Father, if it be possible, take away this cup from me." That was His request, but that was not His prayer. His prayer was, "Nevertheless not what I will, but what thou wilt." The Lord Jesus came out of the Garden with peace which He could share with others. When once He openly yielded to the will of His Father, He was able to face death without any concern.

The question is often asked: If the Lord Jesus knew what the

Father promised Him, why was He distressed? The answer involves an understanding of love. Jesus was distressed apparently because He was to be separated from the One He loved, and to think of such separation would be agony.

The death of Jesus was a *vicarious* sacrifice. The word *vicarious* means "He took my place." I should have been judged for sin; Jesus should have gone free, but He moved over in my place, took my sin on Him, and was judged for my sin so that I could go free. I who deserved to die was allowed to go free, and Jesus who deserved to live came and died in my place. This is the significance of the death of the Lord Jesus Christ. This is the Good News, the Gospel, which we preach over the whole world. It is just as true for everyone and for anyone as it is for me. "Whosoever believeth in him shall not perish, but have everlasting life."

HIS RESURRECTION

The resurrection of the Lord Jesus Christ is perhaps the greatest event in all history. Perhaps I am no different from any other person who is earnest, sincere and honest with himself when I wish that I were better than I am. I would like to be free from the things that hinder, bother, and lead me into trouble. Now I am thrilled to realize it is possible for me to be free. Freedom from everything that hinders or that hurts is made possible by the resurrection of Jesus Christ from the dead.

What actually happened in the resurrection of the Lord Jesus Christ was that a body which died was raised from the dead different from what it was in life. A body that had died was raised into a better life than it had before. The resurrection is not so much that man gets a second start. It is that man gets another start on a different basis, better than anything he ever had before. This is to be seen in the resurrection of the Lord Jesus.

The story of the resurrection is familiar to us all: Jesus was put to death on the cross in the way we call crucifixion. This was not an uncommon event. It was the way all criminals were put to death in those days when Jesus lived. To us it is a cruel, rough way of doing, but the point is that His body was killed and the soldiers checked to make sure He was dead. They pierced His side with a spear to be positively certain He was dead. Then they certified

His body as actually dead. After that He was laid in the tomb. This is the whole story of what happened as far as the action of the soldiers went.

Today the bodies of the dead are buried in graves usually underground. We need to remember that when Jesus was buried, He was put in a tomb which is similar to a vault. It was a cave in the side of a hill, large enough for a man to walk into.

The body of Jesus was wrapped in linen cloth, so His friends could wait until after the Sabbath Day to embalm Him with perfume after the custom of that time. The dead body of Jesus lay in the grave for three days, and when they came to embalm Him it was gone. The grave clothes were lying folded on one side. They did not know what had happened. They thought maybe someone had stolen the body away.

When the Lord Jesus appeared to Mary Magdalene later that morning, she thought He was the gardener. Jesus called her by name, and suddenly she knew who it was. Mary hurried to the disciples and said she had seen the Lord, but they did not believe her. None of them were ready to believe such a story.

That same night, however, while they were all together in a room with the door shut, Jesus appeared in their midst. They were terrified. They thought they saw a ghost, an apparition of some sort. Jesus spoke to reassure them, "Peace be unto you ... Behold my hands and my feet that it is I myself: handle me, and see; for a spirit hath not flesh and bones, as ye see me have." When He saw that some of them still wondered and apparently could not believe, He said, "Have ye here any meat?" The Bible says they gave Him a piece of a broiled fish, and a honeycomb. He took the food and ate it before them. We would call this a scientific demonstration that they could trust their eyesight. They were not being fooled. A man might imagine seeing a ghost, but a ghost would not eat a piece of fish. There must have been a body there to eat that food. After this demonstration Jesus disappeared from their midst.

Thomas had not been with them the night Jesus appeared, and when he was told what happened, he would not believe it. He said, "Except I shall see in his hands the print of the nails, and put my finger into the print of the nails, and thrust my hand into his side, I will not believe." Eight days later they were all together again.

Thomas was present this time. The Lord Jesus appeared, went immediately to Thomas, and said, "Reach hither thy finger, and behold my hands; and reach hither thy hand, and thrust it into my side: and be not faithless but believing." Thomas was completely convinced, and fell at His feet saying, "My Lord and my God."

The Bible does not leave room for any idea other than that the body of Jesus Christ was raised from the dead. While it was the same body with nail prints and spear wound, it was now made of different stuff. Before His resurrection, Jesus did not appear and disappear at will. He did not pass through closed doors. However, after His resurrection He could do these things. This is important because in our resurrection we will be like Him.

Consider also the ascension of the Lord Jesus. His body was taken up away from this earth beyond the clouds into heaven. This brings up questions. I used to wonder: Where would Jesus get oxygen to breathe? What I needed to realize was that Jesus did not have the kind of body that needed oxygen. He did not have the kind of body that needed food. He could eat food, but He did not need it. He had a body that Paul describes as a "heavenly" body in 1 Corinthians 15. After His resurrection Jesus had the kind of body believers are going to have when they are raised from the dead, because the resurrection of the Lord Jesus Christ was the first-fruits of the resurrection from the dead which all believers will experience. All shall be changed as He was changed in the nature of His body.

It is important to realize that all shall be changed, for someone might think that when people are raised from the dead they will be as they were when last seen in this world. At that time they may have been suffering from illness, weak, emaciated by disease. Their bodies may have been very frail. Their resurrected bodies will not be frail. No disease and weakness can come to them. If somebody by some misfortune lost a leg in this world, he will not have just one leg in the resurrection. If somebody by some mishap was blinded, he will not be raised from the dead with eyes that cannot see. Those raised from the dead, having had faith and trust in the Lord Jesus Christ, will have bodies like His body which is called a glorified body. The body that belonged to this earth was ashes and dust, but the body that was raised from the dead was a body of spiritual reality and heavenly substance. This spiritual body could appear and disappear at will and ascend into heaven in apparent defiance of the laws of gravitation.

Another life, better than this one, is available to all who put their trust in the Lord Jesus Christ. Such persons will be raised from the dead. The resurrection brings out the truth that there is life after death. Death is not the final end for anybody. The body will be raised from the dead when the Lord Jesus Christ returns. There is also such a thing as death of the spirit. Death can occur in the whole personality, body, soul and spirit. The spirit can be raised from the dead, and it is so raised when one is born again. The Bible speaks of believers being "quickened" who once were dead in trespasses and sins.

Resurrection, living again after death, will occur to all men, both the just and the unjust. In the case of the believer, the resurrection will be to newness of life. "We shall be like him" (1 John 3:2). How can a person live again? This was very hard for me to grasp when I first seriously considered the Gospel. It helped me to believe this when I reflected on the first birth. The God that made me out of nothing the first time should be able to make me again in the resurrection if He wanted to do so. The God that raises men from the dead is the God who made men out of nothing. He is Almighty God.

HIS ASCENSION

The *ascension* of the Lord Jesus Christ is seldom understood for what it really means. This word refers to the occasion when the body of the Lord Jesus Christ was taken from this world up into heaven. That was truly an amazing event.

In our study of the resurrection we noted that it was the resurrected body of the Lord Jesus which ascended into heaven. In this world His body was composed of the elements of the earth; now it is made of heavenly, spiritual elements. When the Lord Jesus Christ died on Calvary's cross, He went through the experience of human death with an earthly body. When He was raised from the dead, He was raised in a body that does not die. He has a spiritual body which is alive now.

The truth of eternal life is difficult for the human mind to understand; for the mind is, for the most part, limited by the senses. Into this mind is thrust the idea that Jesus of Nazareth, who died and was raised from the dead nearly two thousand years ago, is alive today. The Bible is very simple and clear when it states, "He shewed himself alive after his passion by many infallible proofs, being seen of them forty days, and speaking of the things pertaining to the kingdom of God." At the end of the forty days, while He was speaking to them and blessing them, "He was taken up; and a cloud received him out of their sight."

The Scriptures tell us of two instances in the Old Testament when a human body was taken directly into heaven. Before the flood, it is related that "Enoch walked with God: and he was not; for God took him." The New Testament says, "By faith Enoch was translated that he should not see death; and was not found, because God had translated him" (Heb. 11:5). *Translate* is a very good word to use. If a man speaks in Russian and his words are translated into English, those words are not Russian any more. They are changed. It can be assumed that everything that happened to the body of Jesus Christ at the resurrection happened to the body of Enoch. The Bible does not tell us any more about Enoch than that he was taken into the presence of God. His body was taken from this world and translated from the natural body into a spiritual body.

The narrative describing the departure of Elijah from this world pictures a much more dramatic event. Elijah was with Elisha, who was to be his successor, "And it came to pass, as they still went on, and talked, that, behold, there appeared a chariot of fire, and horses of fire, and parted them both asunder; and Elijah went up by a whirlwind into heaven." There is much about each of these events we do not know, but there can be no doubt as to what happened.

The ascension of the Lord Jesus Christ is presented in a much clearer, precise way because preparation was made for His ascension by the resurrection from the dead. It has been emphasized that the body after the resurrection was of different stuff. This body was taken up from the earth in full view of people and in apparent defiance of the laws of gravity. It is not known that the law of gravitation was broken, because the kind of stuff of which that body was made is not known. Occasionally some magician claims to be able to make a body float. The technical term for that is *levitation*. That is not involved in the ascension. Jesus' body was actually taken away out of this world. He had appeared and disappeared at will for forty days. He could have been taken into heaven at any of His disappearances, but God did not want it that way. God wanted man to see the transition taking place. He wanted a witness to the act of the body's leaving this world and being taken into the other world. God had this thing done when it could be seen so that men could understand it in their minds.

After His ascension into heaven, the Bible refers to Christ as sitting at the right hand of God. The expression "at the right hand of God" does not refer to a location. It is a term of special privilege with God. It is a position of power. Christ is right next to His Father. There are many things about heaven which man does not understand. From what God has allowed to be revealed, it can be said that the Lord Jesus Christ is with the Father. He is in personal fellowship with the Father as one person would be standing or sitting alongside another person in this world. As far as the location of heaven is concerned, that is something which God has kept secret. Here we do well to remember that "The secret things belong unto the Lord our God: but those things which are revealed belong unto us and to our children for ever, that we may do all the words of this law" (Deut. 29:29).

The ascension of the Lord Jesus was witnessed and recorded so that man might know that there is a world other than this one and that Jesus Christ is in it. If I could remember day in and day out that there is a world other than this one, this world would not bother me so much. If I would just keep in mind that there is a life other than this one, this life would not trouble me so much when things go badly with me. This life is not going to last. The other life will last forever. Heaven is real, and every believer in the Lord Jesus Christ is going there. We have that expectation. In that other world there are persons with whom fellowship will be had. God is there. The Lord Jesus Christ is there. The Apostle Paul says, "But I would not have you to be ignorant, brethren, concerning them which are asleep, that ye sorrow not even as others which have no hope. For if we believe that Jesus died and rose again, even so them also which sleep in Jesus will God bring with him."

The promise of God is that all men shall have their bodies raised from the dead. Jesus Christ is now alive at the right hand of God.

Jesus Christ

Man, too, will live again in the presence of God. At the present time at the right hand of God, the Lord Jesus is interceding for us. By His Holy Spirit, He can make me aware of His presence with me now. This means I can become conscious of His presence here in this world. The Lord is really alive and in the presence of God, and His presence is actually with us. In the presence of God, Christ Jesus is waiting to return to this world.

When I keep these things in mind, life in this world can never be the same for me. Just as Jesus Christ was raised from this world and taken into the presence of God, so will all of us who put our faith and trust in Him be raised from this world and taken into the presence of God.

THE HEAD OF THE CHURCH

The Lord Jesus Christ definitely belongs to a certain group of people here on earth. The Bible speaks of Him as being *the Head of the church*. Christ's position as Head of the church must not be thought of as a position to which one is selected. Christ is the Head of the church in the same sense that a human body has a head. This means there is a functional relationship between Christ and His people on earth. The living Lord Jesus Christ in heaven thinks for, guides, and directs the activities of His people here on earth.

Sometimes when meetings are held to decide and vote on some policy regarding something in the church, prayer is made that the Lord Jesus Christ as the Head of the church will give guidance to help the church in making the right decision. That is a very proper prayer, but somehow it does not cover all that the Lord Jesus Christ is doing. He not only overrules to bring the right decisions to pass, but He actually guides the thinking of each member.

When I believe in the Lord Jesus Christ, accept Him as my Saviour, acknowledge Him as my Lord, and am inwardly minded to be obedient and willing to do His will, He sends His Holy Spirit into my heart. The Holy Spirit works in the Christian that which is well-pleasing in the sight of God. When the Holy Spirit is inwardly moving me to do certain things, this is by the will of the Lord Jesus Christ.

The common problem of the average Christian is that, although he is a child of God in Christ Jesus in the Holy Spirit, yet as long as he lives in this world he is a child of his parents and a child of

Adam in the flesh. Every Christian has some inward conflict between being a child of Adam (a child of the flesh) and being a child of God (a child of the Spirit).

The truth of the matter is that even though I am a Christian, I still have what is known as the old man or the old nature, as well as the new man or the new nature. The old nature in me makes me concerned about what I am going to do as a human being. The psychologists and sociologists would try to help me figure out the answer from a human point of view. They claim that if they know where a man was born, whom he grew up with, whom he has been going around with, and what is happening to him at the present time, they can very nearly tell what he is going to do. The Christian with a real relationship with the Lord Jesus Christ will be a puzzle to any psychologist or sociologist on the face of the earth. The Christian is going to do some things for which there is neither rhyme nor reason so far as this world is concerned.

There is no way in human thinking to explain why a person will take money that he has worked for, earned, and saved, and give it to be shared with people in Africa, in Brazil, in Mexico, in Korea. Others would use that money for themselves, but this person gives it to missions because he feels inwardly moved to do it. Sometimes the Christian is conscious of that inward movement. Perhaps in a church service, the words of the sermon prompt one to action. But many times the Christian is not even conscious of what is happening when he finds himself thinking in his heart, "I am going to have to do this." The Christian is being inwardly moved to do these things by the One who is the Head of the church.

Christ is the Head of the believer the way the physical head is the head of the arm, the hand, or the foot. The actions of the hands are decided by the head. The head wills to do and the hands do as they are willed to do, if the man is healthy and well. If a man gets to the place where he cannot move, he is paralyzed; he is sick. Also, if the hands act when the man does not want them to, he has "a case of nerves"; he is really sick. If, however, the members of the body are under control and are obedient to the head, then they act according to the way man wants them to act.

It is the same way between the Christian and the Lord Jesus Christ. If I belong to Christ in a way which is sound and healthy and true, my actions will be motivated and guided by Him. Christians belong to each other as members of Christ's body, and He is the Head of the body.

The Lord Jesus Christ is alive and in the presence of God. He is seated at the right hand of God, having communion with His Father. It is the will of the Lord Jesus to do His Father's will. When the will of the Lord Jesus is manifested in me by the Holy Spirit, I have the desire to be well-pleasing in the sight of God. This desire to be well-pleasing in God's sight is the Lord's moving in me to do this thing. When I try to express my thoughts in prayer, my thoughts may be inadequate, they may even be wayward, and I may not be able to express exactly what I have in my heart; but while I am praying to the Father, the will of the Lord Jesus Christ who is in the presence of God will affect my own praying. The Lord Jesus always says "Thy will be done." In that sense, as Head of the church, He inclines me to do the will of God. The will of the living Lord Jesus Christ is the Christian's motivating power. At this very moment and always, Christ wills to do the will of God, and all I need to do is to yield myself to Him. Christ is now in heaven in the very holy place of God, and there He is as a high priest interceding on my behalf. He not only intercedes on behalf of my sins, He is actually interceding for what I am to do. He is interceding on behalf of each Christian's individual problems.

Let me illustrate it in this manner. Let us say that I am to live through tomorrow. In that twenty-four hours there will be many things which I will face, decisions I must make, situations I must live through. The Lord Jesus Christ, in the presence of God, knows all about my problem tomorrow. He knows the course I am going to take. It is the infinite Lord, who is never weary nor overcome and who shall not fail or be discouraged, who is praying to His Father and prays me into the will of God. When tomorrow unfolds, the only thing I in my human consciousness can contribute is a humble willingness to be obedient and to follow His will. He guides me. I may not always understand why or how, but I can always yield. I can yield in complete confidence because He has planned what will come to me to do. He has prepared the good works in which I am to serve Him. He sets up the situation, and I am moved to do my little part in obedience to Him. That is my place of service.

Often we feel it would be wonderful if every time a Christian did something it amounted to a notable victory. We think it would be a fine thing if every single play made in a game scored a touchdown. We imagine a wonderful way to live the day through would be for everything to be marvelously successful. But things do not work out that way. While the Lord Jesus Christ was here on earth, He was perfect and did the will of His Father at all times; yet He had days of sorrow and grief. If I choose to live along with Him, I too will have sorrows and grief; but I will never be alone. The Christian can rejoice in the Lord because his joy is in Him. Christ is his Saviour and his Lord. Everything is safe in Him, and the Christian belongs to Him. The believer goes through each day walking in the will of God because Christ in the presence of God is interceding on his behalf.

HIS COMING AGAIN

When thinking about the Lord Jesus Christ, it is natural to think of His earthly career. He was born as a babe in Bethlehem; He taught, performed miracles, and did astonishing things; He suffered death. The grave did not hold Christ, however, for the Bible reveals His resurrection, His ascension, and His presence at the right hand of God. And this can seem to be the complete story.

But the Scriptures further promise that the Lord Jesus Christ *will come again*. Christ first came as a servant in humility. He will come again as a king in glory. The prophets foretold that Christ was coming once, and a great many people did not believe it. Christians say He did come; many do not believe it. The Bible says He is coming again, and there are many who do not believe that. All the truths that are in the Gospel—the reality of heaven, God, the soul, eternal life, the resurrection, the ascension, His being at the right hand of God—prepare man to believe that from the presence of God, Christ will come.

Sometimes the second coming of Christ is referred to as the second *advent*. The word *advent* is not a common English word. It means *coming in* or *coming forth*. Some churches recognize one Sunday in the year as Advent Sunday, on which the first coming of the Lord Jesus Christ is remembered. The second advent is His coming again.

He is coming as a person. He will, as Acts 1:11 states, be "this same Jesus" who was seen going into heaven who will come. People often have the idea that spreading the influence of the Gospel is the same as the coming of the Lord Jesus. These two ideas are not the same. When speaking about Christ's coming again, the Bible means to say He will come again in person.

The coming of the Lord may be thought sometimes to be the Lord's coming into our personal experience. This could happen when several people have been planning or working on some projects of service. Maybe they started thinking as human beings, worked along for a length of time, and then paused for a period of prayer. They had been trying to figure the matter out for themselves, but now they wait, as it were, for the coming of the Lord. They ask the Lord to take a hand in this thing and to take over the leadership of it in such a way that they no longer feel they are doing it themselves but He is doing it. The Lord's participation could be thought of in that way, but this is not a fulfillment of the promise of His return. The fulfillment of that promise is that the body which left this world in the ascension is the body that is to return.

When the Bible speaks of Christ's coming again in power and glory, it is made plain that this coming will be greatly different from His coming as the Babe of Bethlehem. On that occasion He came in humility. He had emptied Himself of His glory. Christ was seen in glory on the Mount of Transfiguration when Peter, James and John were with Him. Glory shone around Him. When He comes again He will come in glory.

Poets sometimes describe the coming of the Lord Jesus Christ as the coming of a beggar to the door. It is intimated that the way the person treats a beggar would be the way he would treat the Lord if it were the Lord who was there. We may well appreciate what the poet is trying to say. He may even be attempting to convey the thought the Lord Jesus expressed in "Inasmuch as ye have done it unto one of the least of these my brethren, ye have done it unto me." The idea is that if I neglect to help the beggar, I have refused Christ. If, however, I do help the beggar, then I have honored Christ. The Lord Jesus takes man's rejection or acceptance of the beggar personally. This is the general idea that if a person helps the poor, he is helping Christ; if he ignores the poor, he is ignoring

Christ; because Christ is concerned with the poor. No matter how true such emphasis may be, this is not the meaning of Christ's coming in power and glory.

When Christ comes in power and in glory, He will be here in person. He will be here in a way which the Bible describes as brighter than the noonday sun. There will be nothing of the beggar about Him when He comes in glorious majesty. Some people have seen Christ since He has ascended into heaven. One of those who saw Him was Saul, the Pharisee. You will remember how Saul was on his way to Jerusalem by way of Damascus when "there shined around about him a light from heaven: And he fell to the earth, and heard a voice saying unto him, 'Saul, Saul, why persecutest thou me?' And he said, 'Who art thou, Lord?' And the Lord said, 'I am Jesus whom thou persecutest.' " This experience blinded Saul. John, who wrote the Revelation, saw Christ on the Isle of Patmos and he "fell at his feet as dead." Christ now is glorified and will never be seen apart from His glory.

When talking about seeing the Lord Jesus Christ, a Christian may at times in his enthusiasm say he wishes that the Lord would reveal Himself. From the standpoint of working with men and letting the Holy Spirit minister to men's hearts, taking the humble effort of the Christian witness and turning such into something powerful and strong, this could be all well and good. But, before asking the Lord Jesus to reveal Himself, I should be prepared for something terrific. It would be a light that would blind the eyes. No human being has been able to stand in His presence in glory. It is as if one took an ordinary electric appliance and ran power through it that was a hundred times stronger than it was built to use. That appliance would just burn out. This is exactly how Christ's appearance would affect man. We need not dwell longer on that. When the time comes that the Lord will be revealed, we will be changed. To those who believe, it will be a wonderful, glorious thing; but it will be terrible to those who do not believe; because He will be coming to judge all men, both the quick and the dead.

When Christ comes, He will also receive His own to Himself. Paul says that, at the sound of the trumpet announcing His coming, the dead in Christ shall rise first and then those who are alive and remain shall be caught up together with them and so shall they ever be with the Lord.

The second coming of Christ is something the believer can carry in his mind and cherish. It is in the plan of God. But long ago my father-in-law warned me not to let my mind settle itself only on the time when Christ would come back to this world. He said it would be far more wholesome for me to think in terms of the time when I will go to see Him. The Lord may not come back for a thousand years, but I am going to see Him long before that, because every Christian person when absent from the body is present with the Lord. The Christian is not far from seeing the Lord at any time.

The world is also going to see Him, because He is coming back to earth to show Himself. Every eye shall see Him. "Wherefore God also hath highly exalted him, and given him a name which is above every name: that at the name of Jesus every knee should bow, of things in heaven, and things in earth, and things under the earth; And that every tongue should confess that Jesus Christ is Lord, to the glory of God the Father" (Phil. 2:9-11).

CHAPTER SIX

The Gospel

THE *Gospel* of the Lord Jesus Christ means the *good message,* the *glad tidings,* or the *good news.* The *glad tidings* is taken from the word *evangel* and the word *evangel* is taken directly from the Greek.

When I was just a boy, I used to hear that the church was the place where the Gospel was preached. I did not know what the word *Gospel* was supposed to mean. When I found out that it meant good news, I couldn't understand why they said that, because, as far as I could remember, what I heard at church was what not to do. Why should that be good news?

The preacher seemed always to be criticizing or scolding people. When he told the people they were not doing right, he had preached a good sermon. We knew we were doing wrong, and he kept telling us that we were going to be punished. This made us afraid, but we would go out and do wrong anyway, hoping that maybe he had exaggerated the whole thing. We didn't really pay much attention to what the preacher said. If he was not scolding, he was lamenting about something that was not as it ought to be; or he was pushing us to do something different from what we were then doing. Most of us had the feeling that when we went to church we were going to take a whipping. In church we found out we were supposed to do right; and if we did wrong, we could look forward to going to hell. Nobody I knew except the people in church talked about hell, and the church people did not talk about it much; yet it seemed they should and were supposed to. At least that was the impression I got.

How would anyone get an idea of the Gospel from that? Of course, man should not do any wrong, but we did wrong. Who then could go to heaven? The good people went to heaven, but who

The Gospel

were the good people? Good people were the people who didn't do anything wrong, but such people did not exist. Who, then, would they be? Babies? They have never done anything wrong. Yes, I got the idea that church people thought all babies went to heaven, and also old folks so decrepit that they could not walk down to the corner. Such folks would go to heaven, but who else? Maybe a few sweet ladies and an occasional Francis of Assisi type of fellow whom we had never seen but whom we had read about. Somebody like that might go to heaven. Angels were in heaven, but the farmers I grew up with were not going to heaven. Not any of them. I knew that perfectly well.

Let me share one more childhood impression of the church with you. Regular churchgoers were a glum, stern crowd. The men were strict, and the women, I thought, were a bitter, nasty, nosy, gossipy lot. When we boys went to church, we were threatened and warned. When we did wrong, it seemed as if somebody were gloating over us, and our sure punishment. Now, we were really going to get it! With such thoughts in mind, what would the *Gospel* be? Good news? What would that mean? For whom would be the good news?

I used to think, it would be a laugh if the sinners were the ones who were going to have the good news. I had always heard that the good news was for the good people. I was in high school before I found out that the Gospel *was* for sinners. Did the Gospel mean that the sinners should be good? That would be like telling frogs to fly. To tell sinners to be good is just to fill them with despair. Then what would the *Gospel* be?

Sinners must be told that they can be saved. There is still one step to go, however, because when sinners are told they can be saved, they think they can be saved only if they become angels. They must grasp the idea that they can be saved while they are sinners as they are. The Gospel is for the blind, the maimed, the crippled, the diseased, the paralyzed, and those who cannot talk. When can such people have this blessing? *Now!* Good news to the sinner is that he can be saved *now,* and he can come as he is. He does not have to step over any threshold, climb any stairs or mountains, run any fast mile, or swim any river. He can come *now* to the Lord, and the Lord will save him. I know, by the grace of God, that that is the way the Bible states it. The Bible tells that sinners gathered around the Lord Jesus Christ so much that the church people criticized Him because He was associating with sinners. They described Him as "a friend of publicans and sinners." Why would sinners gather around Jesus? Would they be drawn to someone who was going to condemn them? No. They would gather around someone who could save them and would receive them.

REPENTANCE

There are a number of words to understand in order to get the idea of the Gospel. The first word is *repent*. When thinking of the word *repent* or *repentance,* there are at least two general ideas that are not repentance. *Repentance* does not mean to be sorry for some wrong I have done. It may be quite proper that I should be sorry, but this is not *repentance*. Being sorry for sin does not help. It has no value. It is like crying over spilt milk. Certainly one should cry if he spilt the milk. When I was a boy if I ever spilt the milk, I had better start crying right then and continue until my mother got through with me, because it would be a crying situation. But all my crying would never get the milk back up. There is something about *repentance* far more significant than feeling bad over wrong acts.

Some may think repentance is promising to do good. I do not want to seem to be too harsh, but how much good is it going to do for anyone to promise to do good? I don't know about others, but I can tell about myself. It makes me think of New Year's resolutions. They just don't work out. Why not? Well, consider who it is who says he is going to do good. It is the person who has been doing bad. Why did he do bad? He did bad because he was who he was. He was just a bad guy, and he wanted to do what he did. Men do as they do, because they are as they are. Unless something happens to me, I will always be just as I have been. There is very little more a man can do than he is doing now unless God changes him.

Repentance is primarily a judgment about myself. The expression so often used, which has an awkward translation into English, is, "repenting of our sins." Actually this is not a sound idea. The reason it is so awkward to say is that man does not "repent his sins" nor does he "repent of his sins"; he repents himself. Repentance is a judgment upon myself whereby I admit that I am not good. I realize that I just do not have it in me to do right things as I myself think I should.

Repentance is a very important matter. Because it is not until I am willing to acknowledge before God that I am nothing in myself that I will believe the Gospel. It is when I am willing to empty myself that I am open to receive the Lord Jesus Christ. As long as I have my own ideas, I do not want Christ's; but when I am willing to think that I am not what I should be and I am not going to be what I ought to be, then I am ready to turn to the Lord.

At one time the Lord Jesus told righteous people that the publicans and harlots would get into the kingdom of God before they did! Why was He so harsh with them? Because the righteous people thought they had something in themselves and so would not turn to God for help. Those who understand the Gospel know they have nothing in themselves to merit salvation, and so they are ready to turn to God in repentance. They judge themselves to be incompetent and unfit, and they look to God for help. It is wonderful to know they can have help from Him to save their souls.

BELIEVING

The preaching of both John the Baptist and Jesus of Nazareth was based upon the text "Repent ye, and believe the Gospel." Man must hear something if he is to believe it. Man cannot believe something he has not heard, but that does not mean he will know and understand everything fully when he has heard and says, "I believe." Man can believe what he hears but does not yet know from experience. If he had actually had the experience then he would know, and he would not have to say he believed. There is always an element of looking forward to something which has not been revealed, which has not yet happened, which has not been seen, in believing. Man can look ahead in the promises of God, to what God said He would do for man and he can believe that. He can also look at what the Lord Jesus Christ has done and believe that it is valid for men today. This is taking something to be true which has not yet been demonstrated.

Believing, however, does not make anything real and true. It is one of the sad facts of experience that a person can believe error. To believe a wrong thing is disastrous, just as swallowing poison by mistake is disastrous. A person may believe a glass is filled with milk, but believing the liquid to be milk does not make it milk. The person can give it to a baby, and if by chance it should be a poisonous liquid, the baby would receive it, swallow it, and die. True, it would be a mistake, but the result would be disastrous.

Believing is like swallowing. In believing anyone or anything, a person puts his trust in that person; he commits himself to that thing. If the person is reliable, he is fortunate. If the thing is good, he is again fortunate. In believing, there is always the commitment of oneself to something and reaping the results, whatever they may be.

In the English language, the physical expression *swallowing* and the word *believe* have been brought together. Someone may tell a story, and the listener may wonder if it could be true. Someone else standing by may ask the listener, "Do you swallow that?" meaning "Would you believe it? Would you take as true what this man says?" When one swallows anything, he has committed himself to the consequences of taking the substance into his system. A person can look at the liquid in the spoon as long as he wants to, and as long as he does not take it into his mouth it may be still a matter of opinion as to what it is; but when he takes it into his mouth and swallows it down his throat, he has committed himself to the consequences, whatever they may be. If the consequences are good, the man is fortunate; if they are bad, he is unfortunate. The fact that he thought it was this or that will not change it. Believing that a thing is good does not make it good. It simply inclines one to take it because he thinks it is good.

Believing is not a matter of knowing for sure. Anyone who has been in the business world any length of time will know that believing in the wrong man can hurt you. Because a man makes a good proposition and another man considering partnership with him believes him and invests his money does not mean that the man is honest and sincere. I may believe another man is honest and sincere, but my faith will not make him possess these attributes. If he is a good man, I have lined up with a good man. If he is a bad man, I have lined up with a bad man. Believing always has an element of risk about it.

Many people are inclined to hold back from believing because they think they should come to the place where they finally really

The Gospel

know before they act. However, believing is getting to the place where one has sufficient evidence upon which to risk faith, and then committing oneself to this. Believing always has in it the spirit of *adventure*. The Bible speaks of Noah and Abraham as possessing this spirit. Noah acted in faith when he built the ark before it began to rain; he believed God even though there was no immediate evidence for him. Abraham left his home land and ventured into an unknown country simply because God called him to go. To go, when one does not know where he is going, simply because he has been called to go, that is faith.

There is also an element of *volition* in believing. One says, "I will take this. I choose this." The word *believing* is often used in the phrase *believing on*. Thus I may speak of "believing on God" or "believing on the Lord Jesus Christ." *Believing on* the Lord Jesus Christ is like *believing on* a bridge. Suppose I come to a river and find the water so deep the only way to cross is to go over a bridge. Let us say that spanning the river is a bridge which does not look very safe to me. I am not an engineer, and even if I were I would not know for sure about the present condition of the bridge. Apparently the whole matter of getting over the river will depend on whether or not I will *believe on* the bridge. The only way for me to get across the river would be to trust the entire weight of my car and myself on the bridge. This is what *believing on* the bridge would amount to.

Another illustration might be to think of *believing in* a doctor. Suppose I am sick and I know there are many doctors in the community. Someone draws my attention to a specific one, Dr. Greene, and I decide to make Dr. Greene my doctor. A friend may ask, "Why have you chosen this particular doctor?" I would answer, "I believe in him." "What do you mean when you say you believe in him?" I would answer, "I think he is competent, and he is a very good doctor." Saying that I believe in Dr. Greene is not really going to make any difference in my physical condition. I am only saying that if and when I do go to a doctor I will go to Dr. Greene, but that does not yet mean I am going. The matter of actually letting Dr. Greene be my doctor and *believing in* him is going to require that I go down to Dr. Greene's office and let him treat me. I must commit myself to Dr. Greene. Suppose Dr. Greene is a surgeon and in his examination he finds that it looks as though I have cancer. He tells me that I am to come to the hospital and have an operation. I do not really, in the practical sense, *believe in* the surgeon until I go to the hospital and allow the surgeon to perform his work on me. When I submit myself in this fashion, I am *believing in* the doctor.

Believing in the Lord Jesus Christ has in it that same sort of participation with Him. We need to see this, because very often believing is said to be just a matter of opinion. Actually whether I choose to believe in this or in that is very important. The Gospel is effective and significant only when it is taken in, when it is swallowed. Believing in the Lord Jesus Christ is putting my whole trust in Him, yielding myself to Him, and letting His will be done in my life by His grace and power. Then I can expect Christ's blessing in my life.

It has already been said that one can believe error to one's hurt. When it comes to the Gospel, we do not have to worry. God is reliable. Abraham set the whole pattern for mankind when he acted on the promise of God. The Apostle Paul said, "I know whom I have believed, and am persuaded that he is able to keep that which I have committed unto him against that day" (2 Tim. 1:12).

Let me point out one more fact. Believing does not guarantee that my wishes will come to pass. Believing does commit me to the consequences of trusting in that particular thing or that particular person. When speaking about believing the Gospel, it is still true that if I want to cross the river (this life) and reach the other side (heaven) I must believe on the bridge (the Lord Jesus Christ). "But without faith it is impossible to please him: for he that cometh to God must believe that he is, and that he is a rewarder of them that diligently seek him" (Heb. 11:6).

BORN AGAIN

Being *born again* is what happens to a person who becomes a Christian. It is more than a new birth, more than a second birth, and more than another birth at another time. It is all that, but it is also different. Man is born the first time of human parents and with a human nature. When we say he is born again, we do not mean he is born the second time as a human being and that he has another start for a new life. We mean he was born the first time a human being; but when he is born the second time, he is born a child of God. He is "begotten by the Word of God" and has a new life in him which comes from God.

We can see human nature in a baby. Babies will want everything they can see; they will take anything they can reach; they will hang onto anything they can take; they will try to eat anything they have picked up. What they have, they draw closer and closer to themselves. They do it naturally, and human nature does not change in all the years that follow in their human lives.

A human being reaches out for what he can get and takes it to himself. That is human nature. It is a normal human thing for a man to say when he looks at any prospect, "What do *I* get out of it? What will *I* have to do? How is it going to affect *me?* Will *I* have an advantage if I do it this way?" This is thoroughly human. The ego can be trained, and it is always a good thing to do that. A man can make himself socially good, polite, and courteous. He can be cultured rather than crude. He can be civilized rather than savage. However, he is still a human being and has only human nature.

The Lord Jesus called human nature *flesh*. There are all kinds of *flesh,* both good and bad. There are all kinds of human beings, but none of them will be able to enter into the kingdom of God as human beings. "Flesh and blood cannot inherit the kingdom of God" (1 Cor. 15:50). The Creator, the Maker of all the earth, fixed it so that man would be born once with a human nature which he gets from his parents, in which he becomes conscious of himself and in which he becomes conscious of God. Man has his conscience, which tells him whether he is doing right or wrong, and he feels responsible for his conduct. He is given an opportunity to commit himself to God, accept God's promises, yield himself to God, and receive what God is willing to offer him. He can be saved from his human nature. He can be born again as a child of God. But until that happens he has only human nature, and so is still "in the flesh."

A man is born again as a child of God when hearing the promises of God he receives them and commits himself to them. When the Word of God is spoken to him, he "swallows" it. He takes the Word to himself, saying "This is going to be mine. I am going to commit myself to God according to these promises, whatever the consequences." God does a new work in any man who responds in this way to His Word. All a man needs to do is to open his heart and accept the promise of God. The Bible refers to this new work of God as being *born again.* It is a new creation.

In the new birth, life is not begun over again in an innocent state. Life is now begun in the presence of God by His grace and motivated, inwardly strengthened, helped, lifted, and guided by the living Lord Himself. It is a different kind of life, because now the life of the Lord is in man just in the same way that the life of his parents, his human nature, is in him. Human nature, it has been said, is selfish in its interests. The divine nature which man shares in Christ Jesus after he is *born again* desires to do the will of God. From within, this born-again man wants to be well-pleasing in the sight of God. If he knew what to do to please God and how to do it, he *would* do it for God's sake; and God looking on the heart knows this is true and blesses that person, guides and strengthens him. The second birth is a matter of entering into a new life, a new relationship, with everything that is in Christ Jesus and in God Himself.

This event which Jesus has called being *born again,* the concept of the new birth, is referred to specifically in the Gospel of John. It is also in other Gospels. Matthew states, "No man putteth a piece of new cloth unto an old garment, for that which is put in to fill it up taketh from the garment, and the rent is made worse" (Matt. 9:16). In those days they did not have Sanforized cloth, and if a piece of new unshrunken cloth was put in a hole in old cloth, the new cloth would shrink when it got wet, and this would tear the hole bigger than it had been before. This reminds me of my boyhood days on our farm in Canada. When my parents would buy me a new suit as a boy, they would always buy one that was several sizes too large because during the first rainstorm the clothes shrunk down to your size. It was always a tragedy to buy something just about the right size; because when it got wet, it would shrink so small you couldn't wear it any more. This helps me to understand the parable. Actually the parable is simply saying that the work of God is not a patchwork proposition. God is not going to patch up at a few points. He is going to give the man a new coat. This is a way of saying the believer will be given a new nature.

Matthew uses a further illustration to show the need of the new birth. The Lord went on to say, "Neither do men put new wine into

The Gospel

old bottles (that is, old wineskins); else the bottles break, and the wine runneth out, and the bottles perish: but they put new wine into new bottles, and both are preserved" (Matt. 9:17). The new wine would ferment, the gas would expand and stretch the old wineskins and they would burst. New wine would be put in new wineskins. God does not put His grace in man's old human nature. God works so that man is born again, and then He gives him the grace by which to live.

If the Gospels had been written in our day and time, the illustration used might have been that the Lord Jesus would not repair your engine, but He will put in a new engine. He will not repair the unit in your refrigerator. He will put in a new unit. Your refrigerator unit is one of those things in your home that is not to be repaired. It must be sent back to the factory while the servicemen put a new one in for you. This could illustrate what happens in being *born again*. A new, different, better nature is given to the believer. When a man becomes a Christian, God puts inside him something altogether new. The new birth means that God puts His own nature in a believer. This new nature gives the Christian the disposition to want to be well-pleasing in obedience to God.

The Christian person is still a human being, and so he still has a human nature. But he is also a child of God, and so he now has a divine nature also. That sets up the problem for me as a Christian of how to get along when my human nature is interested in what I myself would like and the divine nature in me is interested in doing what the Lord Jesus Christ wants me to do. The issue for me then is whether to go along with myself or whether to go along with Christ. My personal struggle does not end with my new birth; nevertheless, the new nature now in me is the eternal life of God given to me when I put my trust in Him. It is encouraging to remember that the Bible says, "Greater is he that is in you, than he that is in the world."

RECEIVING CHRIST

Receiving Christ is letting Him into my consciousness to influence and affect me. Believing in Him is a matter of accepting what He has done. Receiving Him is a matter of accepting Him and trusting Him to come into my soul. The Lord Jesus said, "Behold, I stand at the door, and knock: if any man hear my voice, and open the door, I will come in to him, and will sup with him, and he with me" (Rev. 3:20). From these words it should be understood that God actually comes to my heart when I am a believer.

It is often said that when I became a Christian, I went seeking after God. But as a human being I do not start out by searching for God; it is God who searches for me.

I can hear from someone else what Christ has done for sinners, and I can receive it as true in the sense in which I accept information. I can even rejoice to think of what God has done, without definitely taking it for myself. There comes a time, however, when God Himself comes to my heart. When Christ Jesus knocks at the door of my heart and offers to come in and sup with me, this is not my doing. This is something I let God do; when I receive Jesus Christ, I open my heart and let Him in to do His will.

We should notice that God does not force His way in. It is part of the humility of God that He will stand at the door and knock. It is part of the great seriousness of life that I can leave the door shut.

At the same time we should notice that the phrase "the Lord opened their hearts" is used in Scripture to describe *receiving Christ*. Lydia is said to be one "whose heart the Lord opened" (Acts 16:14). The Holy Spirit can show the things of Christ to a person in such a way that that person will open his heart. This is an action, an exercise of the will, of the believer who receives Jesus Christ. "But to as many as received him, to them gave he power to become the sons of God, even to them that believe on his name" (John 1:12). *Receiving Christ* is not something a Christian does which can be spelled out in fifteen, twenty, or a hundred different activities; but it is yielding himself to something God does in him. For me to receive Christ is to let God have His way in my life, according to His promises in Christ Jesus.

Again we can use the illustration of dealing with a doctor. Even when I have chosen my doctor, the matter of letting that doctor treat me is something more. This is letting my doctor come in and act *as* my doctor. When I receive Christ into my heart, I let God work *in* me. I do not have to know what God is doing or understand all His ways. The Lord Jesus said, "If any man will do his will, he shall know of the doctrine, whether it be of God, or

The Gospel

whether I speak of myself" (John 7:17). The willing soul is the one whom God will receive, into whose heart He will come, and whom He will bless.

The word *willing* is a present participle. It is used more often as if it were an adjective. Someone is spoken of as a *willing* person, meaning that he is ready and inclined to act in a certain way. But now look again at the word *willing*. Notice it is I who am willing. If I *will* anything, I am *willing* about it. The willing heart is the heart that wills to do God's will. This means I intend to do what He wants me to do. When the Lord Jesus comes and stands at the door and knocks, the person who *will* open the door to Him is the person who *wills* to have the Lord Jesus Christ come in. I need to open my heart to Him and be willing to have Him come in.

A great artist painted a picture to represent the text, "Behold I stand at the door and knock." He showed a door which was to represent the door of the heart. When the picture was nearly ready for exhibition, the artist called in one of his closest friends to look over the picture. The friend came to see the picture, and after a brief glance said that he supposed some of the most obvious things might skip one's attention. He had noticed that the artist had put no latch on the door. The artist explained that this was not an oversight. There was no latch on the outside, because the door to a man's heart opens only from the inside. This is a profound idea. There is no way of opening the heart of man from the outside. God knocks at the door, but the man himself must be the one to open it.

Perhaps we should also remember that I do not have to clean up inside before I open the door. If I wait until I get things clean, I will never open it. Christ is the only One who can clean you up. When the Lord Jesus comes in, the grace of God, the kindness of God, the love of God, the power of God become active in that human soul. God lifts, carries, and keeps those who let Him have His way.

Receiving Christ is not something that man needs to learn to do or something he must strive to do. Man needs only to open his heart, let Him come in, and receive Him; and this he can do in the simplest way, as a little child. God will work in him "to will and to do of his good pleasure" (Phil. 2:13). This is the good news of the Gospel. Christ will come in.

When a guest comes to the home, the door is opened and he is asked to come in. The host does everything he can to make the guest welcome. He will turn over, as it were, the whole house to that person. It is like that when you receive Christ into your heart.

ABIDING IN CHRIST

Only a Christian could know what the phrase *abiding in Christ* means. The word *abiding* is not a word that is ordinarily used today. It means *living in* or *dwelling in*. A house is referred to as an abode. It is the place where a certain family lives. *Abiding in Christ*, therefore, is a way to say *living in Him*.

When the word *Christ* is used in this way, reference is being made to a pattern of relationship with God. *Abiding in Christ* does not mean that the body of Jesus of Nazareth is here and that the Christian claims he is in it. Also, it does not mean that Christ is some organization on earth that one can join and thus be *in Christ*. *Abiding in Christ* is rather living in a certain relationship with God which Christ Jesus has provided. It is a pattern of relationship which involves certain principles.

Abiding in Christ includes the belief that God is, and that God is Creator, Keeper, Judge, Saviour, and Father. When man has the existence of God in mind, immediately man is responsible to obey Him. God is the Creator; man belongs to Him. Sin is any act on the part of the human being or any condition in the human being, that is a deviation from the will of God.

The word *Christ* used in the phrase *abiding in Christ* means everything that is meant by the word *God*. It also brings to mind that man is a sinner; he has broken the law of God, and is doomed to distress and destruction. Man in himself is lost. However, man need not remain lost, for the word *Christ* further brings to mind that "God so loved the world, that he gave his only begotten Son (Christ), that whosoever believeth in him should not perish, but have everlasting life" (John 3:16). The person who can claim John 3:16 is one who is abiding in Christ. He is trusting in the act of God, who sent His Son into the world to redeem those who have put their trust in Him. Christ comes bringing forgiveness and cleansing—salvation.

Anyone can abide in Christ but not everyone does. *Abiding in Christ* is a relationship man enters into. The Lord Jesus said, "Except a man be born again, he cannot see the kingdom of God"

The Gospel 133

(John 3:3). This means that no one enters this relationship unless he is born again. When a person enters this relationship with God, he joins the company of believers who trust in God by faith. It is possible for a person to be sure that he belongs to God, because he belongs to the Lord Jesus Christ.

To define *abiding* and *belonging* we could have the idea of *resting* in mind. A child rests in his mother's arms. A boy rests in his father's home. In each instance, the idea of belonging is conveyed. The boy belongs to his father's home. He lives in the home; he gets all the benefits of living in the home; he has the fellowship of the people in the home; and he has the protection that comes with living in the home. Everything that goes with having a home is included in the word *abiding*.

When a person is *abiding in Christ,* it means that so far as his soul is concerned he is *resting in* the work of Christ. The idea of *abiding* means *staying* there. It is not just a casual looking-into but "living in Christ." It is not just stepping in on a Sunday morning and staying for a half hour or an hour and then stepping out for the rest of the time. The person who is abiding in Christ is a person who believes in God all the time, believes in the living Lord Jesus Christ all the time, believes in the presence of God with him all the time, and believes in the forgiveness of and cleansing from sins all the time.

If the person who is abiding in Christ is asked about what is going to happen to him tomorrow, he will say he will be taken care of tomorrow. How does he know? Because God is his Father. How does he know God is his Father? The person who is abiding in Christ has an assurance that God is his Father because he is "in Christ Jesus," and God is the Father of the Lord Jesus Christ. Knowing that God is one's Father brings a certain inward quiet confidence, because so far as living is concerned nothing can take the Christian away from God.

This confidence is not limited only to the areas of life involving protection and the forgiveness of sins, but it is true also when it comes to making a choice in life. When confronted with decisions as to what he shall do, where he shall go, and whom he shall go with, the person who is abiding in Christ is conscious of the Lord during this time. There comes a time when a person who is abiding in Christ realizes that there is *never* a time when he can talk to any other person as though he and that person were alone. For a Christian there would always be three—the Christian himself, the person he is talking with, and the Lord Jesus Christ. The Lord Jesus is present, because the Christian trusts in Him.

Someone may suggest the danger that the world may be destroyed and that man might be destroyed. Yes, there is that danger; but the Christian will not be greatly upset. Why not? Because while his body is living in this world, in soul and spirit he is living in the Lord Jesus Christ. The body may be destroyed, but the soul and spirit cannot be destroyed. The body may waste away and be broken, but the soul cannot waste away and be broken.

The person who is abiding in Christ has an outlook and an attitude about life as follows: So far as he is concerned the world is real, and he will deal with it; but he does not belong to it and if it were to be taken away from him, he would be in the presence of God—absent from the body, present with the Lord. There is no decision to make between here and there, because having known Christ and walked with Him, the Christian is in His presence. It is not when the Christian dies that the Lord finds out whether or not he belongs to Him. That has already been settled. Death, for the person who is abiding in Christ, does not have the uncertainty of some terrible examination which he may fail to pass. The person who is abiding in Christ is trusting in the finished work of the Lord Jesus Christ and should he "die before he awakes," he is satisfied that the Lord Jesus will take his soul to be with the Father.

Abiding in Christ has a guarding effect with reference to one's heart and mind as far as the things around him are concerned. The things of this world do not have the same appeal; they appeal only to the part of the Christian that has to do with this world and that is second in importance. The part that has to do with the living Lord Jesus Christ, in whom he is abiding, is far more important. When walking along hand in hand with the Lord Jesus Christ, it does not matter whether he is wearing this or that. It can get to the point where it is not even important whether or not his football team wins on Saturday. He would be glad to have it win, but if it happened to lose, nothing very much would be lost. The Christian belongs to the Lord and the things having primary importance in his life are his dealings with Him.

The people in the world may think that everything just written presents a very unreal situation, but the Christian knows better. It is not the least bit unreal. It is just as practical as it has been set forth. The matter of *abiding in Him* has in it the idea that the Christian is always in a relationship with God which Christ Jesus provided for him.

SERVING THE LORD

Serving the Lord describes the Christian life. This should be used only about Christians; however, *serving the Lord* is not done by every Christian. It is done by Christians who actively, consciously worship and yield to the living Lord and Saviour, Jesus Christ.

Serving the Lord is not a matter of doing what I can to work out a goal or purpose which I think God wants. For example, if I thought all the children of the community should belong to a certain organization, so that I would go out and try to get them all to join, thinking that as they joined I would be *serving the Lord,* I might be *serving the Lord* as I was working, but it would not be because I was working in that organization. *Serving the Lord* is not an outward community campaign. It does not follow that if I work to see that new apartment houses are built where a slum area now exists I am *serving the Lord,* while anyone who is not involved in that activity is not. *Serving the Lord* is not something that can be identified with external activities.

Some people think that serving the Lord means I must go to Africa as a missionary, or I have to preach, or I have to teach Sunday school. Any one of those things might happen, but that is not the same as serving the Lord, because a person whose whole life is taken up with ordinary routine things can serve the Lord. A woman who is working at being a wife and mother and taking care of a home can serve the Lord. This does not mean that every woman who is married and helping her husband is serving the Lord. It does not mean that every woman who has children is serving the Lord. It does not mean that every person who cleans up her house is serving the Lord. It does not mean that everyone who has a place of business and operates that business honestly is serving the Lord. The Bible tells us what it means to serve the Lord: "And whatsoever ye do in word or deed, do all in the name of the Lord Jesus, giving thanks to God and the Father by him"

(Col. 3:17). To *serve in the name of the Lord Jesus Christ* is to be conscious of Him, trusting in Him, and responding to Him while I am going about doing whatever I am doing.

Let us consider the woman who does the daily work in the home. How can she in this serve the Lord? Her daily task is what God in His providence has given to her hand to do. She can accept her tasks in the home as something that God has set out for her. She can actually sweep the floor, wash the dishes, iron the children's clothes, greet the neighbors, take care of the children, discipline the growing youngsters, guide the affairs in the house, and seek to help her husband in his business, as if she were doing it for the Lord Himself. She can have in mind that this is what the Lord wants her to do. She can keep the Lord first in mind and not the children, the neighbors, the husband, or the house.

A man who goes to a place of business where he has a job to perform can accept that work as something which God in His providence has enabled him to have. He can, in this situation, work as though he were working for the Lord Himself. He can be on the job at eight o'clock, because that is the time the Lord wants him to be there. He can work from eight until twelve, because he is doing work that the Lord is going to see. He will go out for lunch and he will come back at one o'clock because that is when the Lord wants him to be there. Throughout the entire day, until the whistle blows at five o'clock, he will continue to work as serving the Lord. That man probably won't hurry away too soon, because the Lord may want him to be there past five o'clock.

Also, such a man will accept the people who are in the office as individuals the Lord has allowed to be there. He may not like all of them. He may not always think every one is doing the right thing, but he will accept all these things as from the Lord. If there is prosperity, he will thank the Lord. If some misfortune or calamity occurs, he will trust the Lord. He is doing *everything* as "unto the Lord." He is not sentimental about it, but deep down in his heart he is conscious that this is the Lord's will.

Everything is all-inclusive; therefore, it suggests that when the man drives his car on the streets, he will drive it as if the Lord were with him. He will deal fairly with everyone, because he is acting in the presence of the Lord. He is an example of a man who is serving the Lord throughout the day.

The Gospel

Everyone finds most of his life already settled for him. There are things he has to do to make a living, and certain things he has to do in the neighborhood if he is going to live there. A Christian will do these activities having in mind that he will be doing them as "unto the Lord." Such a person will take the seven days of the week as from the Lord and will "Remember the sabbath day, to keep it holy" (Ex. 20:8). He accepts the whole week as from the Lord, and he may have in mind that a way to honor God is in proper observance of the Lord's day.

When this person earns money, no one has to tell him to give part of the money to his church. He is inwardly prompted to do that, because the Lord is in his heart and he is living in His presence. When he is serving the Lord with his money, he does not give all of it away. He has to make a living for himself and take care of his family. He knows that, of all the things the Lord gives him, a certain amount is to be given to the Lord. He will understand that God will give him enough so that he can put a tenth of what he receives into the Lord's work, and nine-tenths of what he gets will be adequate for everything he needs. If he should need more money, he will talk to the Lord about it. If he meets a different situation, he will talk to the Lord about it, also. This person is serving the Lord.

Someone may ask this person to teach a Sunday school class; and, if asked, he will ask himself one thing, "Is this what the Lord wants me to do?" If the Lord wants him to teach, he will, whether he feels he can teach or not. He will *try* to do this thing that comes before him. That is serving the Lord.

It has already been suggested that this can come down to personal affairs—for example, in dealing with people. Some persons may be contentious. They want to argue and fuss about trifles. The Christian person in his heart will cry out, "Lord, do you want me to argue and fuss about this thing?" The Lord would say, "No, I want you to give in to it." The Christian serves the Lord and gives in to the man. The man thinks he got away with something. He really did not. The Christian acted the way the Lord wanted him to.

This does not mean that the Lord gives to each man a pattern, or a formula, or puts in his hand a handbook with minute instructions as to what to do so that when the situation comes up he can turn to a certain page and find out exactly what he is supposed to do. One of the problems people have when they come to the Bible is that the Bible does not tell them specifically what they ought to do on the particular street on which they live. No house numbers are in the Bible. One's neighbors are not listed by name in the Bible. The Bible does not state exactly what should be done with each individual person and in each particular situation. It does give certain principles that can be followed, but that is not even adequate because those principles need interpretation. Therefore, God gives to the Christian His Holy Spirit. The Holy Spirit, making the things of Christ real inside the heart of a Christian, makes the Christian conscious of the living Lord Jesus Christ. There is as it were a voice behind him that says, "This is the way, walk ye in it" (Isa. 30:21).

The Christian person, informed as he is, intelligent as he may be, acquainted with things as they are, understanding things in every way, and acting, living, and doing in the world as he should, has in his heart at all times a consciousness of the living Lord Jesus Christ. He responds in all situations as he feels the Lord would want him to do.

These principles concerning work are equally applicable to amusement or entertainment. It may be an old saying, but it has been proved that "all work and no play makes Jack a dull boy." A certain amount of relaxation is necessary and important. A Christian will find when he takes relaxation that he does not feel he is sinning. He does not think he is getting away with anything; for even in his hours of relaxation, he is conscious of the presence of God. Whatever the particular game is that he gives himself over to for relaxation, he is going to play it as if the Lord Jesus were there with him. Actually the Lord is there. If complications develop, the Christian will have within himself the consciousness of the Lord and will be obedient to what the Spirit prompts him to think the living Lord Jesus wants him to do. Such a person is serving the Lord.

The adornment which a Christian woman puts on when she dresses up, which will be perfectly proper for her to wear, will depend upon what she thinks will be pleasing in the eyes of the Lord, who is right there with her and sees her doing these things. Every conceivable thing I do will be affected by His presence in me. "And whatsoever ye do in word or deed, do all in the name of the Lord

The Gospel

Jesus" (Col. 3:17). This is what it means to be *serving the Lord*.

THE BLESSED HOPE

Christians have an idea of what is going to happen, which is called *the blessed hope*. This is a forward look along the lines of the promises of God in the Bible. God knows what He is aiming to do and has revealed some of it to His people.

Life in this world develops in three phases—past, present, and future. My life comes from yesterday, through today, and into tomorrow. We all have feelings about yesterday. Sometimes we have feelings of regret. We all are aware of today; and most of us have some bewilderment and confusion about the future, as we look for tomorrow.

As the Christian looks forward there is in him an element of confident expectation. The Christian believes that it is going to be better tomorrow than it is today. One reason for his thinking this is because he knows God is working. The world warns and threatens that things will be worse tomorrow than they were today. It is a natural thing to feel that yesterday was better, today is bad enough, but tomorrow is going to be awful. Many people live in dread of what another day will bring forth.

This is not true for Christians. It is not that Christians think everything in this world is going to turn out all right. They are not being merely optimistic. Christians believe that Almighty God, working in this world, is a benevolent God. He means well by mankind. The Lord Jesus Christ died for all men. He is now in the presence of God. He is almighty and powerful and He will finally triumph. Regardless of how dark the future may be, there is a glory awaiting in the things of the Lord. This is what the Bible says, and this is what the Christian thinks. In the mind and heart of the believer in Christ there is a forward look that is an upward look in joyous expectation.

Between this life and that final glory, there may be the experience of death. A Christian is normal and natural enough to know that death is an enemy. However, a Christian is not afraid of death, because Christ Jesus died and arose again. Christ has taken the sting out of death. One reason death is so heavy in the consciousness of the average non-Christian is because after death comes the judgment. A person who is thinking about dying is thinking about going into the presence of God and being judged. When anyone feels that way, you can know for sure he has not yet really understood the Gospel.

A Christian may look forward into tomorrow and realize he will stand before God, who knows all about him. The fact that the Christian has sinned will not be a surprise to God. God already knows about his sins, and He has already forgiven his sins. That is what Christ Jesus died for. The Christian is not moving forward into judgment. It is natural for the human heart to feel that way, but the Gospel would tell the Christian that will not happen to him. My expectation is not that one day I will stand in the presence of God, and God will decide whether or not I am good enough to belong to Him. That has already been settled. It was known from the beginning that no man in himself is good enough. But Christ Jesus died for sinners, and He carried away the sin of the whole world and set men free from sin and death. As a Christian I can look forward to coming into the presence of God in all the triumph of Christ's completed work in me.

The wonderful thing in the Gospel of the Lord Jesus Christ is that Almighty God wants to bless and help men, and in order to get that done He sent His son, the Lord Jesus Christ, into the world to save men. The Lord Jesus Christ will bring us through into the presence of God. He will do so in triumph and great glory. The Christian has that expectation.

The Lord Jesus is not done with His work; He is not finished. It is true that with reference to sin He is finished. He finished that when He died for sin on Calvary's cross. However, the evangelism of the world was not finished. God wants the Gospel preached to all nations that everyone should hear the message of the Lord Jesus Christ. This is still going on.

The Lord Jesus is now working to save men "to the uttermost" and that is not yet finished. The Apostle Paul could say after he had been an apostle for many years, "I count not myself to have apprehended: but this one thing I do, forgetting those things which are behind . . . I press toward the mark for the prize of the high calling of God in Christ Jesus" (Phil. 3:13-14). The process was still going on in him. This does not mean that the Apostle Paul had any doubt about his salvation. It does not mean that he was wondering whether or not he would be saved. He knew he was saved,

The Gospel

but he was looking forward to the fullness of the salvation in Jesus Christ as God worked in him to will and to do of His good pleasure.

The operation of God's plan for man and for the world is not finished. The Bible tells us in various ways, but always so that it cannot possibly be mistaken, that the Lord Jesus will come again. The Old Testament predicted that He would come to die. The New Testament promises He will come again to rule. The coming again of the Lord Jesus Christ is part of the Gospel. When the Lord Jesus finished His work on Calvary's cross, He was not through with the task given to Him. When He ascended into heaven in full view of all, He had finished the work of salvation, but not the complete unfolding of God's plan. He is sitting now at the right hand of God interceding for us, but this is not the end. "This same Jesus, which is taken up from you into heaven, shall so come in like manner as ye have seen him go into heaven" (Acts 1:11). The Lord Jesus Christ, when He comes again into this world, will complete the plan of God. Then the things that God wants to have done will actually be accomplished as the Lord Jesus Christ manifests the glory of God in full view of the whole creation.

The coming again of the Lord Jesus Christ has been referred to by many people as *the blessed hope*. It is *the blessed hope* with reference to the Lord Jesus Christ's presence. But there is a certain element of *the blessed hope* in every expectation of what God will do. The word of the Lord Jesus says, "Let not your heart be troubled: ye believe in God, believe also in me. In my Father's house are many mansions: if it were not so, I would have told you. I go to prepare a place for you. And if I go and prepare a place for you, I will come again, and receive you unto myself; that where I am, there ye may be also" (John 14:1-3). That is a blessed thing. It is a wonderful expectation. In the first epistle of John we read, "It doth not yet appear what we shall be: but we know that, when he shall appear, we shall be like him; for we shall see him as he is. And every man that hath this hope in him purifieth himself" (1 John 3:2-3).

The Christian has the confident expectation that he is going to meet the Lord face to face. I do not know for sure that I will be here alive on the earth when the Lord Jesus comes. Some persons will be. I may have fallen asleep in Jesus, but just as surely as God is in heaven and the Lord Jesus comes, I will be raised to meet Him. This is the scriptural promise, and the Christian can cherish the blessed hope of expectation of meeting the Lord.

Songs have been written about the blessed hope. "When we all get to heaven, What a day of rejoicing that will be!" "When all my labors and trials are o'er, And I am safe on that beautiful shore, Just to be near the dear Lord I adore, Will through the ages be glory for me." There are many such songs which Christians have used to express their expectation that God will one day manifest His glory, take them to Himself, and vindicate every one who has put his trust and faith in the Lord.

When the Lord Jesus comes again, He will come suddenly. It will be in such a time as man thinks not that He will come. No one, by any manner of investigation or examination or reason, can possibly say when that day will be. The day and the hour is not known to any man, but God knows. In the fullness of time God will again send forth His Son. What is so important to the Christian is that He will come to bless and take him to Himself.

The blessed hope, when it is cherished, fills the heart with a confident expectation that the future is in the hands of God. When the Christian looks forward to the future, to death and life after death, there is in his heart a confident expectation that God will do him good. Through the Lord Jesus Christ, God has prepared the way so that the Christian is going to come into His presence in glory.

RESURRECTION

The Christian believes in "resurrection unto eternal life." The idea of *resurrection* is more than that a person is going to live again. That much is true, but resurrected people will live on a different level. Being raised from the dead is not a matter of having another chance to do the same thing. Rather, it is a privilege of living in a situation better than anything ever experienced before.

Jesus of Nazareth is the supreme example. The Son of God took on human flesh and in that flesh He died. When God raised Him up from the dead, it was confirmed to the whole world that what the Lord Jesus had said was true. As He raised up the Lord Jesus Christ from the dead, so He will raise from the dead anyone who believes in Him.

There are instances of resurrection in the New Testament other

The Gospel

than that of Christ: for example, the widow's son, the rich man's daughter, and Lazarus. These resurrections, however, were not like the resurrection of the Lord Jesus Christ, and they are not like our resurrection. Each one of these people died again. But when a believer is raised in the Lord Jesus Christ, there will be no second death.

What the resurrection really means is that when a man has lived his life, God will bring this man to life again in a body prepared for him by Almighty God. It sounds incredible, but this is what the Bible teaches; it is the very essence of the Christian Gospel.

When the Lord Jesus Christ was asked to give the people some sign that would show them that He was the Son of God, He told them the only sign would be the resurrection of His body. One fact He expressed over and over again was "Destroy this temple (His body), and in three days I will raise it up" (John 2:19). He was referring to His physical resurrection, but the spiritual truth is even more profound. His resurrection shows the power of God to raise the dead, but the spiritual truth is that a person living as a human being can pass through the experience of death in human nature to be raised from the dead and to live in the nature of God. This is "resurrection unto eternal life" and it takes place as soon as the person turns from the things of this world and yields himself to the Lord.

The Bible speaks of the existence one gets from his parents in this world as "life," but when it speaks of the life that comes into a person who believes in the Lord Jesus Christ, which is the "life of God," it calls it "eternal life." Eternal life does not mean life in this world going on forever. It means this life coming to an end—dying —and a new life from God that never ends because it is from God. The body will pass through the resurrection sometime in the future and it will be changed. The soul also passes through the resurrection but that happens while I am still living in this world. My soul is raised in newness of life the moment the Holy Spirit of God comes to dwell within me.

And now, consider again the resurrection of the Lord Jesus Christ. When He was killed on the cross at Calvary, His body died. On the day that Jesus was crucified there were two other men, two thieves, crucified with Him. Those three men were crucified the same way, and they died in the same way. The Bible does not tell how the soldiers undertook to check on the death of the two thieves, but in order to make sure that Jesus was dead, they pierced His side with a spear. That pierced body was raised from the dead.

But when it was raised from the dead it was different. The resurrection body was enough like the human body that they could recognize Him. The nail prints were in His hands. The wound was in His side. It is commonly thought that this was for identification purposes, and that Almighty God left them in Him as marks of His great suffering for mankind. But the resurrection body apparently was made of different stuff.

When the Bible tells of resurrection, it is understood that men's bodies will be raised from the grave and brought into the presence of God. As discussed in Chapter Five, we should understand that the people who are raised from the dead are not going to look the way they looked when they died. If some person suffered in those last days and lost weight until he was weak, frail, and emaciated, he is not going to look like that when he is raised from the dead. If someone was unfortunate enough to lose a limb and lived his days one-armed or one-legged, when he is raised from the dead he is not going to look like that. When he is raised from the dead, he will be as he was originally designed. Not only will the body look different, but it will be made of something different and it will be complete.

The human body is made of the dust of the earth. It is composed of chemicals that are found in the world (carbon, oxygen, hydrogen, nitrogen, iron, sulphur, etc.). All these things belong to this world, and all these things will perish with the world. So will the earthly body of any person. The body will be raised from the dead, but the new elements which will then be in the body will be everlasting elements of a spiritual, heavenly nature.

A man can have an architect draw up a design and plan for a house. He can build that house with wood, or he can build it with stone. It will not make any difference as far as the shape of the plan is concerned. The windows, doors, roof, and everything will be the same shape according to the plan. The body's structural principle is like that plan, and that is what is going to be raised from the dead. It will die no more because the stuff that it is made from will not be temporal. In 1 Corinthians, Chapter 15, Paul says that there is a natural body and there is a spiritual body. The heav-

The Gospel

enly body is also called a glorified body. This body will not experience pain, suffering, and death. The reason may very well be that the stuff of which the body is made is different. That is the kind of body the Lord Jesus Christ had when He ascended into heaven.

The new life that is going to be lived in Christ Jesus is different from this life on earth. Heaven is different from earth. It is a whole lot better. The resurrection is unto eternal life. If I have an understanding of "the resurrection of the body," I will also have in mind the resurrection of the soul in which I am raised in newness of life. If I reckon myself indeed to be dead to sin, crucified with Christ, and raised in newness of life, I will mortify my members here upon earth that I might put on the spiritual ways of living and the things that belong to the Lord Jesus Christ.

Every Christian person has the expectation that he is going to be different. Someone may come to a Christian person and say to him, "Well, I don't see that you are any different from other human beings." That is true now. He is not any stronger, taller, or bigger than other people, but one of the things the Christian can know is that he is not going to be as he is now all the time. When his body begins to wear away, his eyes lose their sight, his muscles are no longer strong, and aches and pains many times bother him, the Christian has an inward, secret, joyful hope: he knows that he is going to leave this body behind.

The Christian may have personal traits and characteristics that are the same as they were before he became a believer. It may seem that he is always going to be that kind of person. That may be true in this world, but one of these days that body is going to be put six feet under and left right there. He is going to live forever in the new body that will be given to him in Christ Jesus. The Gospel of the Lord Jesus Christ promises that the Christian will share the "resurrection unto eternal life" wherein he will live a new, different life in Christ to the glory of God.

CHAPTER SEVEN

The Holy Spirit

THE Bible teaches us to put our trust in God, that we may rest in Him. In the Old Testament the emphasis seems to be upon the one God, or—as we might say—upon all of God as one God. The people had dealings with God, and God had dealings with them. In the Gospels—Matthew, Mark, Luke, and John—attention is focused on Jesus Christ. In the Book of Acts and in the epistles, attention is focused upon the Holy Spirit. And so over the Bible as a whole we think of God as Father, Son, and Holy Spirit, whom we call "the triune God."

Throughout the earthly ministry of the Lord Jesus Christ repeated reference was made to the coming of the Holy Spirit, and it was distinctly noted that He had not yet come. The Holy Spirit had been promised in the Old Testament, but He had not yet been "poured out" while the Lord Jesus was alive. John explains, "for the Holy Ghost was not yet given; because that Jesus was not yet glorified" (John 7:39).

The presence of the Holy Spirit in the hearts of the disciples was considered so important by the Lord Jesus Christ that He said, "It is expedient for you that I go away, for if I go not away, the Comforter will not come unto you" (John 16:7). In these words the Lord Jesus is saying simply that it would be a good thing for His body to be taken out of this world, because that would make it possible for the Holy Spirit to come into their hearts. To have the Holy Spirit in the heart would be a greater benefit than to have Jesus of Nazareth Himself present in the body. When we have the Holy Spirit in our hearts, we have an advantage over the disciples who walked with the Lord Jesus Christ in the days of His flesh. To be sure, the disciples saw the Lord Jesus Christ. They saw what He did, heard what He said, observed Him in His conduct. They would form some opinion about Him but they could be wrong. However, when the Holy Spirit is in our hearts, He thinks the very thoughts of God in us. This is even better than to see the Lord Jesus Christ in His human body.

Although the disciples had been with the Lord Jesus Christ during His three years of public ministry, they were told not to begin their ministry to all the world until they had received the Holy Spirit. Jesus had personally taught them; He had worked His miracles before them; and He had shown them many things in the length of time He was with them. Yet He commanded them not to start on their mission to the world until the Holy Spirit came upon them. It seems plain they were not ready to go until they received the Holy Spirit, who would give them power and so make their witnessing effectual.

THIRD PERSON IN THE TRINITY

When we think about the Holy Spirit as God, we think of Him as the third person of the Trinity. As such, He is thought of as a person. This is not an idea which we can grasp easily. When I try to understand about God in heaven, I say to myself that God is high and holy and lifted up and transcendent, far above everything. Even though I have not seen God, I can somehow think of Him like that. When I think about the Lord Jesus Christ, about God being in human form, I can comprehend this even though I am astonished. When I hear that Jesus Christ was raised from the dead, I am amazed. When I am told His resurrection body was taken up into heaven on the day of ascension, I am deeply impressed by the wonder of it. To think He is now at the right hand of God strikes me with awe. Yet, somehow, all this fits together. But when I think about the Holy Spirit and am told that "He is in us," I find it very hard to grasp.

I could think of the Holy Spirit as being in heaven in the very presence of the glory of God, but to think that the Holy Spirit is in the church (not in the church building, but in the church people), that He is in the believer, that is hard for me to get into my mind. I have learned to understand one reason this truth is so vague. The Bible tells us the Spirit shall not speak of Himself (John 16:13). While the Holy Spirit is doing His work, He shows men the things of Christ. When the Holy Spirit is working in the heart of a Christian, the mind is filled with thoughts of Jesus Christ. If I am going to think about the Holy Spirit, I must take myself in hand and make special effort. I need to turn my mind definitely to thoughts about Him, because as I normally think about God and try to understand Him, my mind is led to focus upon the Lord Jesus Christ. The Holy Spirit in my heart takes the things of Christ and shows them to me.

The Holy Spirit is not actually a name. The word *spirit* is sometimes used for *ghost*. The words *ghost* and *spirit* as used in our English version of the New Testament are interchangeable. The word *ghost* is not commonly used in our speech because people have associated that word with certain things we do not commonly believe, such as phantoms and ghost stories. The word *spirit* is preferred by us in common speech. God is a spirit; the angels are spirits; and Satan is a spirit. There are good spirits and bad spirits. This one is called the *Holy* Spirit, but God is holy and there are holy angels, so there is nothing unique in the words *spirit* and *holy*. Anything special about this title would be in the definite article *the*. We say *the Holy Spirit*. By *the* Holy Spirit we mean the third person of the Godhead, as when we say "Father, Son, and Holy Spirit." He is actually unnamed even as He is unseen. Apparently He personally wants to be unnoticed because He wants to show us the things of the Lord Jesus Christ.

What is meant, then, when we say that the Holy Spirit is a person? When we considered God as a person, we emphasized the fact that a person is a being who can think, feel, and will. It is hard for me to think of God or of the Holy Spirit as being a person, because I am inclined to think of persons as having the appearance of human beings. It is natural for me to think a person has a body, but a person does not have to have a body. God does not have a body such as men have and yet He is a person. Satan does not have a body as men have, but he is a person. Gabriel, the angel, who talked to Mary, did not have a body. Michael, the archangel, who wrestled with Satan over the body of Moses, is a person but does not have a body such as men have. The Holy Spirit does not have a body, and yet He is a person—which means He can think, feel, and will.

How do I know He can think? The Bible states that Paul and his party were "forbidden of the Holy Spirit" to go into Asia (Acts

The Holy Spirit

16:7). At a meeting of the early church the Holy Spirit said, "Separate me Barnabas and Saul for the work whereunto I have called them" (Acts 13:2). At various other places in the New Testament, the Holy Spirit is referred to as saying or speaking. This indicates that He can *think*.

The Holy Spirit can also *feel*. Paul wrote, "Grieve not the Holy Spirit of God" (Eph. 4:30). The fact that the Holy Spirit can be grieved shows He has feeling.

The Bible also tells us the Holy Spirit has a will. He gives gifts to the church by selecting and giving certain abilities to serve as He sees fit. When He forbade Paul to go into Asia, the Holy Spirit told Paul what Paul should do and what he should not do. It was the Holy Spirit that decided what Paul should do. When the Holy Spirit told the early church to set aside Barnabas and Saul as missionaries, He was deciding who should go where and do what in the Lord's service. All this would show He is what is meant by a *person*.

Some years ago, I had a friend who was suffering from a sickness which made him feel very weak. His blood pressure was low. It affected his heart action, and it gave him a general feeling of psychological depression. He was an intelligent man and a Christian. He knew his physical state caused his depression. He knew too that the Lord could help him. He tried to understand and believed the Holy Spirit could give him joy.

This man invited me to come to his home. There he explained his condition to me. He said he believed in the Holy Spirit of God, but he had difficulty in realizing Him, in being aware of Him, and he felt the need to be aware of Him. Although he felt depressed, he understood from Scripture that he could have joy spiritually because he believed in the Lord Jesus Christ and he believed he belonged to God. He had the assurance that when he left this world he was going to go to heaven, but he wanted to have some of the joy of the Lord in his heart now. He knew he could have it if he could just think of the Holy Spirit as the Bible told about Him.

We tried to figure out how a person could think about the Holy Spirit as a person when He cannot be seen. I suggested to him that he could suppose he was in a house and in another room was one of the members of his family. He wouldn't hear the person; he wouldn't see him; that person might not talk, but he would know someone was there. This would make a difference. Then he realized he could think of the Holy Spirit as being behind him. He would not be able to see Him, but he would know He was there.

Several weeks later I went to see my friend again, and he told me that he had been greatly blessed. My friend said, "I never feel alone, and it is a great blessing to remember that God is with me at all times."

Many Christians have worked out some similar procedure to let them be aware of the presence of the Holy Spirit. Sometimes a man will pull an empty chair beside his bed to help himself become conscious of the Presence of the Holy Spirit. This is called "Practising the Presence of God." It always brings much blessing to the soul.

IN THE OLD TESTAMENT

The Holy Spirit of God is often mentioned in the Old Testament. At the very beginning, in speaking of the creation of the world, the record says "the Spirit of God moved upon the face of the waters." Sometimes this is translated to say "the Spirit of God brooded upon the face of the waters." In the Hebrew the expression that is used for *moved* or for *brooded* is *outstretched wings*. These may be thought of as wings such as a hen would spread out over eggs which she was hatching. In that sense the word *brooded* is used. Or they can be the outstretched, fluttering wings of a bird. The whole idea is that the Holy Spirit was moving, fluttering, brooding over the face of the waters.

Something of the same function that the Holy Spirit performed in the creation of the world is performed in the re-creation of a sinner, the regeneration of a soul. The Holy Spirit moved over the world when all was still darkness. So when the sinner's inward soul is without form, void, empty, and dark, the Holy Spirit can move over him and say, "Let there be light." "The entrance of thy Word giveth light." As the Holy Spirit is involved in the creation of the world, so is He involved in the re-creation of every person who believes in the Lord Jesus Christ.

The Old Testament relates many instances where the judges and prophets were guided by the Holy Spirit. There is one interesting expression with reference to Gideon. The King James version of the Bible says " the Spirit of the Lord came upon Gideon" (Judg. 6:34). Another translation that can be made of this passage is

The Holy Spirit

that the Holy Spirit "clothed Himself with Gideon." This means that God took Gideon, worked in him, and used him as an instrument for the leading of God's people. The Bible says that when Saul became king, "the spirit of God came upon him and he prophesied among them" (1 Sam. 10:9).

It is important to note the language used in the Old and New Testaments. In the Old Testament, the Holy Spirit is spoken of as *coming upon* individuals. In the New Testament, and since the Day of Pentecost, the Holy Spirit *dwells in* individuals. In the Old Testament, the Holy Spirit *came upon* human beings and used them. In the New Testament the Holy Spirit *dwells within* the believer and motivates him to do the will of God from his heart.

Consider the following expression used in the New Testament about an Old Testament event, when it says, "the Holy Ghost spake by the mouth of David" (Acts 1:16). The prophets in the Old Testament were actually moved and used of God when the Holy Spirit came upon them and had them doing what He wanted them to do. This is what Peter means when he spoke of how the Scriptures were written: "Holy men of God spake as they were moved by the Holy Ghost" (2 Pet. 1:21).

In all the writings of the prophets, beginning in Isaiah, and especially in Jeremiah and Ezekiel, the idea is brought out that God would do a new thing in the world. Until that time God's way of dealing with the world had been to show forth His promises and His law and call on men to trust in Him and to walk in His way. It is recorded that men did not of themselves walk in the way of God, and it was obvious that they could not walk in the way of God. Being sinful, their human nature did not have the disposition to want to walk in the way of God.

In the time of the prophets, God began to reveal to His people that He was going to save them and bless them in a new way. He would put His Spirit within them. Isaiah refers to the time when "the spirit be poured upon us from on high" (Isa. 32:15). These promises were *the new covenant*. They were intimated in Isaiah and are made plainly in Jeremiah, Ezekiel, Amos, Micah, and Joel. It is made clear how God would "pour out his spirit upon all flesh" (Joel 2:28). "And I will give them one heart, and I will put a new spirit within you; and I will take the stony heart out of their flesh, and will give them an heart of flesh" (Ezek. 11:19).

Another way in which the Bible says that God would put His spirit within them is that He would write His law upon their hearts. "But this shall be the covenant that I will make with the house of Israel; After those days, saith the Lord, I will put my law in their inward parts, and write it in their hearts; and will be their God, and they shall be my people" (Jer. 31:33). In Old Testament times the law of God was put on tablets of stone. The person who wanted to walk with God would see the commandments, and then in his own heart and mind he would decide to do those commandments. But his performance would always be inadequate. Sometimes he would not fully understand what God wanted, and then again, even if he did, he did not really want to do what God directed him to do. The human heart was simply not minded to walk in the ways of God. Therefore, God said He would write His law on their hearts and in that way He would make it so they would want to do His will.

In New Testament times, instead of seeing a written description of how they ought to live, men feel an inward impulse to want to do the things of God. This is the work of the Holy Spirit within the heart. When the Holy Spirit is thus working within our hearts and we want to do the will of God, then we will really obey Him. But this will be God working in us "to will and to do of His good pleasure."

In Old Testament times when the Holy Spirit would come upon a man to move him to do the will of God and completely dominate him, it would be said that the man was "filled with the Spirit of God." This was the case at the beginning of the New Testament account. John the Baptist, although his story is told in the New Testament, in many respects can be understood as the last of the Old Testament prophets. When John the Baptist lived, the Lord Jesus had not yet died. John lived and died before Pentecost, and he never saw what would happen when God would come to dwell in the hearts of people. Yet John the Baptist was filled with the Holy Spirit from his birth. This is what the angel promised John's father, "and he shall be filled with the Holy Ghost, even from his mother's womb" (Luke 1:15).

John the Baptist was like an Old Testament prophet, completely dominated by the Holy Spirit of God. He was really a godly man, and yet John predicted, "but one mightier than I cometh, the

The Holy Spirit

latchet of whose shoes I am not worthy to unloose: he shall baptize you with the Holy Ghost and with fire" (Luke 3:16). John's baptism was an outward mode symbolizing the truth that God would bless the individual soul. As the rain falling from heaven falls on the ground and makes the earth "bring forth and bud" so the grace of God would come upon the heart and make the heart respond to God in faith and obedience. John said that he baptized with water, but that the Lord Jesus Christ would baptize with the Holy Spirit and with fire. *Fire* is the word used for *judgment*. What John, in his baptism, merely indicated was going to happen, the Lord Jesus actually brought to pass.

When the Lord Jesus was baptized, the Holy Spirit descended from heaven in bodily form as a dove and abode upon Him (John 1:32). John saw the Holy Spirit fill in unreserved measure the human form and frame of Jesus of Nazareth. In some special way, God came to be with His Son, the Lord Jesus Christ, to be His companion, and to be with Him all the remaining time He was here upon earth.

So far as other people were concerned, the Holy Spirit was not given while the Lord Jesus was alive here on earth. He Himself promised that the Holy Spirit would be given after He was gone into heaven. Then He would be in the hearts of believers like "a well of water springing up into everlasting life."

It is understood that springs come from water high up in the mountains. The water seeps out at a certain place in the valley below and creates a spring. The Holy Spirit's home is in heaven, and He comes down from God, just as the water comes down out of the mountain, and shows up in the heart and life of the believer. This is the source of the Holy Spirit within the hearts of believers in Christ.

PENTECOST

Perhaps everyone is acquainted with the fact that the Holy Spirit came at Pentecost. The word *Pentecost* actually means fifty days. It was used by the Jews to refer to harvest time. They allowed fifty days from the time when harvest began, when they brought in their first fruits, until they would celebrate Harvest Home. The whole period was called *Pentecost,* but the last day was *the day of Pentecost.*

This is the idea in mind when the Bible says, "And when the day of Pentecost was fully come . . ." (Acts 2:1). Beginning with the resurrection of Jesus Christ as "the first fruits" of God's work of salvation and counting the forty days in which "he showed himself alive by many infallible proofs," and the ten days of prayer meeting in the Upper Room, it was the full fifty days of the harvest period of Pentecost when the incident of the coming of the Holy Spirit took place.

This use of the word *Pentecost* brings to our minds the idea of *harvest,* as if the coming of the Holy Spirit into the hearts of the believers is the completion of the work of God, which He does in saving souls through Jesus Christ. It would seem that having the Holy Spirit within our hearts is the fulfillment of what Christ Jesus came to do.

The Book of Acts tells the story of what happened (Acts 2). Without any intention of taking anything away from this account in any way, let me share with you something from my personal experience in reading it. When I first became a Christian and read the account of Pentecost, I had trouble about the wind. I was just practical-minded enough that I could not see how a mighty rushing wind could be in a house with the doors shut. I do not know how long it was before I found out that the story did not say there was a mighty rushing wind, but there was "a sound" *as of* a mighty rushing wind. The sound which they heard affected them. I was also troubled about the tongues of fire. But the story tells us they were not tongues of fire, but they were tongues "like as of fire." They are sometimes called fiery tongues. They looked like flames. What could they be? How could they look like fire if they were not fire? Perhaps you have seen trolley wheels go over a crossing of the wires at night. There are electric flashes. That is not fire, but it looks like fire. Lightning is not exactly fire. Nothing is burning, but it looks like fire. I am not going to say what this particular phenomenon was, but apparently it was not anything burning. However, it was "like as a fire." The account tells us also that the "sound like as of a rushing mighty wind" and the "tongues like as of fire" were outward signs that impressed everyone who was there.

There were other events in Scripture very similar to this. In the Old Testament, the tabernacle was the place where God would dwell with His people. When everything had been built as required,

The Holy Spirit 155

the sacrifice had been offered, and the blood had been sprinkled, a glorious light filled the tabernacle so that no one could go in. It is called the "Shekinah Glory of God." It was an outward, visible manifestation that God gave His approval and had come to dwell among them.

Later in the history of Israel, when the people became settled in the land, they built a temple in the city of Jerusalem. When everything had been completed, the sacrifices offered, and each detail of ritual performed, the people waited before God. The Bible records that "the cloud filled the house of the Lord, so that the priests could not stand to minister because of the cloud: for the glory of the Lord filled the house of the Lord" (1 Ki. 8:10-11). This was a way of emphasizing and outwardly showing that God approved the way they had done everything, and it confirmed their expectation that He would come and live with them and from then on would be in their midst.

The tabernacle and the temple were the dwelling place of God in those days, where He met His people, but God no longer dwells in tents and He "dwelleth not in temples made with hands" (Acts 18:24). The tabernacle and the temple are symbols of what Christians are. The disciples of the early church actually were to be the "habitation of God." It can be thought that as the Lord Jesus called His disciples together He was assembling the elements of the temple of God. He brought them together as David collected the material and Solomon built the temple. After He had brought them together and had taught and shaped them for three years so that each one would have His place in the fellowship of the kingdom of God, then the sacrifice was offered. The Lord Jesus went to Calvary's cross and His blood was shed in the presence of God. Having done these things and then having spent forty days to teach the disciples the things of the kingdom of God, He ascended to the Father. The disciples then spent ten days in prayer, during which time they corrected some things that were wrong among them and waited before God. When everything had been done as the Lord God had commanded, He suddenly manifested His presence in glory, and that was Pentecost. The Shekinah Glory of God in the real temple of God is the Holy Spirit filling the soul of man and is God's way of approving something He is going to dwell in.

RECEIVING THE HOLY SPIRIT

It is both astonishing and wonderful to think that the Holy Spirit of God can be received into the heart of a human being. The Bible teaches that every Christian person can have the Holy Spirit in his or her heart and experience. But apparently there is something to be done to bring this to pass.

A rather strange incident is recorded in the Book of Acts. The Apostle Paul came to certain disciples who had not received the Holy Spirit. The story is told in Acts 19:1-7. This incident is amazing. These were people who were believers, and they were well enough known as believers that the apostle came to them as if they were brethren of his. After he had been with them for some time he asked them, "Did you receive the Holy Spirit when you believed?" What made him ask that question? One cannot tell by looking at a person whether he has received the Holy Spirit. The Spirit is invisible. Yet, there must have been something different about these believers, because we have no record that Paul asked that question of any other group.

When I first read that for myself, I wondered what would have happened if I had met the Apostle Paul. Would he have asked me, "Did you receive the Holy Spirit when you believed?" I wondered whether he would notice anything missing in my life and in my fellowship with him that would make him ask that question.

I am going to suggest that something was really lacking in this group. They said they had been baptized with John's baptism. John the Baptist preached about sin and that men should repent. Men should realize their own weakness and sinfulness and believe in the Lord Jesus Christ. I believe that as long as Christian people (I use the word *Christian* in the broad sense) are impressed and depressed with their own weakness, they have not had the fullness of the Gospel of the Lord Jesus Christ. Of course, men should be depressed about their weakness, but if they receive the Lord Jesus Christ, they would not be left with their weakness. I am weak, but my hope is not in me. My hope is in Him and in Him I rejoice.

The Bible does not say it, but I am inclined to think that when that group of believers met together they possibly deplored their weakness, felt their sinfulness, and wished to God they were better; and that went on, and on, and on, and on. What Paul probably

The Holy Spirit

looked for and listened for but never heard was the joy of rejoicing in the Lord. They did not seem to be sure that their salvation was safe and secure in the Lord Jesus Christ. I think they probably were more depressed with the idea that they were wrong than they rejoiced in the idea that He would save them. If the Holy Spirit had been in them, they would have been talking and thinking about the grace of God that is in Christ Jesus.

Any time I have a serious burden about my own personal weakness, I can thank the Lord because I am halfway home. I repent myself; I admit that I am not good; I know that I am a sinner; and I realize my weakness. That is all good, but it is halfway. I have emptied my heart. Now I need to receive the truth of the Lord Jesus Christ and let the whole Spirit of God show me that Jesus Christ "is able to save them to the uttermost that come unto God by him" (Heb. 7:25). He is available to every Christian and He is available to me.

In the Book of Galatians believers in Christ are told, "Because ye are sons, God hath sent forth the Spirit of his Son into your hearts" (Gal. 4:6). This gives us to understand that God gives the Holy Spirit to the person who is a believer in the Lord Jesus Christ. The question could be asked, "Does that mean that every believer has the Holy Spirit in the fullness of His function, and so on?" I will now try to answer this and to show there is something the believer must do if he wants the fullness of the Spirit in his own heart.

God sent forth His Son to redeem men to be His children. But is everyone redeemed? God gave His Son to die for sinners. Are all sinners saved? No? Which ones are saved? "As many as received Him," these are saved. God sent His Son to die for all men, but "as many as receive Him" have the benefits of that death. God sends His Holy Spirit into the hearts of His children and in the same way as many as receive Him will be the ones who will have the blessing of the Holy Spirit in their lives. One might ask, "Can the Holy Spirit be in my heart and I not have received Him?" Apparently, "Yes." His coming into my heart is God's work but my receiving Him is my personal response to His coming. Some people think that the reason the world cannot receive the Holy Spirit is that the world is wicked. That is not true. They might think that the reason the world does not receive the Holy Spirit is that the world is sinful. That is not true. If sinners could not receive the Holy Spirit, Christians could never receive Him. Believing sinners *can* receive the Holy Spirit. They are sinners, but they believe in Him. God makes the Holy Spirit available to every one who believes in Him and in the Lord Jesus Christ. If any man sees Him and knows Him, he can receive Him.

How can one see a spirit? To see the things which are invisible is to understand, to perceive. The person who does not understand about the Holy Spirit will not be able to receive Him or know Him. The word *know* is used to convey the idea of esteem or appreciation. Because the world does not understand about the Holy Spirit and does not appreciate or esteem Him, the world cannot receive the Holy Spirit.

What does that say to the individual? If a man does not understand the Holy Spirit and does not esteem Him, then the Holy Spirit cannot be operative in him. Although the Lord Jesus Christ died for everyone, as long as people do not know about it, they will not be able to have salvation. It is when they understand about Him and receive Him as their Saviour that the blessing takes place.

Think back to those people whom Paul went to see at Ephesus and of whom he asked the question, "Have you received the Holy Ghost since you believed?" Their answer was, "We have not so much as heard whether there be any Holy Ghost." They had not been *told*. In our present day, this could be likened to a person who goes to church and listens to preaching and Bible study. If the preaching and Bible study do not tell about the Holy Spirit, people could go to that place and listen in that place and yet live without the blessing of the Holy Spirit for they would not understand about Him and would not recognize Him for what He is.

Paul further asked them, "Unto what then were ye baptized?" They said, "Unto John's baptism." This was all right so far as it went, but John himself told his disciples that Christ would do more for them. Paul told them about the Lord Jesus Christ and baptized them in His name, and they received the Holy Spirit.

There is something men can do about receiving the Holy Spirit. They must be conscious of His presence. They must appreciate Him for what He is. Perhaps the following illustration will help in understanding what it is to receive the Holy Spirit.

Suppose you were expecting someone to visit you in your home.

The Holy Spirit

You were looking forward to having a guest come to spend the week end. You have a little girl five or six years old, who comes in from the front room and says, "Mrs. So-and-so is here." You would say, "What do you mean she's here?" "She's in the front room," the child replies. You say, "Why, she couldn't be in the house; I had the door locked." The little girl says, "I opened it, and I let her in." In that situation, what should you as the lady of the house do? If the guest you were expecting is already in the front room, you must go and receive her. What does receiving her mean when she is already in the front room? It means going in, recognizing her, facing her, speaking welcome to her, and making her at home. Usually it would mean showing her to the room where she is to stay.

That is very similar to what is involved with a Christian person who wants to have the blessing of God in the Holy Spirit. He must make the Holy Spirit at home in his heart. He must understand literally that God has come to be with him and, looking into His face, he must give Him not just one room, but a passkey to every room in the house. The Christian must let the Holy Spirit come in to dwell with him, to show him the things of the Lord Jesus Christ and to help him respond to the will of God in his own living.

BRINGING MEN TO CHRIST

The Holy Spirit, working in the heart, brings men to Christ. Human beings are not believers when they are born into the world. I became a believer when I became aware of God, whom I had never seen.

A very small child pays no attention to objects or to people. Gradually, however, the child learns that objects mean certain things, and he or she comes to know and appreciate some people and to fear others. As time goes on, the child also learns that there is a loss when someone is absent. Later in life, a person becomes aware of people, relatives and loved ones, who live a great distance away and cannot be seen. But it is still more difficult for a person to come to know God.

God shows Himself in nature. I can get an idea of God by looking at the stars above me. I can also come to know God through the truth of the Gospel. God judges sin. Those who have done wrong are sinners in God's sight and will come under His judgment.

The Gospel tells us, however, God will forgive sins. This forgiveness is worked out through His Son, the Lord Jesus Christ. The sinner must turn to God, come to Him, and believe that Christ Jesus died for him. But this is not a simple thing to do. It is not easy for a person, who knows he is a wrongdoer, to believe that Christ Jesus would die for him. It takes inward help even to think about it. This is part of the work of the Holy Spirit.

One way God brings men to think about coming to Him is by permitting them to have certain kinds of trouble. People can have so many difficulties that in desperation they will seek help from somewhere, no matter where. They will even turn to God and call upon Him. And so God lets things happen to a person's life. God is constantly working on people through natural events, commonly called "acts of God," to get them to think about Him. An "act of God" is something which happens in the physical world that men cannot stop. It might be a hurricane, an earthquake, or a great fire. Any of these may result in great destruction and usually takes many human lives. Such sudden drastic calamities cause human beings to stop and think.

But the Scriptures also show that the Holy Spirit works on the heart, the mind, and the conscience, interpreting these events to individual people. Because of the work of the Holy Spirit, human beings suddenly become conscious of the fact that they are not right in the sight of God. In order for this to happen, they must be aware of several things. They must believe there is a God and they are responsible to Him. They must understand and recognize that they are not acceptable to God, for they have done wrong in His sight. The Holy Spirit, working on the heart, inclines a person to be conscious of the reality of God and makes him appreciate the Gospel. He is ready to believe that God is holy. This inward working of the Holy Spirit will show a man to himself in such a way that he will know he will be judged by God. Many people will bear testimony to the fact that in the midst of some great trouble the first thing they thought of was the wrong they had done. This consciousness was the working of God by His Holy Spirit, because "he will reprove the world of sin, and of righteousness."

The heart will become aware of the fact that God is holy and that He desires men to be like Him. This would not especially impress some people. They would think this is simply another human

The Holy Spirit

idea. However, if the Holy Spirit has been able to work in my heart when I hear these words, I will feel them to be true; and I will have a desire in my heart to be right in God's sight.

The Holy Spirit inclines people to be conscious of judgment to come. When the Holy Spirit is active in me I know that one day I am going to have to face God and that God is going to deal with me. God will punish sin. This impression in the heart is the result of the Holy Spirit's interpreting the affairs of life.

When an accident occurs, one person may think it is just an accident and someone is probably to blame. Another person will think it happened in this way for a purpose. This latter person is being influenced by the Holy Spirit, who brings to mind the things of God and inclines people to think of the judgment to come.

In bringing men to Christ, the Holy Spirit not only blesses natural events so that men are reminded of God, but He leads Christians to witness to other people. The New Testament relates in detail the meeting of Philip with the Ethiopian eunuch. The angel of the Lord told Philip to go down through the desert from Jerusalem to Gaza. As Philip traveled through the desert, he met a man from Ethiopia who was returning to his native country after having been to Jerusalem to worship. The man was sitting in his chariot reading the Bible and had come to a passage in Isaiah. As we read the entire story, it seems obvious that it was not Philip's idea to go down through the desert nor was it his idea to go to the man in the chariot. He did these things because he was inwardly led to do them. Philip may not even have been conscious of the Holy Spirit's guidance. However, when he would look back afterwards on those events and interpret what had happened, he would, no doubt, readily admit that the idea of taking the trip to Gaza was not really his own nor was the idea of meeting the man from Ethiopia something he had in mind. Yet the Holy Spirit used him.

A further illustration from the New Testament involves Peter. Cornelius, a centurion of the Italian band and a Gentile, wanted to know the way of the Lord. He was a devout man, he gave alms to the poor, and he prayed to God always. God spoke to Cornelius in a vision and told him to send to Joppa and find a man called Peter, who would tell him what to do.

While the servants from Cornelius were on their way, Peter also had a vision. Peter was told in his heart that he was to go with his servants, doubting nothing. Through the vision, the Holy Spirit had prepared Peter to understand that the Gospel of the Lord Jesus Christ was for Gentile as well as Jew. He was to go and preach to Cornelius and his household. The result was that these Gentiles were led to the Lord and became believers.

It seems clear that the household of Cornelius believed because Peter preached to them. Peter would never have preached to them if he had been left to make this decision for himself. The Holy Spirit opened the way for Peter, and he was obedient to the Spirit. The Holy Spirit had given Peter the grace and the message, and as Peter obeyed the Spirit, men were brought to Christ.

The Holy Spirit arranges to bring together the things that will bear upon a certain man's heart in such a way that that man will be brought to the place where he will believe in the Lord Jesus Christ and commit himself to Him. Thus the Holy Spirit works in the unbelieving person to bring that man to Christ.

IN BELIEVERS

After I become a Christian, there are still many things for me to learn. I must learn about Christ's daily guidance and His unceasing intercession to God on my behalf. As I read in the Bible what Christ Jesus did while on earth and what He will do, the real meaning is brought to me by the indwelling Holy Spirit of God. By the influence of the Holy Spirit, I am made to feel that I am actually participating in the events of the narrative. If I am reading the story of the Lord Jesus Christ's healing the leper, the Holy Spirit working in my heart can persuade me that if I had been there as a leper the Lord Jesus Christ would have cleansed me. I can then interpret this to mean that if there is something wrong with me now, I can turn to the Lord Jesus Christ for help.

The Scriptures tell of several instances where the Lord Jesus opened the eyes of the blind. The Holy Spirit will make me so conscious of this miraculous work of Christ that I will feel that had I been blind Christ would have opened my eyes. It is not a far step to realize that when I am blind spiritually the Lord Jesus will open the eyes of my understanding.

The Holy Spirit makes me conscious of these things, showing me the things of Christ and leading me in the course of my experience in life to put my complete trust in the Lord Jesus Christ. This is what Peter means when he says, "Casting all your care upon him; for he careth for you" (1 Pet. 5:7). Through the Scriptures the Holy Spirit leads me in my mind into the will of God and guides me in my affairs so that when I am wondering what I should do on a given day I will pray to God. God, through the Holy Spirit, works in my heart, and as I pray I am guided into the will of God.

It is possible to come to God in prayer with our minds in a state of confusion. Then as we wait before the Lord, thinking on the things of the Lord, the Holy Spirit reveals God's will to our hearts and minds. The Holy Spirit enables us to see the truth about things. We can look at them free from selfish ideas, because the Holy Spirit helps us to act with spiritual intelligence, following the example of the Lord Jesus and desiring to be well-pleasing in the sight of God. This will help us get a true view of anything we are considering.

Because of the Holy Spirit, my heart can be aware of the love of God. The love of God is seen in the cross of Calvary. When I have yielded my heart and mind to the indwelling Holy Spirit of God, He will show me more of the meaning of the death of the Lord Jesus Christ. I will be filled with gratitude and a desire to be well-pleasing in God's sight. I will obey God then, not because I am compelled to, not because I am afraid not to, but because I inwardly want to, because the love of God is shed abroad in my heart by the Holy Spirit. The Holy Spirit has shown me how God in Christ Jesus loved me first, even before I knew Him, and as a result I love God and I love other people. The great work of the Holy Spirit is to spread abroad the love of God in the heart.

In my spiritual experience, the Holy Spirit will guide me to speak to certain people. I will find it in my heart to visit certain people who are sick, and I will be guided to talk to various persons concerning spiritual things.

As I go about my daily living, I will have the feeling that I am being led by the Holy Spirit. He does not stand with a pointer in front of me to give directions. He is not a signpost. The Bible puts it this way: "And thine ears shall hear a word behind thee, saying, This is the way, walk ye in it, when ye turn to the right hand, and when ye turn to the left" (Isa. 30:21). When I am yielded to God and am trusting the Holy Spirit in me to help me, I will get in my mind ideas of what I ought to do.

The Holy Spirit not only guides me to talk to, to visit with, and to pray for certain people; but He enables me to do special things. Some Christians are given the understanding to explain things to people, others are helped to guide people, and still others are moved to exercise themselves in prayer so that certain answers come in such a way that other people will think about the Lord. I may become involved in a conflict with someone else. The other person and I are openly against each other. The Holy Spirit can make me mild-mannered and gentle throughout the whole difficulty. My actions and attitude could be a surprise to all who know about our quarrel and might make a good impression upon others who may be watching what is going on.

The Holy Spirit helps me to be strong and effectual in praying. From time to time, questions arise concerning *what* should be done and *how* it should be done. The Holy Spirit will give to certain people the capacity to see what ought to be done. Such believers will then make good leaders. Others may be given the ability to give public testimony. When they talk about the things of the Lord Jesus Christ, they can speak freely. In such ways the Holy Spirit not only guides the believer into the will of God, but He helps him to do what God wants him to do.

In His work in my heart, the Holy Spirit produces certain results which are called the "fruits of the Spirit." He affects me in such a way that I am inclined to act more and more the way God wants me to act. People who are led by the Holy Spirit and obedient to the will of God are spoken of as "spiritual" people. A believer in the Lord Jesus Christ becomes spiritual when his consciousness is affected by and yielded to the Holy Spirit.

The opposite of being spiritual is to be "carnal." A carnal person's thoughts, his ideas, and his way of doing things are just like the ways of other human beings. He does whatever he thinks is to his advantage. Carnal conduct can even be for good reason, but it remains carnal when it is carried on in human strength.

On the other hand, when I am led by the Holy Spirit of God I have an inward dependence upon the Lord Jesus Christ. I believe in the living God and I personally trust in Him. The Holy Spirit will guide me to put my whole confidence in the Lord Jesus Christ, will direct my choices as to what to do, and will strengthen me to

The Holy Spirit

do God's will. Fruitfulness will follow in my life in a way that will be to the glory of God.

Not only does the Holy Spirit make me fruitful in my conduct, but He keeps me thinking about Christ. As long as I am thinking about the Lord Jesus Christ, the Holy Spirit is having His way in my heart. The Holy Spirit does not lead me to think of Himself, but He takes the things of Christ and speaks to me about them. In this way I am being guided by the Holy Spirit to do God's will.

IN THE CHURCH

In addition to the Holy Spirit's work in the world and in the believer, there is a sense in which He works in the church. Every congregation has the Holy Spirit working within it in various ways. By putting within the hearts of certain people a willingness to serve, the Holy Spirit is working to provide leadership in the church.

The Sunday school must have officers. Someone must undertake the responsibility of doing the work of the superintendent. This job will take time and thought. There will be times when it will take faithfulness and a good deal of patience to serve as superintendent of the Sunday school. The Holy Spirit puts into the heart of someone the disposition to be willing to accept this responsibility, and also gives to that person the disposition to carry out the task. The man who makes a good superintendent is one who does this work, not for the sake of the congregation, nor for the Christian Education Committee, nor even for the Sunday school, but for the sake of the Lord Jesus Christ. It is possible for him to have that outlook, frame of mind, and attitude when the Holy Spirit is working in the heart.

The Sunday school will also need teachers. Generally speaking, Sunday school teaching is not very encouraging. The teacher cannot always be sure the pupils will come. If they come, the teacher cannot be sure they will listen; and if they listen, no one can be sure they will do anything about it. A new lesson must be prepared each week, and every Sunday the teacher must be present in class. Sometimes it is difficult to get along with the persons the teacher is trying to teach. Also, it is not always easy to get along with other people who are working in the Sunday school. Some of them have queer ideas when they want this, that, or the other thing done.

Parents are not always cooperative or sympathetic with the teacher. It is discouraging when a teacher is trying to get the children interested in what is being done in Sunday school and then the parents take them off to the beach or to the lake and break up the program. Under such circumstances, it would be a very easy thing for me to get tired of teaching Sunday school. However, the Holy Spirit can affect me so that if I am asked to teach, I may be willing to accept the responsibility; and if I once undertake it, I may be faithful in doing the work. In this case I do it not because of the children, or the parents, or the church, but "as unto the Lord."

The man who takes the responsibility of the office of deacon in the church will have many things to discourage him. When he speaks to people about how they should support the Lord's work, they may not like to hear him; and when he goes to them and asks them to give more liberally, they may not like to see him. Some deacons have quit. They have figured it out that if church members are not any more interested in the church's work than that, they don't have to be interested either. Such a frame of mind can be understood from a human point of view, but of course it is not a spiritual attitude. The Holy Spirit will move a man to do the best he can as unto the Lord whether other people are doing it or not.

It is the Holy Spirit who makes a faithful elder perform his functions, thinking always of the spiritual welfare of the people. Many times people are not interested in, and do not care about, the spiritual welfare of the church. Yet it is the elder's responsibility to try to keep things in the church going along in the way the Lord would want. How can the church get elders to accept responsibility for the spiritual life of the people? It is possible because the Holy Spirit of God, working in the heart, makes a man willing, able, and faithful so that he will try to do these things.

The Holy Spirit empowers people to do specific work in the church. Men and women will be willing to take on work to do because the Holy Spirit is working in their hearts, showing them the things of Christ and reminding them of what Christ has done for them. They are moved in thanks and gratitude to be willing, ready, and eager to do the will of God.

When a particular congregation feels that nobody wants to do anything in the church, this means that all their members are acting like human beings. Human beings do not want to do anything

The Holy Spirit

in the church, for they have too much to do already. It is probably quite true that the average person has more to do than he can do. Certainly the average woman has more to do than her hands can hold. When the church comes along with something else for her to do, she feels she just cannot add this. She hasn't been able to do what she is supposed to do without doing this extra thing. And it is the same with men. When asked to help do a certain piece of work in the church, they can honestly say they cannot now keep up with their business. They are worn out already. When they come home they need rest. The reason they don't come to church on Sunday is that they are so worn out by Saturday that if they are going to go back and hold their job on Monday, they have to rest all day Sunday. Sunday is a day of rest, anyway, and that is just what they need to do. Chances are, they told the truth. By Saturday noon they are worn out, and they don't feel like doing anything until Monday. For some of them, it will be even later than Monday before they feel like doing anything. Certainly they do not think they can take any time out on Sunday to go to church or to do anything in the church. All that is the matter with those people is that they are human beings. Even if some of them were invited to go to a party, a big game, a fishing trip, or a duck hunt, they would be too tired. It is true some would go, but others would say they were not interested. When once they get home and get their shoes off, they cannot be budged to take part in what they feel is merely extra things. From a human point of view, such people have their reasons, good reasons. How will those people ever care about the church? How will they ever care about spreading the Gospel?

The Holy Spirit can move that kind of people actually to undertake to do work in the church. The truth of the matter is that when any of them will take time to take care of their souls they are often stronger for the rest of the week. However, it takes faith to believe that, for it will not appear that way unless the heart is moved by the Holy Spirit to start and to follow through in the things of the Lord.

The Holy Spirit moves the people of the church to worship God. When everyone in the congregation wants to sing, it means that hearts are full of praise to God, and want to express their joy. Some congregations do not want to sing. The members have the feeling that after all there is a choir. Let the choir sing. Such people will just stand through the service of song and wait until it is finished without taking any part. They do not feel like praising God. They have not been moved by the Holy Spirit. What is true concerning congregational singing also applies to prayer. When a prayer meeting is announced, some people will say at once, "Just count me out. I won't be there." Humanly speaking, I would never be interested in praying; but, spiritually speaking, I find I am. I wish I would pray more. When the Holy Spirit works in my heart, He moves me to be willing to worship the Lord and to do things for the Lord's work. I find myself willing to take part in the Lord's work, willing to follow others who are doing the Lord's work, and willing to give of my money to the Lord's work.

When a congregation does not want to sing, pray, and give, the Spirit is not working in them. When the feeling comes to my heart that I should do something about it, the Holy Spirit is then working in me.

FRUITS OF THE SPIRIT

The Holy Spirit comes to work in the heart of the individual believer and in the church as a whole. The result of the work of the Holy Spirit can be seen in certain fruits. The Bible teaches, "But the fruit of the Spirit is love, joy, peace, longsuffering, gentleness, goodness, faith, meekness, temperance" (Gal. 5:22). These fruits of the Spirit will be found in the life of each Christian.

When the Holy Spirit works in the heart, He shows me what Christ has done. The Holy Spirit reminds me that Christ Jesus died for me and that He is now at the right hand of God interceding on my behalf. The Holy Spirit further reminds me that God has accepted me through the Lord Jesus Christ. As these ideas and truths are kept before my mind, I am affected "Because the love of God is shed abroad in our hearts by the Holy Ghost which is given unto us" (Rom. 5:5). When the love of God is shed abroad in my heart and I really seek to be well-pleasing in His sight, results, known as fruits, follow in my daily life.

The first of the fruits of the Spirit to be mentioned is *love*. Love is not so much an emotion and a sentiment as it is a direction of activity. The man who loves God will seek to please God. The one who keeps the commandments of God is the one who loves Him. Loving God is not a matter of looking at His beauty and admiring Him, although this is very important. Adoring and worshipping God are also very important. Loving God, however, is seeking to do His will and having a desire to be well-pleasing in His sight.

Love is not only directed toward God, but it is also shown in concern for my neighbor. Loving my neighbor does not mean that I am delighted at every thought of him or approve everything he does. Even if I were unhappy about him I could still love him. We show love for other persons when we love as God loves. "For God so loved the world, that he gave his only begotten Son, that whosoever believeth in him should not perish, but have everlasting life" (John 3:16). This is a way of saying that God so loved people that He took His *own* Son, and gave Him to die for their benefit. And this shows us what it means to love other people; it means we will take of our own to help them in their need.

A certain man, a lawyer, came to the Lord Jesus Christ and asked, "And who is my neighbor?" The Lord Jesus told him the parable of the Good Samaritan (Luke 10:30-37), which shows what is meant by love for one's neighbor. The Good Samaritan loved the man whom he found in the ditch. Now let us see just what this meant. The man had been traveling from Jesusalem to Jericho when he fell among thieves. They stripped him of his raiment and left him half dead. A priest came by and looked at him, but passed by on the other side. A Levite came along and looked at him, but he, too, passed by on the other side. When the Good Samaritan saw the man, he was moved with compassion for him and *helped him*. He took of his *own* first-aid equipment, poured oil in his wounds, gave him wine to drink to refresh him, set him on his *own* beast of burden, brought him to an inn, and took care of him *himself*. Since it was necessary for the Samaritan to continue on his way the following day, he gave the innkeeper money to pay the man's room rent and gave him instructions to care for the man and whatever expenses were incurred he would repay the innkeeper when he passed through at some later time. That is love; that is not sentiment. We have no idea whether the Good Samaritan liked the man or not. Love is not to be shown only to people I have seen before and like, nor is it to be given only to those described as "one of ours," persons related by blood. Love is something to be given to any and every human being. Through the work of the Holy

Spirit in my heart, I see the needs of others. I want to help the other fellow; and so I take of my *own* and *give* to the one in need. Such conduct on my part is pleasing to God and it is helpful to other human beings. This is the result of the Holy Spirit's working in my heart.

Another fruit of the Spirit which the Christian will have is *joy*. When I have *joy*, I feel good about things. The Bible often speaks of *joy* and *rejoicing*. Joy is sometimes expressed by such words as *gladness, mirth,* and *cheer*. The word *rejoice* means calling to mind the joy that I have in my heart. When I say *re-*joice I mean to bring my joy to mind over and over again.

What can I have joy about in the Lord? I can have joy in the Lord since I am forgiven my sins, since God is taking care of me, and since the Lord Jesus will never leave me nor forsake me. Christ will be with me all the time. If I have joy in the Lord for this reason and I recall my joy tomorrow and the next day, then I am *rejoicing*. The Holy Spirit will help me to do this more and more. When I remember how the Lord is watching over me, I can have joy in all things, including adversity, suffering, and affliction. The Book of Acts tells of the incident when the apostles were brought before the council. They were badly treated and beaten but "they departed from the presence of the council, *rejoicing* that they were counted worthy to suffer shame for his name" (Acts 5:41).

The third fruit of the Spirit is *peace*. Peace is a condition and state of mind in which I have no contention, no conflict, and no strife. A great deal is said in our day and time about living in peace. Many people are in favor of peace. The United Nations is a *world* peace organization. The word *peace* as it is commonly used today seems to describe a situation in which people do not fight. This may not be really peace at all. To be able to hold myself in so that I do not blow my top may be admirable in me but it does not show the peace of God.

To understand the peace of God, picture the Lord Jesus standing in Pilate's courtroom. The soldiers had just mocked Him, they had plucked His beard, they had spit in His face, they had buffeted Him, they had placed a crown of thorns on His head, and they had dressed Him in a purple robe to make fun of Him as pretending to be a king. If any merely human being were given that sort of treatment, he would have been wild with rage or with fear, or both; but the Lord Jesus stood in their presence at peace. Pilate looked at Jesus and could not understand Him. Pilate said, "Knowest thou not that I have the power to crucify thee?" It did not seem possible in Pilate's mind that anyone could realize the danger Jesus of Nazareth was in and not be upset by it. But when the Lord Jesus stood in Pilate's courtroom, was He at peace because He was exercising self-control? Did He really feel like fighting, but had the will power to hold Himself back? The only way to understand the Lord Jesus Christ is to say that He was *inwardly* and *altogether* at peace. The reason these wicked and violent things did not disturb Jesus was that He had been in the Garden of Gethsemane, and He had had a long prayer session with His Father. He understood it was His Father's will that these things should be, and so He endured everything patiently. Later, when He was on Calvary's cross, He could pray, "Father, forgive them; for they know not what they do" (Luke 23:34). Jesus was free from violence and retaliation, because He had dealings with His Heavenly Father which gave Him victory over anything that man could do to Him.

I can actually have something similar to this when I am filled with the Holy Spirit of God. The Holy Spirit will bring to my attention the things of Almighty God in such a way that the things of this world will not trouble me. Then I can enjoy peace, a fruit of the Spirit.

We have not the space to study each of the fruits of the Spirit, but this much about *love, joy,* and *peace* will show how it would be with the other fruits. When the Holy Spirit in my heart shows me what God has done for me, is now doing, and will do for me, I am filled with ideas and feelings which are called the "fruits of the Spirit."

CHAPTER EIGHT

The Christian

THE word *Christian* is first used as a noun. It is never used in the Bible as an adjective. Expressions such as "speaking a *Christian* word" or "doing a *Christian* deed" are not found in the Bible. The word *Christian* is used only three times in the Bible. In the phrase "the disciples were called Christians," the word *Christians* is plural. Individually, each disciple was a Christian.

Citizens of America are spoken of as Americans. Each individual is an American. Because there are Americans in the world there is an American way of life. We speak of American habits and American ideas, but that is all secondary. There must first be Americans before there can be American ideas and an American way of conduct.

A man can be a Christian and not look and act like one. A person can be a Christian even though he has not yet learned to walk in the ways of a Christian. Many years ago, I became a soldier in Canada. I walked into the recruiting office, signed a paper, and walked out a soldier. I knew nothing as yet about soldiering. I did not know how to march, how to clean a rifle, or how to keep my tent. I had no knowledge of army regulations. But I was a soldier. I became a soldier by signing an agreement stating that I would serve in the Canadian army for the duration of the war and six months thereafter.

Two people marry. They have the certificate signed by the minister and the witnesses, but the man may not as yet act like a husband. He may become a father, but he may not act like a father. He may act like a stranger, even if he is a father.

HIS FAITH

Normally speaking, a Christian will grow in faith and under-

The Christian

standing; and he will begin to act like a Christian *after* he has become one. A Christian is a person in whom God is working by His grace, according to His promises in Christ Jesus. There is no such thing as a Christian in whose heart God is not working. The Christian acquires certain characteristics as God works in his heart. He will develop Christian faith. He starts out by believing in the Lord Jesus Christ. Christian faith is believing in Christ and committing oneself to Him in all aspects of life. The Christian believes in Christ as He is presented in the Bible. The Christian believes that Jesus Christ is the Son of God, and that as the Son of God He did, does and will do certain things.

When it is said that a Christian believes in God, it means that he believes in the God of our fathers, the God of the Bible, the God and Father of our Lord Jesus Christ. He believes that the whole universe was created by God, but he believes far more about God than that He is Creator. He believes the Creator is a Person and that this Person is holy, just, and good. The Ten Commandments are His law. However, believing these truths does not make a man a Christian. The Christian believes that God was in Jesus Christ and that Jesus of Nazareth, who was born in Bethlehem, who lived thirty years on earth, who died on Calvary's cross, and who arose from the dead, was the Son of God. A Christian believes that God was in Christ Jesus "reconciling the world unto himself" (2 Cor. 5:19). He specifically believes that God is his Father.

It is a common thing in our day and time to assume that the Fatherhood of God refers to God's kindness to all people. God is kind to all people as Creator, Keeper, Provider, and Sustainer, but He is the Father, in a special way, of those who believe in the Lord Jesus Christ. When the Christian considers God as Father, he is thinking of the One who begets him. The Christian is born again of God. What the Christian believes about God in a special way is that God as the Father of the Lord Jesus Christ becomes his Father. The Christian is adopted into the family of God as His child. "And I will be a Father unto you, and ye shall be my sons and daughters, saith the Lord Almighty" (2 Cor. 6:18).

The Christian also believes certain things about Jesus Christ. It is not enough for a Christian to believe that Jesus of Nazareth lived, that He was a good man, that He was the Son of God, or that God was His Father in the sense that He is everybody's Father.

The Christian must believe that Jesus Christ is God. When the Christian worships God the Father, he worships God the Son and God the Holy Spirit. He accepts Jesus Christ and believes Him to be his sacrifice for sin. He believes that because Jesus Christ died on Calvary's cross God will forgive the Christian; and so he will say that Christ's death has brought him forgiveness from sin. He believes that the Lord Jesus Christ is his Saviour day by day *now* because *He* is alive in resurrection power. The Bible teaches that Christ Jesus is "also able to save them to the uttermost that come unto God by him, seeing he ever liveth to make intercession for them" (Heb. 7:25). The Christian also believes that Jesus Christ is the Lord of his life, so that every day his life is directed by Him. A person who becomes intelligent about himself as a Christian understands that the living Lord Jesus Christ will guide him, and so he prays to God to find out what the Father wants him to do, and counts on the Lord Jesus Christ to guide his steps. Jesus said, "I will never leave thee, nor forsake thee" (Heb. 13:5). He said, "I will come again, that where I am, there ye may be also" (John 14:3). He said to go into all the world and preach the Gospel to every creature and "Lo, I am with you alway, even unto the end of the world" (Matt. 28:20). The Christian also believes that Christ Jesus is the coming Judge of all the world, but that He will always be the Companion and Friend of those who put their trust in Him. The Christian has the comforting assurance that "whosoever will" may put trust in the Lord Jesus Christ and be saved.

Concerning the Holy Spirit, the Christian believes that He is a Person, that He is God, and that He has been sent to believers in a way that can be learned, even if the believer never fully understands. The Christian believes that God has given the Holy Spirit into his heart so that He dwells within him and the believer's "body is the temple of the Holy Spirit" (1 Cor. 6:19). He believes that the Holy Spirit as a Person can be grieved. As a Person, the Holy Spirit is also to be obeyed. The Christian wants to do what he is inwardly led by the Holy Spirit to do. He comes to understand that the Holy Spirit uses the Word of God as "the sword of the Spirit" (Eph. 6:17). The Holy Spirit makes the Scriptures alive to the believer and thus guides him in the revealed will of God.

What else does a Christian believe? He believes all things that

The Christian

the Scriptures teach. This will include believing that Jesus Christ is coming again. He believes that all men will stand before God to be judged. He believes that Almighty God is over all things—His eye is on the Christians and He will not let them be destroyed. The Christian understands that death is not the end of anything. He has found out through Jesus Christ on Calvary that death does not stop the soul and that the believer will go right on into the presence of God. He believes that the Lord Jesus Christ is alive and waiting for him. The Christian understands that he can call upon God and that God will answer him because of what the Lord Jesus Christ has promised. The Christian expects to go to heaven to be with the Lord.

REGENERATION

Regeneration is something very important in a Christian's life and experience. When we are thinking about Christians, we need to remember that everybody is not a Christian. No one is born of human parents as a Christian. It is not a matter of background, or family, or community which makes me a Christian. All kinds of people can be found in any society, good and bad, beautiful and ugly, kind and cruel, civilized and savage. But Christians are found only among those who have heard the Gospel.

A Christian has been "born again" (Chapter Six). "Born again" means that I have experienced a spiritual renewal—*regeneration*. When I am regenerated, something new has been begun in me. There are differences of opinion as to when regeneration happens. Some people think that it happens before I believe, while others think that it takes place after I believe in Christ. They may have different ideas about the time when it happens; but all agree that if I am to be a Christian, I must be regenerated. Actually it is when I am regenerated that I really become a Christian. It is because I am regenerated, which means "born again," that I am able to walk with the Lord and to be with Him.

Regeneration may take place in me in such a way that I do not notice it as it happens. This need not puzzle me. When I was born the first time, I did not know it. It is like that in regeneration. It is quite possible for God to begin working in me before I am conscious of it.

Another word that is often used to refer to this phase of Christian experience is *conversion*. The word *conversion* is used very little in the Bible. The general idea in the word is that of being *turned around*. It is as if when I was going north I turned and started going south. So I was going away from God, and now I am going to God. This involves a change of attitude in my heart, a turning around in the way in which I want to go. Speaking of my conversion, I could say something like this: "I was converted at 8:30 p.m. on October 12, 1915." I would be saying that at that time I changed my mind and turned around with reference to the Lord Jesus Christ. However, many people cannot name the exact date on which their conversion occurred. In my case, I was looking toward God and the Lord Jesus Christ, and I wanted to come to Him for weeks before I could see my way clearly. I suppose that in my case the word *illumination* would be better. *Illumination* can be used to refer to the experience of the heart, mind, and consciousness when I saw the truth which before was hidden from me. I suppose I had been converted earlier. Only God, not I, knows when I was regenerated. But something must have happened to me before this, or else I would not have had that new disposition within me which made me want to come to God.

When I was born as a child, I had a human nature. Human beings behave in various ways, but, generally speaking, they are selfish. Starting as a baby, I reached for things to *take*. If I live to be eighty, I will still be reaching, a little bit slower perhaps, but still reaching. I will not be able to grab quite so tightly, but I can take hold and I am going to hang on to everything I have. This is human nature, but it is not divine nature. When I am born again, it is to the praise of God and to the joy of the Christian that I will find within me promptings to want to do what is pleasing to Him "who loved me, and gave himself for me" (Gal. 2:20).

As a Christian I want to be pleasing in the sight of God. Instead of just taking things for myself, I find joy in *giving* to others. This is not something that I can learn as a human being. My human heart will be struggling with the thought: why should I be giving to someone who has never given anything to me? After all, it would be natural to seek to make a profit on any deal. But as a Christian I have the disposition to give to another person because I care about that person, and that person needs what I am giving. This act of giving is a response to the grace of God—God cares. The man I am helping may not be lovely, but God loves him, and God wants me to do for him. He is not good, but God wants to save him. God is like this because of His grace. This is the new disposition that I have when I have been born again. This may not always show up immediately in one's attitude toward other people, but it will come.

Regeneration is the method by which God changes me. I am born again from within; I belong to God, and now I want to be well-pleasing in His sight. As a new creature I grow by feeding on the promises of God, considering the grace of God, worshipping the Lord Jesus Christ, and walking with Him. In this new nature I want to be with God and His people. I want to do God's will and share in God's work, helping to spread the Gospel and seeing other people saved. This is the divine nature which was in the Lord Jesus Christ, who came "to give his life a ransom for many" (Matt. 20:28). When I become a Christian, I find that this new nature is beginning to influence my ideas and to affect my actions.

JUSTIFICATION

Justification is a common word used in speaking of the Christian experience. It is a Bible word. In order to understand the word *justification,* it is necessary to understand the word *just.* The English word *just* has in it a very simple idea. When a man is *just,* he is right. He is what he ought to be.

God is just. God is always fair. He deals with every man alike. There are no favorites with God. He is not one way one day and another way another day. He is the same all the time. He is exactly what He is in Himself, and He is always that way. You can depend on Him.

No man in himself is just. Human beings are devious. If God is like a straight line, man is not straight. If God is exactly perpendicular, man leans to one side or the other. Men who break the law are described as being crooked. They are not just. If they were just, they would be straight; but they naturally deviate from the law. When we say "All have sinned," we mean that all have deviated from the straight. All have transgressed. They have all failed and "come short." "All we like sheep have gone astray" (Isa. 53:6).

The whole Bible teaches us that God wants to have fellowship with man. But God is holy and just, and man is not. Man is a sinner, and God's holy eyes are such that they cannot look on sin. God can deal only with just men. That creates a problem. If God cannot have fellowship with a sinner, and "all have sinned and come short of the glory of God," how can God find anybody with whom he can have fellowship? Humanly speaking, there would be no man with whom God could live. This is where the Gospel brings relief. The Lord Jesus Christ came into the world to save sinners. He is able to take unrighteous people and make them righteous: unjust people and make them just. He is able to take sinners and make them fit for God. To be *justified* before God is to receive complete forgiveness of all sins and to be permanently reinstated to a place of favor and privilege with God.

The word *justify* is ordinarily used in the following manner. When someone does something he should not do, he is called in and asked to give a reason for his actions. When he begins explaining, He is trying to justify himself: trying to make himself what he ought to be by arguing that he did not do wrong at all. But this is not the way God justifies. God does not say that whatever I have done is all right. God admits that what man did was wrong, but He can fix it so that the wrong which the man did will not stand between man and Himself. This does not mean that God will excuse man or alibi for him. Sin is awful in the sight of God, but God is able to remove that sin. He is able to carry it away through Christ, who is the substitution for sinful man. Christ is the sacrifice for sin.

Sacrifice means that the penalty of death which should have fallen upon the sinner falls upon a substitute. In the Old Testament a lamb was the sacrifice. The death that should have come to the sinner came to the lamb, an innocent animal, and the man was set free. In God's dealing with man this principle is always true. God will let someone else pay the sinner's bill. When the sinner's name comes up in the presence of Almighty God, the Lord Jesus Christ steps in, and bears the sin in His own body so that man goes free. The result is that man is then treated by God as if he had not done anything wrong. God knows he did wrong. The man knows he did wrong. The Lord Jesus Christ knows the man did wrong, but the man is made *just* in the sight of God.

A word which means much the same as justification is *reconcilia-*

tion,* the method by which Christ Jesus brings a sinful man to the Father. *Reconciliation* is not a matter of affecting the emotions and the mind. Christ is reconciling me to the Father when He brings us together in such a way that the holy Father can deal with me as if there were nothing against me before Him. The reason I do not have anything against me is that the Lord Jesus Christ paid my fine. I am not justified because of anything I do, but I am justified because of what Christ Jesus did.

Having been justified before God and reconciled to Him through the Lord Jesus Christ, now that I am a Christian, I have a change in attitude. I am grateful to God and I want to bow down and worship God with thanksgiving and praise. As a Christian I am also guided from within by an impulse to serve God, "to will and to do of His good pleasure."

SANCTIFICATION

Sanctification refers to what God does in and for the believer. God does things for all people everywhere. He is the Creator of the whole world, and His grace and providence overrule throughout everything. His sun shines on the good and the bad, and His rain falls on the just and the unjust. There is not a human being on earth who does not have dealings with God. But God has prepared special things for those who will commit themselves to Him through believing in Jesus Christ. God will work the wonders of His grace in Christ Jesus for me if I will yield to Him.

Sanctification is the work of God in which the believer is set apart for God alone.** When any object of any kind is set apart for an exclusive use, it is *sanctified*. The Bible speaks not only of human beings as sanctified, but also of buildings, vessels, utensils, and days.

What is the meaning of the word *sanctuary?* The word *sanctuary* designates a room, a building, set apart for the exclusive use of worshipping God. The Sabbath Day is a *sanctified* day. A day cannot have morals; a golden vessel cannot have morals. Being *sanctified* is not a matter of morality. Being *sanctified* means being set apart for a particular use.

* This is also discussed in Chapter Three, p. 71.
** This is also discussed in Chapter Four, pp. 82-85.

Some people may have a few *sanctified* items in their homes. These are the few items which are used for a certain purpose and are not used for anything else. Do you have in your kitchen a special cup or a particular knife that you have set aside for one specific purpose only, and it is not to be used for anything else? What you have really done is to *sanctify* that article. As simple as it sounds, that is what *sanctified* really means.

When I recognize that I have been bought by the blood of the Lord Jesus Christ, I am not my own, I belong to God and am to be used for nothing but for God's purposes alone—this is what is meant by my being sanctified. Any man that is so set aside for God is a *saint*. The word *saint* is the noun of which the word *sanctified* is the verb. *Sanctify* is to set apart for a special use, and the man who is so set apart is a *saint*.

In our common language, we are inclined to speak of a person as a saint if he has achieved a high excellence of spiritual performance. But actually anyone who is set aside for the exclusive use of God will get to be a better man. It will not be long before all manner of moral virtue and spiritual excellence will be found in anybody who is set aside only for the use of God. Whenever anyone turns his mind and heart over to God and seeks to please Him, and has nothing in mind at all except that God's will be done, others will soon see moral excellence, personal virtue, and spiritual excellence in that person. When others see this, they say of such a person, "Why, he is a real saint." And we can understand what they mean, but that is not the true meaning of the word.

A person first *becomes* a Christian and then God begins to work in that person so that he can *act* like a Christian. In sanctification, God sets me apart for Himself. He wants me to serve Him. He wants to be the sole owner of my heart and mind. When I turn myself around to God, wanting above everything else to please Him, God will make me into a person who will act as if I belong to Him. Moral, ethical and spiritual virtues begin to appear in me.

If you live in that way for a length of time, you will become conscious of God. You will want to please Him. He bought you with His blood; He saved you from your sins; He is going to deliver you from going to hell; and He is going to bring you to heaven with Him. There is nothing now between you and the Father in heaven, and you can really and truly come into His presence at any time.

As you do that, it will affect you in such a way that you will change your ideas. You will have new notions and new thoughts, in which you want to please Him.

When all these results are added up, they are called *holiness*.* The English word *holy* can well be understood if the word *wholly* is remembered. *Entirely* is the meaning of the word *wholly*. I used to think that the word *holy* referred to a person who lived an exceptionally godly life—a person who was just perfect. If such were the case, how could anyone be holy? Yet we are told to be holy. Shall we think that God is asking me to do something that I cannot do? Who then can be saved? But by *holiness* we mean that I am *wholly, totally* given over to God. I can take that step on any day in my Christian experience. After I have surrendered to God as a sinner, certain changes will follow; but I repeat: What makes me *holy* even while I am yet a sinner is that I turn myself over altogether to God.

This is a wonderful thing. I can turn myself over to God just as I am. Suppose I am not much; I can turn that over. Suppose I am not even a faithful person; I can turn that over. God will straighten me out. I must turn myself completely over to God as I am, trusting in nothing else except God and yielding myself into His will. Certain results will follow in me and those results will be *holiness*. *Holiness* is the consequence of being *holy*, which is a matter of giving myself totally over to God.

I can start from anywhere in life. The Scriptures say: "Let the wicked forsake his way, and the unrighteous man his thoughts: let him return unto the Lord, and he will have mercy upon him; and to our God, for he will abundantly pardon" (Isa. 55:7). Anybody any time can turn himself entirely over to God. The act of yielding to God is being "sanctified in the Lord." Belonging to God is being a *saint*, being entirely His is being *holy* and the result in one's life will be called *holiness*.

GLORIFICATION

In addition to justification and sanctification, a third word used to describe what God does for a Christian is *glorification*. To understand the word *glorification*, one first must have a clear idea of

---

* This is also discussed in Chapter Four, pp. 85-87.

the word *glory*, because glorification is that work of God in a believer which results in the glory of God. We use the word *glory* very little in everyday talk, and so it may sound strange to our ears. But what it means is not so hard to understand. Any time I reach my goal, any time I manage to do what I want to do, any time I succeed in any effort I have undertaken—such are times of glory for me. The Hebrew word has in it the idea of harvest, especially the *joy of the harvest*. I grew up as a boy on a farm. I learned the hard way that farmers suffer many disappointments. Sometimes our harvest was poor and for a whole year we would suffer because of the shortage of money that resulted. Yet harvest time always seemed to be a time of rejoicing and gladness. The work of the whole year was now to be rewarded with the harvest. This was *glory time* for the farmer.

There may be even more meaning to this word in the way it is used in the Bible, but this will do to give us an idea of what is meant by the *glory* of God. God has in mind to bless us. He works in us to that end. When He succeeds in His work and actually produces in us the performance of His will as it was done in Christ Jesus, He is glorified in us. "Herein is my Father glorified, that ye bear much fruit" (John 15:8).

To many people the word *glory* may possibly mean something only in heaven. The Book of Revelation does show us that heaven is filled with God's glory, but the glory of God is also to be seen on the earth during our lifetime.

In the Westminster Shorter Catechism, one of the questions is, "What is the chief end of man?" The answer is, "To glorify God and to enjoy Him forever." Personally, for many years I had in mind that that meant that after man died and went to heaven he would join with others to increase the glory of God. I didn't know how it would be done, but I thought saved men would glorify God by somehow increasing the magnificence of the glory of the light that shines around the throne in heaven. But the chief end of man "to glorify God and to enjoy Him forever" takes place in this life. Man does not have to wait until heaven for this to happen. Some people are waiting for heaven for everything they are to get. But the glorious fact is that we do not have to wait until we leave this world to share in the glory of God. Some of that can happen here now.

The Christian

The Christian is to bear fruit here on earth. Christ Jesus said, "I am the vine, ye are the branches. He that abideth in me, and I in him, the same bringeth forth much fruit" (John 15:5). The glory of a wheat field is the bushels of golden grain. The glory of an apple orchard is the barrels of ripe apples. The glory of a man is the prime fullness of his strength. The fulfillment of anything is the glory of it. God is glorified when His plans work out and when what He does pays off in results.

God did not send His Son into the world only to save men from hell in the future. God could have fixed it so that I would never go to hell by simply not making me. In that case the Lord Jesus would never have had to die. But if God wanted me for Himself, and created me so that I would be with Him in eternity, and if it happened that I would be condemned to destruction because of my sin and so I would need to be saved, then Christ Jesus died not only to save me from hell but to take me to heaven.

A housewife goes to the hardware store and buys a kettle for cooking purposes. She takes it out of the store. Now no one can use it for carrying nails and bolts. The housewife has bought the kettle, and it is now hers. She has bought it to use and not merely to put on a shelf to show her neighbors she has a kettle. However, until something is put into the kettle, and it is used for cooking, its purpose has not been fulfilled.

Christ Jesus came into the world and died for me to save me from hell and to save me for heaven. The important thing is that I should belong to God and let Him have His way in my heart. When I let God have His way in me to work out His purposes through me, I will show His glory. He will produce in me the fruit of the Spirit. The word *fruit* is singular, and it means at least nine different things. A person cannot have one and not have the other eight. Anyone who has *love* in his heart will have *joy,* and anyone who has *love* and *joy* will have *peace*. The person who has love, joy, and peace will be inclined to be *long-suffering,* and the long-suffering person will be *gentle*. The gentle person will be *good,* and a good person will find that he can trust God. A *trusting* person will be *meek,* and a meek person will have *self-control* (temperance). These nine fruits of the Spirit are like grapes on a stem; when the stem is picked up, all the grapes are picked up at the same time. The fruit of the Spirit, these nine aspects of a Christian's nature, is the result of God's working in the heart. Man does not aim at these things; he does not try to do them. They simply are his if he belongs to Christ and yields to the Holy Spirit.

There are many, many people who wear themselves out trying to enjoy themselves. Sad and bitter is the dark brown taste they have in their mouths the next day from trying to enjoy themselves. Joy is the gift of God for those who commit themselves to the Lord Jesus Christ. He will *give* joy within that will bubble up in the heart. There are times when a Christian feels so good he will not be able to understand what is happening to him. He realizes his circumstances and knows that at that particular time he ought not to feel good at all; but he does. The reason for this is that the Christian has an inner quietness and peace. He has a confidence which is his strength. He has a love spread abroad in his heart in such a way that he feels good all over. This is not his own doing. God does it in him.

Were you ever in love? You will remember that nobody could make you mad then. Nothing made you downhearted or gloomy. The sun shone a little brighter; the flowers smelled more fragrant and everything was sweeter in the days when you first found love. A Christian person falls in love with the Lord and never gets over it. This love grows and grows and grows. The more there is of love in the heart the less a man cares about what happens on the outside. People may say such a man does not have good sense. He acts as if there is nothing the matter when he may be in real trouble. He does not seem to notice his hard circumstances. He has the fruit of the Spirit in him—love, joy, peace, etc. This is the result of God's working in the heart, and such results glorify God.

Glory will come in heaven. The Christian may look forward to it. There will be joy, peace, gladness, and singing. But this can be his earthly experience also, if he will yield himself to God, and let God have His way in his heart to work out His will in that life to His own name's honor and glory. That is what we mean by *glorification.*

COMMUNION

There are at least two ideas that come to our minds when we speak of *communion.* The first is that of the *Communion Supper* and the second is the *communion of saints,* mentioned in the Apos-

The Christian

tles' Creed. The Sacrament of the Lord's Supper is referred to as the *Communion Supper* because at the Lord's table the individual Christian enters into the close, intimate relationship with Jesus Christ which we call *communion*.

When Christians profess their faith, using the words of the Apostles' Creed, they say they believe in "the communion of saints." By this term they refer to the fellowship of believers with each other. Wherever Christians gather together in the name of the Lord, there is what is meant by the *communion* of saints.

The word *communion* commonly refers to daily experience with the Lord. It is a face-to-face, person-to-person relationship. The prefix *com* means "to come or bring together," and the word *union* means "as one." *Communion,* therefore, means "to bring together into one." This is to be seen when two little girls skip down the street together. They skip along arm in arm and exactly in unison. They may be said to be skipping in *communion*. Sometimes as boys walk along they put their arms around each other, and they walk exactly in step, foot by foot, step by step. Perhaps you have experienced sitting with a friend and after a time of silence you began to talk and your friend said that she had been thinking about that very thing. That shows that you and your friend were in communion with each other. Communion is an intimate relationship where two or more people feel alike and act together.

Communion is in evidence when people are singing. When a great many people sing the same words at the same time on the same pitch, they are singing in unison. Singing together in the different parts assigned to different voices is singing in harmony. However, this enters into the meaning of communion, for in it is involved everything that would convey the idea of blending together and doing the same thing at the same time. The word *rhythm* is also helpful to the meaning. In the army, men are trained to march, because it is a fact that if a man marches in step with other men, he can walk longer and with greater ease than if he is walking on his own. The rhythm will carry a soldier on after he is tired out. In *communion,* the Christian is in step with Christ.

The same thought is illustrated by two young people in love. They think the same things, they feel the same way, and there is a certain joy and sweetness of fellowship between them. What causes it? It is the joy they have in being with the particular person whom they happen to be with. It happens with husband and wife. The Scriptures say, "They shall be one flesh" (Gen. 2:24). The ambition of every young couple thinking of getting married should be that they will live in communion with each other. When husband and wife live in communion, there are two equals living together. If a young man were thinking of getting married and came to talk with me about it, I would urge the young man to remember that from his wedding day on he will never be able to be by himself. In everything he will do, he will have a partner. This means that his thoughts, ideas, and actions will not be his alone. There will be another person sharing with him in all these things. When two people are in communion, they experience an increased dimension of joy and strength. It is more than fellowship, for communion describes the relationship of two people being together as one.

In the Christians' relationship with the Lord Jesus Christ, even more is true. Christians are together with Him like husband and wife—He is the Bridegroom and they are the bride—but there is a difference, because He is the Lord and they are the servants. He is the "head of the body," and the Christians are the members of the body; and yet they are both in one body and they belong together.

The experience of communion is developed and strengthened by the practice of worship. In worship the person focuses the attention of his heart and mind upon the one to be worshipped. In worship a person looks upon some one person and prefers that one above all others: that one comes first. Not only is that one preferred, but he is adored. When I think only of one person and give him my adoration, I enjoy and appreciate that person's beauty, and he becomes very valuable to me. This is what I do when I worship the Lord Jesus Christ. I bow down before Him in my heart and gaze upon Him. I consider the things which He did. He healed the leper; He opened the eyes of the blind; He forgave the woman taken in sin; He was patient with the woman at the well. He went into the house of Mary and Martha and raised Lazarus from the dead. He knew He was going to raise Lazarus, yet at the graveside He wept in sympathy with these people because of their sorrow and grief. In this way I think on the actions of Christ. I watch and gaze upon them. I esteem those truths as the most important things in the whole world and in that way I worship Christ. Worship leads me to say, "I'd do anything for Him." The experience of worship contributes to communion.

• Gazing into the face of the Lord Jesus Christ and letting everything that is within my heart esteem and appreciate Him will lead to prayer. In no other exercise can I have fellowship with the Lord as much as through praying. Christ Himself is constantly praying for me and for others. In my time of communion with the Lord, I will be moved to act as Christ acted when He was here upon earth.

Whenever I tell people about the Lord and invite them to come to church, I am doing what Christ did, and in this way I am walking with Him. Helping the poor, caring for the sick, and visiting the infirm or those who are in trouble is what Christ would do and when I do these things I am walking with Him. Anything I do by way of service to Christ in which I move in His will is communion with Him.

The Lord Jesus worshipped the Father. The Lord Jesus Christ looked out upon human beings and felt sympathy for them. The Lord Jesus undertook to win people to God. If I do these things, I am like Christ. When people rebuked, reviled, and persecuted Him, the Lord Jesus opened not His mouth. If I am patient under persecution, I am like Christ and in that I have communion with Him. The Lord Jesus gave everything He had—He gave Himself—on behalf of other people. If I do this, I am like Him.

When people discredit the Bible, when they criticize Christianity and make fun of the things of God, when they slander the Lord Jesus Christ, I may take this to heart as though they were criticizing, slurring, and casting shame upon me. In communion I share with Christ. Anyone who repudiates the Lord Jesus Christ repudiates me. The glorious part of communion is that if I walk with Him here in this life He will keep me with Him in the world to come.

GROWING IN GRACE

When a person becomes a Christian, he starts living a new life. The new Christian, being young in faith, is referred to as a *babe* in Christ. After a baby is born, it is natural for it to start to grow. All parents try to make sure that their child is growing normally. In the life of the Christian, the idea of growing is also very important. The term commonly used in speaking of the Christian's increase in knowledge, understanding, and practice of spiritual truths is "growing in grace."

In this world, living things never start out full-grown. Apple trees begin as seedlings and grow to be apple trees. Horses begin as colts and grow to be horses. Dogs begin as puppies and grow to be dogs. People start out as boys and girls and grow to be men and women. Shortly after a baby is born, it is given a name. Suppose the baby is a boy and he is named John Brown. John Brown grows as any normal boy will grow. When he is five years old he will be much taller and heavier than when he was born, but he is still John Brown. When he is ten, fifteen, twenty years old, he is still John Brown, but he has grown into the possibilities that were in him when he was a baby. Christians start as *babes* and they grow to be in the fullness of the stature of the Lord Jesus Christ (Eph. 4:13). They are Christians all the while, but they grow.

All living things grow, although they may not grow for the entire length of their lives. Some things grow until they are full-grown. A boy does not grow for forty years. He grows for about twenty years, and at the end of that time he has reached his height and is thought to be full-grown. Apple trees will grow, and they will start bearing apples after a couple of years, at which time they are considered mature apple trees. They may live for twenty years and have good seasons and poor seasons. New branches will come out, old branches will break off, but the apple tree is a mature apple tree all that time. But a Christian should never stop growing. From the time a person is born again, there should be growth. Even though a person may be considered by other people to be a mature Christian in terms of his understanding of Bible teaching, there is still room for growth and development, for the riches of God's wisdom extend beyond any goal that man may ever attain.

Everybody knows that all babies do mainly three important things. They eat, sleep, and grow. All three are necessary for the baby to grow normal and healthy. The prayer of all Christian parents for their children is that they would be healthy and grow and be and do the best they can. A person grows by taking food into the body. The food is assimilated, making strong bones, muscles, tissues, and nerves. If a baby does not receive sufficient food, its growth will be stunted. It will not grow to full proportions. Sickness can also stunt a child's growth.

The Christian

I have a brother who was sickly until he was eleven or twelve years of age. Our father was five feet ten inches tall and all our uncles on our mother's side were six feet tall or more, but my brother is a good deal shorter than I am, and I am scarcely five feet ten inches tall. People speak of my brother as a short man. He has breadth, but he never grew very tall. I think he never grew to his possible size because of his time of sickness as a child. This is the sort of thing that sometimes happens with Christians. After I become a Christian, I need to feed on the Word of God that I may grow and develop in my Christian life. If anything interferes with my Bible study and my prayer life, I may never be all I could have been in the Lord.

The Book of Hebrews sets forth the idea of what the milk of the Word is. It has to do with great doctrines—repentance, faith, forgiveness of sins, cleansing, the filling of the Holy Spirit, judgment, heaven. These are things a young Christian should learn. When I become a Christian, I need to think about heaven. I am saved from hell, but I am saved to heaven. God will judge me. I will be forgiven by the *grace* of the Lord Jesus Christ. Christ's blood was shed for my sins. God gives His Holy Spirit to me. I am to believe in God. I am to count myself in the presence of God at all times. I am to judge my daily life in the presence of God. That is milk. A young Christian needs to think on those things. In so doing, he will grow into the fullness of the stature of Christ.

It is a sad experience to see a child that has never matured. Such a child may be twelve years old, but have the mind of a three-year-old. Even though the body may be healthy and strong, the mind may not be developed. Everyone will pity this child and sympathize with the parents. What happened? We say this is a case of retarded development. The child simply did not grow up.

This is what it is like when Christians do not grow up. Christians should encourage one another to "grow in grace and in knowledge of the Lord Jesus Christ." *Growing in grace* does not mean that the Christian becomes sweeter, more gentle, kind, loving, and peaceful as time goes by. These things will take place, because they are the fruits of the Spirit. But to *grow in grace* is to become more and more conscious of the presence of the Lord. Every moment of every day the mature Christian remembers that Christ is his Saviour. The reality of Christ's death and the forgiveness of God enter into the Christian's mind in such a way that he wants to be obedient and well-pleasing in God's sight. This is maturity.

Some years ago a missionary who was a former student of mine wrote to me and asked, "What can I do to feed my soul while I am on the mission field? I believe all the Gospel, I preach it, I teach it, and I want to help the natives to come to know it; but I find myself inwardly feeling weak, and I do not feel that I am as strong as I could be. For that reason, I know I need to grow in spiritual things." My answer to that young man was, "Read and study the Bible." By this I meant: Read the Old Testament instances of how God dealt with His people. Read through the life of the Bible characters and watch what happened when they walked with God and also watch what happened when they disobeyed God. Notice what happened when they needed help and when, how, and for what they prayed. Then notice how God answered their prayers. By doing this, the missionary would be feeding on the Word of God.

Just as one takes food—bread, meat, fruit, and milk—into his body, and the body grows and becomes strong, so it is with the things of the Lord Jesus Christ. I will grow in grace and knowledge of the Lord Jesus Christ by feeding upon the Word of God and taking into myself the truth of Christ's death for men, Christ's resurrection from the dead, Christ's promise that if men believe in Him they too will be raised from the dead, Christ's presence with God, Christ's continued praying for believers, and Christ's giving of the Holy Spirit to Christians, enabling them to walk with Him day by day. In this way the grace of God will abound in my heart and so I will become a healthy, strong, constantly growing Christian.

SERVICE

The word *service* is best understood when it is remembered that the person who serves is a servant. A servant is one who waits on another. It may be stated very simply that a servant is one who runs an errand. A servant is someone who will do what he is told. The trouble with some servants is that they want to become bosses and do as they see fit, instead of doing the service which they should do.

Some years ago when I was a schoolteacher, I attended a meeting at which the speaker was the man who was acting as principal of a school attached to the New York Stock Exchange. This particular school is for the purpose of training the pages, the boys who run errands at the Stock Exchange. The boys are chosen from all over the United States, and obviously are chosen only because they are the very smartest boys. They are put on a salary basis immediately; and they draw full wages while they attend orientation courses at this school. The principal asked us what we thought was emphasized in the school courses during this period. We had no idea and yet we were surprised when he explained that the courses are especially designed to drill the boys to do *exactly what* they are told *exactly when* they are told to do it. They have assignments that require them to do things at precise moments. They are given some simple thing to do at a minute and a half after 10 a.m. and they must do it right at that time. They are graded on their promptness and accuracy in carrying out detail. The principal went on to say that the biggest difficulty with these smart boys is that they find it hard to do *exactly* what they are told. They all have ideas of their own.

We can see how this fits in the Christian life. The Lord Jesus said, "I am among you as he that serveth" (Luke 22:27). He also said, "My Father worketh hitherto, and I work" (John 5:17). "The Son can do nothing of himself, but what he seeth the Father do" (John 5:19). These sentences bring out the idea that it was Jesus of Nazareth's peculiar, personal ambition to be totally obedient to His Father in heaven. Christ Jesus gave Himself in unqualified, unreserved loyalty and obedience. This is for us the essence of Christian service.

Many people have the idea that if a person is going to act like a Christian and serve like a Christian he must do certain things. However, it is not *what* I do, but *how* I do anything that is my service to the Lord. If I am going to do the service of the Lord, this will not primarily mean that I must go three doors down the street and talk to a neighbor about Christ; it is not that I must teach a Sunday school class; it is not that I must keep the house clean. The first thing I am to do is to yield myself as willing to obey the living Lord. The Lord is not going to ask me to climb the highest mountain, swim the widest river, or run the fastest mile.

He will ask me to do something that I can do. Usually it will be a simple thing, and often it will be so humble that I will not want to do it. I might want to do something important. I would not want to just give in and give up all the time. But that may be exactly what the Lord Jesus would want me to do, because that was what He did when He was here. He yielded Himself; He didn't take anything for Himself; He emptied Himself.

The Christian's service will move toward *good works*. When the Bible says *good works,* it means works that are of good report, actions which people talk about as *good*. The Christian will have in mind that he will do whatever is good for others, because that will be honoring to the Lord Jesus Christ.

Paul had no special zeal about how he would act at any time except that he would always act in obedience to his heavenly Father. In this way he was willing to be "All things to all men" that he might always render the service expected of a Christian in any situation in which he happened to be. Whatever was required in that situation, he wanted to be found faithful to his obligation, honest in the sight of all men, and of good report—acting in a way that people would accept.

In my service as a Christian, I will show certain characteristics. I will always show respect to those who are over me. I will not be disobedient to those in authority. It is not befitting for me to break any law of the land, whatever that law may be. As a Christian I not only yield to those who are in authority and respect those who are over me, but I show the same regard for those who are on a level with me, or over whom I might have authority. The Christian will have consideration for all people in any service he performs.

If I were living in an apartment house and I happened to have my radio tuned in loud, I would immediately think of all the other people in the apartment house. Therefore, not wanting to disturb anyone, I would turn down the volume on the radio. If I owned some chickens and I moved into a community in which there was no definite law stating I could not have chickens but the people of the community did not want chickens around, as a Christian I would not insist on having chickens. I would do without them, or I would move out into the country. If I had a dog that barked late at night, I would get rid of him. A barking dog might disturb someone who is not feeling well and needs sleep. It is not that important for me to have a dog, but it is important that I consider the needs of other people who live near me.

Some people may wonder whether or not a Christian should be expected to act in that way. I would ask them what they think the local preacher ought to do in such a situation. That is a good way for people to decide what ought to be done. If they heard that the preacher lived at a certain place and that he had a dog that barked late at night, would they think he ought to keep that dog? We know very well they would say he should not. They might think their reason is that he should act that way because he is a preacher. They really mean because he is a Christian.

I can remember when our four children were all small, but yet old enough to enjoy games. On Sunday afternoons they would have their usual hilarious enjoyment of some game in the back yard. Our children were about 4, 5, 6, and 7 years of age and usually six or seven neighbor children the same age and size would come over to play with them. One Sunday we received a phone call from the neighbors, who requested that we quiet the children a bit. The neighbors were trying to sleep. We were embarrassed because we had not thought of the neighbors, but I am glad to say they never had to phone again. What our children were doing was certainly innocent enough. After all, it was just a group of children playing in their own yard. But we didn't own the whole town, and some of those children could make enough noise to reach over the whole town. Our children simply had to take up a more quiet Sunday afternoon activity.

Christian service means that I will honor those who are above me, I will consider those who are equal to me, and I will show charity to the poor. This type of behavior will adorn the Gospel and lay up treasure in heaven. It will be my "reasonable service."

CHAPTER NINE

The Church

IN our discussion of the church, it is inevitable that we should repeat some of the material which appears earlier in this book. The subject of the church in the final analysis covers or touches every aspect of the Christian's relationship to God. When the Bible uses the word *church,* it means something different from what is meant in everyday use of this word. In any ordinary conversation I might use the word *church* to mean a *building,* as when I would say, "There are three churches in our block." The Bible does not use the word *church* in that sense. I could also use the word *church* to refer to a *denomination,* as when I would say, "The Baptist Church has many congregations in this city." The Bible does not mention denominations at all. I could use the word *church* to refer to a *cultural factor* at work in the community. In this way I could say, "The church opposes vice and the sale of alcoholic beverages." But the Bible never uses the word *church* in that way. I could use the word *church* to refer to all public activities of Christians as a group in society. In this way I could say, "The church was certainly weak in the community where I grew up as a boy." The word *church* is never used that way in the Bible. Or I could use the word *church* to refer to a *cause.* And so I could say, "I am certainly in favor of promoting the church." By this you would understand that I am in favor of anything that produces the good and the moral. But again it is not used in that sense in the New Testament. I could also speak of the *church* as "the pillar of society." I could say, "Our American society rests upon the home, the church, and the school." And everyone would understand that I meant to say that the *church* is one of the factors which build up our civilization. This would be understood by my hearers, but the New Testament never uses the word *church* in that way.

The Church

Each of the uses which I have mentioned above is meaningful. Each means something in our modern language, and it is possible to see how each idea is related to the true *church* as set forth in the Scriptures. But not one of these ideas is what the Bible means when it uses the word *church*.

ECCLESIA

The word *church* was originally a Greek word, *Ecclesia*. It was used in the New Testament, and it gives the real meaning of the church because it means the "called-out ones." This really describes the believers in Christ. Believers in Christ are actually the "called-out ones" and so are called the *Ecclesia,* which is the Greek word we translate as *church.*

The question might well be asked, *called out* from what? The Bible would answer, "called out from the world." This does not refer to a change of location. The Scriptures say that believers are "in the world but not of the world." The church remains in the world, but actually is not part of the world. How can this be? The church may be likened to a boat in a lake. The boat is in the lake, but it is not of the lake. The only reason the boat is of use is because it is not part of the lake; for the minute the boat and the lake become the same thing, the boat loses its usefulness. It is only while the boat can ride on and over the lake that it can be useful.

So it is with the church. The church is in the world, but it is not of the world. The church is called out of the world so far as its nature and life are concerned. That does not mean that the church is a part of the world which has been made over—refined, moralized, spiritualized—so that it is the part of the world which is moral and spiritual. It is something taken *out of* and *away from*. But now our thinking must be directed to Biblical expressions, because in trying to understand the church as the *called-out* ones the question could well be asked, "Can we be sure that this is the meaning of the word?"

The Bible is filled with illustrations of *called-out* people. Consider first, Noah. In Noah's time, the judgment of God had gone out; and the whole world was to be destroyed by water. But Noah was *called out* of that destruction. God told him what to do, and he carried out God's command in the building of the ark to the saving of his family. Although the flood came, it did not destroy Noah because he was *called out, singled out, separated* from the rest of the people by the fact that he did what God told him to do in the making of the ark.

Secondly, consider Abraham. Abraham is the classic example of faith. Christians are called children of Abraham and the whole of Scripture would point to Abraham and say, "There is a man who believed in God." But what did Abraham do when he believed God? When we read Genesis 12:1 and Hebrews 11:8, we find that Abraham left behind everything that was his own and came into a new country where he had never been. The word *Hebrew* in the Old Testament and the word *Ecclesia* in the New Testament are similar in their meaning. The word *Hebrew* means *over*. The *Hebrew* is a man from *over yonder,* an immigrant. A man may be spoken of as going "over the hill" in the sense that he is going away. In a rather peculiar yet significant way, Abraham was the world's first recognized immigrant. He left his own country and "came out" into a new country.

Both Noah and Abraham begin to point to what is meant by the church. In the New Testament, the church is not only spoken of as *called out* in the word *Ecclesia,* but Christians are called *strangers and pilgrims* (Heb. 11:13; 1 Pet. 2:11). The believer in Christ is distinctly told that he does not belong in this world but that his citizenship is in heaven (Phil. 3:20). The word *stranger* has a very broad meaning, and the word *pilgrim* is rarely used in present-day speech; so perhaps the word *tourist* will give a clearer idea of what we mean. A *tourist* is a visitor; he is passing through the community; he does not belong there. He obeys the laws of the community but he is not part of the community. Any member of the true *church* is a *tourist* in the world.

The Book of Exodus (Chapters 1-14) tells of Israel's bondage in Egypt. The time came, however, when those people were *called out* of Egypt. This whole story sets forth the very basic idea that I will have to "come out of" and "away from" the situation that I am in as a human being before I can "come into" the blessing of God.

If I become a member of the church through faith in the Lord Jesus Christ, then I really belong to Him. I will experience being "called out of" myself to "come into" the things of the Lord Jesus

Christ. The Lord Jesus Himself said, "If any man will come after me, let him deny himself, and take up his cross, and follow me" (Matt. 16:24). As a Christian I am distinctly told to reckon myself "indeed to be dead unto sin that we may be alive unto God."

In these various scriptural uses it seems clear that the word *church* refers to people who have been "called out of" anything that is natural and ordinary with them, "into" something that God wants them to be. We can see that the primary meaning of the word *church* is the *called-out ones*. This is not something church members should seek to become. This does not mean that after being a member of the church for a certain period of time a person finally becomes separated to Christ. This is the way it all starts. I begin to be a Christian by being separated to Christ. But can I begin to be a Christian without any experience or preparation? It is very much like getting married. Folks can get married without any former experience. They can get married without knowing anything about it, and many do get married without even thinking much about it. When a couple gets married it simply means that out of all the group of girls that used to live in that neighborhood, this one girl becomes the bride of this one boy. In that sense, she is "called out of" all the girls in that community to be the wife of this particular man. In the same sense, the church is "called out of" all the world to become the Bride of Christ. A young couple can be married without having had any previous experience, but everyone would agree that once they get married they have experience, and experiences follow. Marriage is real from the very outset. So it is in the matter of being in the church.

Since the word *Ecclesia* is being considered, it would be well to mention the adjective *ecclesiastical*. We use this word when we say about some man: "He is an ecclesiastical officer." Or we may say, "That is an ecclesiastical organization." The adjective *ecclesiastical* means far less than the word *church*. It is about twice removed from the original idea. It refers to the church organization and that is the church at its poorest. The church is at the best level in the heart condition of the people. We have the beginning of the church when the individual soul receives the Lord Jesus Christ. We see the church more really when the individual

Christian worships the Lord Jesus Christ, and we see the church at its best when the individual Christian does the will of the Lord Jesus Christ and feels personally responsible to Him.

When the church is set up as an organization and becomes a public group, it always has people in it who do not really belong to it. There can be people voting on ecclesiastical problems who are not really Christians, people not really dedicated and yielded to the Lord. While the word *ecclesiastical* does belong to *Ecclesia* by way of its origin, it is only in this sense that it refers to the church organization. The scriptural meaning of the word *church* is far more fundamental and basic in Christian experience than the organization which, of course, comes later. The matter of being "called out to be with Him" points to the vital heart of the true church of God.

THE BRIDE OF CHRIST

The Bible sometimes speaks of the church as the *Bride of Christ*. This is one name for the church that the whole world would understand. The writers of the New Testament may well have had in mind that the word *bride* would be understood by people in any culture and in any society. A bride is one who belongs to her husband, and in that sense the church belongs to the Lord Jesus Christ. This is meant to be very exclusive. The church belongs to the Lord Jesus Christ as she belongs to no one else. The church is a group of people who are "called out of" everything that is natural to live only in the Lord Jesus Christ. They belong to Him in a way in which they belong to nothing else. When I am a member of the Bride of Christ, there is no organization that I belong to, there is no society that I am a member of, there is no culture in which I am related, there is no family into which I was born, there is absolutely no other relationship that is now to be considered equal to my relationship to the Lord Jesus Christ. I belong to Him more and differently than I belong to anything or to anybody.

When a woman marries a man she belongs to him, and when a man marries a woman he belongs to her and these "twain become one flesh"; they forsake all else that they should belong together. When the Bible speaks of the church as the Bride of Christ, it has in mind that these individual Christians belong to

The Church

Him *first* before all others. When our Lord Jesus Christ was here upon earth, on one occasion certain people came to Him and said that His mother and brothers were outside and wanted to talk with Him. "But He answered and said unto him that told Him, Who is my mother? and who are my brethren? and he stretched forth his hand toward his disciples, and said, Behold my mother and my brethren! For whosoever shall do the will of my Father which is in heaven, the same is my brother, and sister, and mother" (Matt. 12:50). In that way, the Lord Jesus Christ Himself showed how exclusive and completely absorbing this relationship is in which the Bride of Christ belongs to her Lord.

When we think of a bride we have in mind immediately that she is loved by her husband. It may be that different husbands love to a different extent; but so far as any one husband is concerned, all the love in his heart goes out to his bride. Just as the bride is loved by her husband, so the church is loved by the Lord Jesus Christ. This places a significance upon the church and upon its members. If I am a member of the church, I am a person who is loved by the Lord Jesus Christ.

A bride begins a new life with her husband. Wife and husband will live together as neither one of them lived before. They are going to have fellowship in things that neither of them has experienced before. They are going to have experiences together that are part of a common life. The same is true with the church. To speak of the church as the Bride of Christ means that I as a Christian am going to enter into a fellowship and relationship with the Lord Jesus Christ that I have never had before and that will shut out all others and open up new experiences for me such as I never could have by myself.

When we say that a certain woman becomes the bride of a certain man, we mean that she becomes a part of him and the two of them become the beginning of a home and the beginning of a family. So, too, with the church. When the believer in the Lord Jesus Christ receives Him and enters into fellowship and relationship with Him, the Christian becomes part of something that never existed for him before. This is going to lead him into experiences that he never had before.

When the church is called the Bride of Christ, we emphasize the *personal* nature of the relationship. When a man gets married, no other man but *that* man gets married; and when a girl gets married, there is no other girl but *that* girl who gets married. It is very personal. In this sense, it is a personal matter when I receive the Lord Jesus Christ. Nobody else in the church, or in the community, or in that church service has the experience that I have. I have an experience that is altogether *personal* and altogether *singular*.

Being a member of the Bride of Christ is also a *total* relationship. When a girl gets married, she gets married *in toto*. When a boy gets married, he gets married *altogether*. It is possibly true there are boys and girls in the world who do not fully realize this. They seem to imagine they can get married and still be what they were. This is one thing, however, they will certainly find out. It is quite possible they will be better than they ever were, but they will surely be different. The same is true with reference to becoming a Christian. Something happens to me when I become a member of the church, the Bride of Christ: something that is complete, and total, and final. When I become a member of the Bride of Christ I enter into a relationship that is intended to be forever. In the Bible, marriage is considered to be permanent. In the world, marriage is often entered into as a temporary arrangement; but even so, when husband and wife come together and they "twain become one flesh" something happens to each of them that changes them forever.

When we speak of the church as the Bride of Christ, we mean that the church is loved by the Lord and that she loves the Lord, in an exclusive way. The Bible teaches again and again that it is the will of Almighty God that the church shall belong to Him only. In speaking about this, James uses very blunt language. He says, "Ye adulterers and adulteresses, know ye not that friendship of the world is enmity with God?" (James 4:4). That language is used to refer to this very relationship and means that when I come as a bride to the Lord Jesus Christ and then let my heart be diverted to anything else in the world, I am guilty of spiritual adultery. It is like the woman who marries a man and then lets her heart be turned aside to other men. That is not the way it should be either with human relationships or with the church. As the Bride of Christ, the church shares all Christ is. When a girl marries a man, she shares whatever he is and has. He gives her his name; she comes into his home, and from that time on he is Mr. So-and-so and she is Mrs. So-and-so. They work together. The bride may herself have nothing and the groom may be a millionaire; but the moment she marries him she is a millionaire because she has and shares everything that he is and has.

The Bible speaks of Christians as being "heirs of God and joint heirs with Christ" (Heb. 8:17). All that Christ has the Christian shares in the sense that the Christian belongs to Him and His Bride and is involved in all that He does. When I live truly in this fashion, I will be interested in winning souls because the Lord Jesus is interested in winning souls. The Lord Jesus is interested in going to the ends of the earth to win the heathen people to God; therefore, the church is interested in going to the ends of the earth to win heathen people to God. I share all that He does. I do not just reap the benefits of belonging to Christ, but I actually participate in what is going on in the same way the bride participates with her husband in the life that he lives.

We could also say that the church gives her whole heart to her Lord. Her heart is what He wants. If I have money, or means, or prestige, I can give all that, but the main thing Christ wants is my heart, my mind, and my strength.

In all this discussion we can see that the expression the *Bride of Christ* gives an idea of the proper mind of a Christian. As a Christian, I should be thinking that I am married to the Lord Jesus Christ and have entered into total communion and companionship with Christ Jesus as my Beloved. This is final, so that I am not looking for anything else. It is personal, so that with the living Lord Jesus I seek to be in constant communion. It is a case of feeling together, of being together, of thinking together, and of walking together, with Christ Jesus.

We should keep in mind that when we say the church is "thinking together with the Lord Jesus Christ," we do not mean that the church had any original contribution to make that would affect His mind. It is not exactly the same as when we think about a husband and a wife in this world. Man and wife, both being human, are obviously on an equal basis; but when we speak of the church as the Bride of Christ, we remember that the Lord Jesus Christ is in Himself God and the church is not. Actually, the church becomes His body and so enters into a real relationship with Him. In this way the church will think His thoughts after Him, and His thoughts will become her thoughts; His feelings will become her feelings. Something like this happens time and again when people get married. When husband and wife live together in a normal marriage relationship, the one begins to think and to feel like the other. That is the way it is with the church— the Bride of Christ.

THE BODY OF CHRIST

The church is often spoken of in the Bible as the *body of Christ*. When this term is used, the emphasis is upon the obedience which the church should exercise and the service which the church should render. The word *body* is intended to refer to just the same function that our bodies have. When we say the church is the body of Christ, we mean the church is in relationship to Christ as my body is in relationship to me.

What, after all, is my hand? It is a part of my physical body. My hand does things which cannot be done by my ear, my foot, my lungs, or any other part of my body. It is that part of the tissues, muscles, and bones of my body that is designed for use when I want to shove, carry, pick up, or write something. If my hand is going to be a real hand, it must obey me. If I want to pick up something, I have to grasp it and hold it. If I want to carry something, I have to hang on to it. If I want to lay it down, I must let go of it. If I desire to place an object that is lying on one table on another table, my hand must move where I want it to move. If my hand is going to be useful to me, it must be obedient to me. My hand, in itself, will not have any thoughts of its own. It must do what I want to do with it.

The church as the *body of Christ* is in just such a relationship to Christ. It does not figure things out for itself. The church does not decide what it is going to do. The church tries to do in obedience what the living Lord wants it to do at any time in any place. When I believe in the Lord Jesus Christ and belong to the church, the body of Christ, I am to be an obedient member of His body. Then, as part of the body as a whole, I am to be obedient to the Head.

When trying to understand obedience, we may remember that there are times when hands do not do as they should. There are

The Church

unfortunate people whose hands have become paralyzed. Very often a paralyzed hand stays small; in time it withers, and loses all its strength. The same is true with the church if it will not do as the Lord wants it to do. When we use the word *church* we must keep in mind that the church is the individual Christian belonging to the Lord Jesus Christ. Whatever happens to the church starts in the individual believer. If I as a Christian do not respond to the will of the Lord Jesus Christ and do not do what He wants me to do, then that relationship will shrivel like a withered hand. In the story of the miracle of the healing of the man with the withered hand (Mark 3:1-5), a picture is given of any Christian who does not obey the Lord. The church must respond to her Lord's will in the same way the hand must respond to the person's will.

There may be aspects of the spiritual experience that are involuntary and over which a person has no control. There are organs in the body whose actions are involuntary and over which a person has no conscious control. The heart beats without the will's being involved. The blood circulates in the body unconsciously. The liver, the lungs, and other inner organs go about their work without the person's deciding about their function. In spiritual experience, the Lord Jesus Christ may accomplish some things in men even when they are asleep. As the body lives while the person sleeps, so the spiritual experience would go on even when the person sleeps. God will do even more than men can ask or think and He will work out His will in our lives, even though part of what He does never comes to our conscious attention. But the body is to be the means by which the person operates. With the body the person performs the daily tasks, whatever they may be. So, too, the Lord operates with the use of His body.

The believer in Christ may ask, "What would the Lord Jesus Christ want me to do?" He is not left entirely to his own imagination. He can turn to the Gospels—Matthew, Mark, Luke, and John—and there find out what the Lord Jesus wants His followers to do. The Lord Jesus said, "as my Father hath sent me, even so send I you." It is not to be thought that the Father stayed in heaven and sent the Lord Jesus down into this world on an errand by Himself. While there is a sense in which it may be said that

God sent forth the Son, it must be remembered that there was never a time when the Father was not with the Son. The Son went out in obedience to the Father, but He could at any time lift His eyes up to heaven and speak to His Father: "Father, I thank thee that thou hast heard me" (John 11:41). As Christ stood before the world, He could say, "I and my Father are one" (John 10:30). He further said that He did nothing of Himself, but "My Father worketh hitherto, and I work" (John 5:17). The Lord Jesus Christ testified to the whole world that at all times there was the very closest communion between Himself and His Father. Although to the human mind it might at first appear that God sent His Son away from Himself, God went with Him. It is in this fashion that the Lord Jesus said, "even so send I you." He sends the church out into the world but never to go alone. The great commission of the Lord Jesus Christ was, "Go ye therefore, and teach all nations . . . and, *lo, I am with you alway,* even to the end of the world" (Matt. 28:19-20).

At one time it was my expectation to go to the mission field. My father-in-law questioned me as to why I was going. The best reason I finally discovered for my going to the mission field was to have fellowship with the Lord Jesus Christ. If I did not go, I would not be with Him. Later, the best reason I could give for going into the pastorate was that if I did not take this work I would not be with Him. The best reason I had for talking to a soul to see if he could be won to Christ was that if I did not go and talk to that soul I would not be in fellowship with the Lord. My father-in-law tried to bring to me the idea that when the Lord Jesus said, "Lo, I am with you alway," He did not necessarily mean "Lo, I am following after you." It could very well mean "Lo, I am going before you." The verse says, "I am with you *alway,* even unto the end of the world." Going before would be the normal way in which Christ would do it. When He was with the disciples, He always led them; and when He is with present-day Christians, He will also lead them.

The church, then, is going to be led by the Lord Jesus Christ. Believers are not left entirely in the dark as to what that leading will be. Matthew, Mark, Luke, and John tell what Christ did. It is astonishing that there is no record of the Lord Jesus Christ's doing anything that ordinary human beings do. The Bible does not

The Church

say that He built any fortune; it does not say that He built any buildings. It does not say that He painted a picture, or that He wrote a poem, or carved a statue. He never led an army. He wrote no music. What did He do? *He came to seek and to save the lost.* He came to win men to God, and He did that as no one else ever did. That shows exactly what the church should be doing. It is the only thing, really and truly, that the church should actually be doing in the world. Christ has not changed His mind. During the time that He was here on earth, He did His work; and now that He is gone, He is not going to do something else. No, He did what He had to do, and now He will send us to do the same. "As my Father hath sent me, even so send I you."

Christians, being members of His body, will not be led through the same physical experience that He was led through; but the spiritual experiences will be the same. This could be pointed out in many different ways. If the Lord Jesus Christ wants to do anything in our community today, He will do it through His believing people. If He wants to talk to somebody who is not in communion with His Father in heaven, the only way that He can talk to that person is through a believer who will go and speak to that person.

When Paul had seen the Lord on the road to Damascus and was left blind in the house of Simon on the street called Straight, Ananias was sent to him and was told to speak to him and baptize him and give him his sight. Ananias needed to go in order for Paul to have the benefits intended for him. That is a way of saying that there will be no one invited to church unless the members of the church *go* and invite them. No one will be taught the Gospel unless believers teach them. That is how the Lord Jesus Christ wants to do it. Believing people—the church—are members of the body of Christ, and as such they are His means of working in this world.

MEMBERS ONE OF ANOTHER

The Bible speaks of the church as being *members one of another.* Notice, however, that this expression follows the phrase *one body in Christ*—the *body of Christ.* The attention is now focused upon the *relationship between Christians.* We have seen that the term *body of Christ* means the relationship of the individual church member to the Lord as being similar to the relationship of a member of the human body to the head of the body. Christians are primarily members of His body. In the second sense, and involved in that idea, they are members of each other; but we should remember that they become members of each other as they become members of Christ. Christians are members of the *body of Christ* in what they do and in how they obey. As members of Christ's body, Christians are guided through communion with Him that they should follow as He leads, and do what He wants them to do.

Now we shall see that individual believers, Christians, as members of Christ's body are also *members one of another*. They are *members one of another* mostly in experience; however, they do not learn from one another what they ought to do, for that is learned from the Lord. But while they are doing what the Lord wants them to do and while they are doing these things together, they have the experience of being *fellow members of His body— members one of another*.

With reference to his inner feeling, the believer is first of all conscious of the Lord, but if any one member is disobedient to the Lord there is set up in the heart of fellow believers sadness, distress, strain, and uneasiness because this fellow Christian has not obeyed the Lord. All will feel his guilt and his responsibility. They sympathize and share in his feeling. Paul makes this clear when he states, "And whether one member suffer, all the members suffer with it; or one member be honoured, all the members rejoice with it" (1 Cor. 12:26).

It is very important that members of the church, Christian people, should be aware of this fact that they have such a real relationship with each other. They belong to each other not because they are led by each other as to what to do, for each believer is led by the indwelling Holy Spirit of God. But whatever results from the service of anyone, the consequences of obedience or disobedience, these are shared with each other. If some one member of the church has been led of the Lord to serve Him in a marked way or if one member of the church gives liberally to missions, the whole church is lifted by such service. If one member of the church is moved to engage in evangelistic activity, seeking to win souls, the whole church is conscious of it. Every member of the church may not approve it, but all members will be aware of it and the entire tone of the church will be affected by the fact that one member is doing something.

In the same way, if there are members of the church who do nothing, taking no part in evangelistic activities at all, the tendency will be for the whole church to do nothing. Even those who would be minded to do something will feel it hard to do anything because there does not seem to be any support. There will be individuals who will carry on visitation in spite of disinterested members, but such will feel the drag of those who will not visit. It is a bit like being in a company of people where everybody is tired; you, too, will soon feel sleepy. However, if you were in the company of people who were alert and bright and interested, you too would become more wide-awake. This does not work actually 100 per cent, but it is a tendency. If one member suffers, all other members suffer with him. If one member is hurt, all the members are hurt; and if one member is blessed, they are all blessed. They share; they are *members one of another*.

Because Christians share this mutual relationship with each other, the individual should keep in mind that if he wants his own spiritual life to grow, he needs to be interested in other Christian people. Any one Christian person will find that his own relationship with the Lord will not prosper unless he gives actual and intelligent attention to other Christians with whom he is associated. Sometimes he will see in them things that should be prayed for; he may see deficiency; he may see faults. The Scriptures tell him to do this. Members *need to do* this or else their own spiritual life will falter.

Being *members one of another* carries in it the meaning that Christians are all related to each other. Therefore, a genuinely sincere Christian should have in mind that any other genuinely sincere believer in any church or denomination is his personal brother. This will mean that if a Christian in a community is a member of the Presbyterian Church because he wants to be a member of the Presbyterian Church and if there is a Methodist Church in the community, he should pray for that Methodist Church. There may be an Episcopal Church, a Pentecostal Church, a Salvation Army Church, or a Roman Catholic Church in the community, and the Christian should keep in mind that among all these congregations there could be someone who is actually his brother because that person names the name of Christ. When a Christian approaches the Lord, maintaining communion with Him, he could have in mind that if for any reason he feels sluggish in his relationship with the Lord, it might well be that the body of Christians in that whole community is just slow; they are cool and he needs to pray for all of them. They may not all warm up at the same time, and it may be that revival will start in his own heart. When a revival starts in my heart I should be very careful that I do not let myself be moved into isolation and away from other people. I should remain concerned about them, for if they belong to the Lord Jesus Christ it should be my desire that what is happening to me would happen to them. This is the attitude that is grounded in the truth that Christians are *members one of another*.

Because Christians are *members one of another,* they will do certain things with each other. In the Book of James, the Christian is told: "Confess your faults one to another, and pray for one another, that ye may be healed. The effectual fervent prayer of a righteous man availeth much" (James 5:16). Many Christian people will have in mind that other members will not always confess their faults to them, so they will have to pray for them even though they have not confessed their faults. The matter of being conscious of the faults of other Christians can be very normal; but I should take care that such knowledge does not degenerate into criticism. It should move me to prayer. As the Christian becomes aware of the needs of others, he should pray about them. Christians are *members one of another*.

When the Christian learns something about the Lord Jesus Christ, he will want to share it with others. If one Christian has some understanding about Scripture, he will try to impart it to other people, bringing out of his treasury things new and old. Christians will also give to each other of their material things. When the Christian becomes conscious that some other member of the church is in need, he will feel inclined to share with him. Christian people will visit the sick and help those who are in trouble and those in need in the congregation, because they are members one of another.

By working for each other, Christians are helped to respect one another. Being members of the body of Christ and members one of another means that when I become a Christian I belong to fellow Christians and I belong to the Lord. Upon observing members in the early church, the pagan people said of them, "Behold, how they love one another." That comment has been used as sarcasm in our present day, but it is true that Christians do care for each other. Christians should strive to "love one another," so that the statement may be no less true now than when it was made concerning the first-century church.

THE HABITATION OF GOD

The Bible teaches that Christians should not "forsake the assembling of themselves together." In this way, the writer of the Book of Hebrews puts it upon my heart and mind that I should meet in fellowship with other Christians. The reason I should do this is simply that we are all members of the church.

In what we have said before, we have pointed out that as a Christian I am a member of the "body of the Lord Jesus Christ" and belong to Him; and, also, with reference to other Christians we are "members one of another" and belong to each other. Now we shall see that as Christians we not only are to *belong to* each other but also we are to have *fellowship with* each other. We are to have *communion* with each other, and this is what happens when we come together in church meetings.

In the New Testament, we can see this idea plainly because many of the epistles were written to churches rather than to single individuals. Much of the explanation of the Gospel was given to Christians as a group. The Book of Romans was written to the Christians who were in Rome; the Books of 1 and 2 Corinthians were written to the church of God in Corinth; the Book of Ephesians was written to the believers at Ephesus. Each of the church epistles of Paul was written to some congregation, yet it is known that the truth comes to the believer *individually*. I must as an individual receive the Lord Jesus Christ and must myself belong to Him; however, I am to have this individual experience in fellowship with other Christians. While the Lord does deal with me in my own heart and I have a person-to-person relationship with the Lord so that I become a member of the body of Christ before I am in the church as members one of another; yet when the Lord would teach and bring ideas to me, He speaks to me when I am in the church. So we can see why the messages in the epistles are directed to what is called the *church*.

The *church* in itself is never anything but the company, the fellowship, of believing people. In fact, I receive an understanding of the Gospel when I am in company and in communion with other people. This is actually helpful for the soundness of my spiritual experience, because the very nature of man is such that "it is not good that man should be alone" (Gen. 2:18). This is not only true for me *personally* and *socially,* but it is true for me *spiritually.* When I am together with other Christians, I am stronger; and I am also kept from personal peculiarities.

We notice as we look around at people we know that when people live with other people they are likely to be normal. But if anybody lives by himself and is alone a lot, there is a tendency for that person to become queer. Such a person can actually become unbalanced. Certain things in which he has a personal interest get bigger and certain things in which he is not personally interested get smaller, until his judgment and his conduct are simply not sound. Living together with other Christians in the Lord is important because in being together with others we keep a better balance. One person may be more interested in one aspect of the truth; another person may have greater interest in another aspect so that together they balance each other. Suppose there is a congregation with three members named Tom, Dick, and Harry. When they all meet together, Tom emphasizes what he is interested in, Dick emphasizes what he is interestd in, and Harry emphasizes what he is interested in. The result is that Tom, Dick, and Harry have more together than if Tom were alone, or Dick alone, or Harry alone. God has arranged it this way so that no one should have the total responsibility for all that he has. Some of what I have as a Christian comes to me from other Christians.

When a group of people are going to live together, they must have some kind of order. If not, they will become a mob, and that is not far away from a riot. Whenever people gather as a group, some form of leadership is needed. This is what the Bible teaches about the church. When Christians come together, *gifts* are given to them wherein God helps them along with their living together. The *gifts* are "apostles, prophets, evangelists, pastors, and teachers" (Eph. 4:11). An *apostle* is a man who serves other people; a *prophet* is a man who teaches other people; a *pastor* is a man who watches over other people; a *teacher* is a man who gives ideas to other people. Every one of these *gifts* is exercised with other people, and this shows that God has in mind that some individuals should serve others by helping them in their faith and life. Such servants are given special abilities "for the perfecting of the saints, for the work of the ministry, for the edifying of the body of Christ: till we all come in unity of the faith . . . unto a perfect man." The Bible says that Christians coming together "are built upon the foundation of the apostles and prophets, Jesus Christ himself being the chief corner stone; in whom all the building fitly framed together groweth unto an holy temple in the Lord: in whom ye also are builded together for an habitation of God through the Spirit" (Eph. 2:20-22). The expression "fitly framed together" brings out that one person will be given one kind of ability, while another will have a different ability. So there will be some who can interpret well, some who can perform and carry out practical activities, some who pray well, and so on. But working together they all help the church to grow.

When I think about anything being "fitly framed together," I think of a house. In order for a house to be "fitly framed together" it must have walls, a roof, and a floor properly arranged. The whole house cannot be walls nor can it be all roof. If it were all floor, it would be a patio and not a house. To be a house it must have doors, windows, and some wall space. It could not be all doors. Between doors and windows there must be wall space. The general idea is plain enough that it takes all these different parts to make a house. So it is with the church, the fellowship of Christians. All members must function with each other and "those members of the body, which seem to be more feeble, are necessary" (1 Cor. 12:22). This is what Paul meant when he wrote, "All the building fitly framed together groweth unto an holy temple in the Lord."

Peter says the same thing. In speaking of Christians, he says, "Ye also, as lively stones, are built up a spiritual house . . ." (1 Pet. 2:5). The word *lively* means *living*. Here Peter is bringing in the idea that Christians are more than individuals, more than just single persons. They are persons in action. In their action they should be together as Christians. What does the word *stones* mean? Stones are the material from which the temple is built. When Peter says "a spiritual house," he means what Paul means when he says "an habitation of God." They both are referring to the church. Apparently they want us to get the idea that it is God's plan that the church as a group of people should be *gathered together,* and also they should be *structured together* in the sense that each will have his own function to perform. As an individual I will have some part to play, some function to perform; and the strength of the church will be determined by the manner in which I and others like me perform our particular functions.

The important thing for a brick in a wall is that it should remain a brick and stay in its place. The brick must not melt away or fall out of place. If the brick does not stay in its place, the wall will collapse at that point. Staying in place is just what many Christians need to do as church members. They need to be simply what they are and be faithful to that.

Being "fitly framed together" can be illustrated by a person's hand. The hand is composed of five fingers, and yet the hand is more than just the five fingers. The hand can do some things which no one finger could do. But for it to be a hand, the five fingers must each one do its part. The thumb must act like a thumb and the little finger must act like a little finger. If for any reason all the fingers should do the same thing in exactly the same way, it would not be a hand; it would be a flipper. A hand must be flexible, and the only way it can be flexible is for each of the fingers to do its part. So it is in the church; all the members "fitly framed together" can do much when each one does his part and lets the others do their parts.

THE TEMPLE OF THE HOLY SPIRIT

The Bible speaks of the church as being the *temple of the Holy Spirit.* We have been thinking of how the church, builded together, is "an habitation of God." This can be called the temple of God. And that means there will be a time when the Lord Himself will come to dwell in it.

The tabernacle in the days of the Exodus of Israel was the first dwelling place of God among His people. When it was finally completed and every part of it had been put together according to the specifications which God Himself had ordered, there came a time when it was filled with the glory of God (Exod. 40:34). This is

The Church

called the "Shekinah Glory of God." The same thing happened when the temple of Solomon was built. When every part of the temple had been completed, and all the furnishings had been put in place, when the priests had been sanctified, the sacrifices offered, and the people waited before the Lord, suddenly the glory of God burst forth and for seven days no one could go in or come out of the temple (1 Ki. 8:11).

In the early church the Christians were to learn that in their communion and fellowship together, they were the temple of the Holy Spirit. The Bible teaches that the Christian's body is the temple of the Holy Spirit, but there is also a strong emphasis that the Holy Spirit dwells in the hearts of His people when they are in fellowship with each other in a way that He cannot dwell in their hearts when they are not in fellowship with one another.

When the Holy Spirit came on the day of Pentecost, He came to the group. The church was together "with one accord (of one heart and of one mind) in one place" (Acts 2:1). The expression "one heart and one mind" means exactly what "fitly framed together" means. All Christians had the same ideas. This does not mean that they were all alike. Peter was still Peter; James was still James; John was still John. Each one of the apostles retained his own nature and remained his own size, so to speak; but there was a union and a communion among them. There was a unity into which the Holy Spirit was given.

When the Lord Jesus was here on earth, He said, "For where two or three are gathered together in my name, there am I in the midst of them" (Matt. 18:20). The Lord Jesus Christ comes to dwell in the hearts of believers. But is there ever such a fullness of the presence of the Lord in the heart of the believer when he is alone as there is when he is in company with other believers? I think not. This is a way of saying that when the Christian joins in the fellowship in a Christian church and shares in the communion, the worship, and the service, there will be a certain richness, a certain fullness, a certain enlargement of his experience he could never have when he is alone. We should notice that in every instance where the coming of the Holy Spirit is recorded in the Book of Acts it happened at a time when a group was together. Each time it is stated that "they were *all* filled with the Holy Ghost."

Individuals *can* be filled with the Holy Spirit, for the Bible says that Peter was full of the Holy Spirit when he stood before the council (Acts 4:8). Paul was also filled with the Holy Ghost when Ananias was talking with him (Acts 9:17). But just now we are noticing that at Pentecost, *all* the disciples were gathered together when the Holy Spirit came. The "habitation of God" had been built and the Holy Spirit came to dwell in the building that had been prepared. Any time Christians come together and have communion and fellowship with each other as believers, they can be sure the Holy Spirit of God is with them.

This truth means something for the church. When thinking of Christians as being members of the body of Christ, each one a stone in the wall of the temple, all builded together, and "an habitation of God," it should be remembered that because God is holy and will now dwell amongst them, Christians are to be holy. Paul has this in mind when he says, "Wherefore come out from among them, and be ye separate, saith the Lord, and touch not the unclean thing; and I will receive you. And will be a father unto you, and ye shall be my sons and daughters, saith the Lord God Almighty. Having therefore these promises . . . cleanse yourselves from all filthiness of the flesh and spirit, perfecting holiness in the fear of God" (2 Cor. 6:17-7:1). This idea of the believer's being the temple of the Holy Spirit will move all Christians to have a feeling that their daily life should be affected. There will be things that will be unfit for them, unclean, unsound, and improper simply because God is in their hearts.

The Holy Spirit comes to be in the heart of the Christian primarily to witness. Whenever the Holy Spirit was given in the New Testament, there was always some form of action. He was never given merely for the individual to enjoy so that the Christian could be happy in himself over what God had done. The Holy Spirit was given for service. There was always something for the Christians to do that would help other people.

Christians are to serve both God and man. Christians are to serve the Lord. They are also to serve each other. And there is a responsibility of the Christian to render service to the people on the outside. The Holy Spirit given to the Christian moves him to act in all these directions.

Toward God, the Christian is moved to worship. When the Holy Spirit is in the heart, the Christian is moved to prayer. The Lord

The Church

Jesus taught His disciples to pray "Our Father." The word *our* is social; it implies a group. One cannot say, "Our Father," unless he has some other people in mind; otherwise, he would say, "My Father." It is recognized that for the individual Christian there is a sense in which he can pray to God as "My Father." That is private, personal, very important, and very real; but when the Lord Jesus Christ taught this prayer, he was teaching a group. He uses the words, "Our Father, which art in heaven, hallowed be thy name." And, "give *us* this day *our* daily bread and forgive *us our* trespasses." Always there is the plural, which means not so much being in the physical presence of others as conscious of the fellowship of others. The Christian is aware of others when he worships, because the Holy Spirit is given for function and performance in the group.

The Scriptures do not encourage believers to think that the individual is called out to serve alone. It is group performance, even though I may have my own responsibility in that performance. I may have to stand out on my own, but I am bringing all others with me when I come into the presence of God. In serving God I am led to prayer and in serving other people I am led to communion and service.

In this fellowship with other Christians in the Holy Spirit, there is comfort for the soul. Every Christian will know in his own spiritual experience that there is great strength in having fellowship with even one other Christian person, for "where two or three are gathered together" the Lord is present. It is when I share with others that I get more comfort from the promises of God. In sharing with other people I am built up in the edification of the Spirit and with reference to service. God has aranged to come and dwell in the hearts of His people when they are in fellowship with each other.

AGAPÉ

The Bible speaks of the church as the gathering of believing people which should be a *community of love*. In the Greek, the word *agapé* is used. It is difficult to translate into English because when translated it becomes a word that can be used for so many different things. The Greek word *agapé* gives the idea of the church's being "gathered together in fellowship" when the Christians will have a "love feast" or a "love communion." It is a time when they all become aware that they belong to each other.

When the word *love* is used in the Bible, it does not mean the inward feelings which we call emotions. There are words in the Bible which mean that: such as *compassion, pity, honor,* and *respect.* But this is not really what is meant by the word *love.* There is scarcely any action one can put his finger on and say, "This is the act of love." Love in itself is not special conduct. Love is a quality that can be seen in any conduct. One man will support his family, and do so in love. That will mean that he supports his family because he seeks to help them and he wants to do for them. Another man may support his family because he wants other people to think well of him. When people work at their daily labor by which they earn their living, whether it be in the office, in the factory, or on the farm, one could ask, "Why are they doing this? What is their objective?" If they are working because they either want to please God or they want to help their fellow man in some way, they are doing their work in love. But if they work for their own advantage, this is not done in love. The word *love* refers to the intent of one's action.

What we are thinking about can be seen in the story of the Good Samaritan (Luke 10:30-37). No doubt the Samaritan was moved to compassion, but this is not why the Lord Jesus told this parable. The story did not end when he looked on the man who was left wounded by the roadside and felt compassion. It goes on to tell that he took of his own things and gave to this other man to help him. Love is to be seen in this: that he took of his own and gave to the other man because he needed help. The Samaritan was motivated, aroused, stirred by compassion, to be sure, but the *actual performance* when he took of his own and gave to the wounded man was *love*. The Bible states: "For God *so* loved the world, *that he gave* his only begotten Son." This passage does not draw any attention to God's feeling. It simply tells us what He did. Love is action.

Living in this *community of love* is not a matter of Christian people's getting together, looking into each other's faces, and being so pleased with each other that they think that they are the sweetest, nicest people in the world. Doing something for such people would be no great virtue because one would be doing something

The Church

for people whom he likes. But when the church has this *agapé* (sharing with each other) it means that the strong, the weak, the rich, the poor, the big, and the little care for each other and do things to help each other.

The *communion of love* may be compared with what happens when one brings in his poor relations and includes them in the family situation. In the *communion of love* I am willing to include in my group those who are disobedient and cantankerous, even though some might have to be disciplined. They will be cared for; they will not be shut out. All will be brought into the group. The word *agapé* brings in the idea that *all* Christians belong together to this one group. When we say each one is interested in the other we do not mean that each one approves the other, agrees with the other, or thinks that the other is perfect. We mean that each one admits that he belongs to each other Christian who is present and the other believer belongs to him. This will mean that when the church gathers together in this *agapé* feast (love feast) it is going to take note of the weak members. It is going to take note of the slow ones, because the church is not going to be able to move any faster than its slowest member. It is not going to do any more than the weakest person can share. The very essence of this *communion of love* is going to be that the strong must bear the infirmities of the weak and not act to please themselves.

The important thing about the group of believers is that they are linked together. This may be pictured in an outward way by mountain climbers in the Swiss Alps. We understand such climbers have the custom of tying a rope from one to the other, so that if any one person falls other people on the rope will be able to hold him and keep him from destruction. This is an almost perfect illustration of what is involved when the church is considered as a *community of love*. It is not a community of mutual approval. When Christians gather together, this is not a time to flatter each other. It is the time when they realize that Christians belong to each other and each one is interested in one another. It will cause one person to inquire about another person. That is part of the *agapé*. If one member has been talking too much, other Christians will find it out, and they will do something about it.

It is very important for the new Christian and the young Christian to join an established fellowship of Christian people. Normally speaking, if the congregational life of the church is what it should be, the congregation as a whole will be interested in each individual member. That means that if there is a member of the church who is sick, the rest of the church will visit him; if there is a member of the church in trouble, the rest of the church will join in and will share in that trouble; if there is a member of the church who is in need, the rest of the church will share with reference to that need. There is this sense of communion that is to be activated by a sincere interest in each other.

The entire fellowship of the church which is brought out in the communion of love is pictured for us at the Lord's Supper, where all the church gathers together in fellowship around the table in the warm, informal, spontaneous fellowship of eating together. Believers are to eat together of Christ's broken body and are to drink together of His shed blood, which means that they are as a church to think together that their salvation comes from Him. In the Apostles' Creed, Christians confess their faith and say they believe "in the communion of saints." The "communion of saints" underscores the fact that all believers are to belong to each other and to have fellowship with each other. This is true not only from person to person, but it should be true from church to church with the result that there should be in the spirit of any one congregation and denomination a feeling of belonging to other congregations in other denominations, for believers are all one in the Lord.

NOT OF THIS WORLD

In trying to understand the church according to what the Bible teaches, we must consider that it is *not of this world*. Something is true about the church that can never be understood as part of this world. By *this world* we mean human beings living according to the senses. This world is what they hear, see, taste, smell, and touch. The whole outlook of human beings is the way the world affects *them*. When they organize any part of the world, it is *for themselves*. It is the most natural thing in the world to look out for one's self. A man thinks: "I like this; I don't like that. I go here; I don't go there. I like this one; I don't like that one. I have this fellowship; I don't have that fellowship. I will be willing to do this, because I think I will get something out of it. That is the way I see it." In the thinking and consciousness of the world, *I* is the central

The Church

point and from that all other things diminish in perspective. The farther away from *me*, the less important anything is. When *I* have no connection with it, it has no meaning to *me*. This is the general point of view in the world, and on it the world is built. John, in writing about the world, says, "For all that is in the world, the lust of the flesh, and the lust of the eyes, and the pride of life, is not of the Father, but is of the world" (1 John 2:16).

It has been noted in our discussion about the church as *Ecclesia* that the church is "called out of" the world. Christians are reminded that they are "in the world but not of the world." A good way to approach the phrase *not of this world* as it refers to the church, is to look at the Lord Jesus Christ. While it is true that the Lord Jesus Christ appeared in human form, the entire record in the New Testament makes it obvious that He was *not of this world*. That is one reason why the virgin birth is important. He was not born the way other people are born. He was "born not of blood, nor of the will of the flesh, nor of the will of man, but of God" (John 1:13). This Child was not conceived when a man and woman came together, but it was God who moved in "the fullness of time" (Gal. 4:4), and came to Mary telling her that she was going to become the mother of the holy One who would be called the Child of God. From the time of His birth, throughout His life, His death, and His resurrection, there is no part of the Lord Jesus Christ that can be thought as only human. He had a human form in the sense that His appearance was like a man, but His origin, His power, His performance, and His death were more than human. When men see the death of a human being with his body being placed in the grave, it is natural to think this is the end; but it was not the end of the Lord Jesus Christ. God raised Him from the dead. He was in the world and looked like a man, but He was *not of the world*.

Before leaving His disciples, the Lord Jesus Christ said to them, "As my Father hath sent me, even so send I you" (John 20:21). This word still goes out to the church, and the only way to understand this fellowship which is called the *church,* the *body of Christ,* is that its origin is not human. Whatever else might be said about the church, it did not come into existence because good people got together and figured it out. Well-meaning people who understood the social nature of man did not decide that it would be a good thing if all the good folks would join themselves together and make themselves into this company. The origin of the church is in the will of the Lord Jesus Christ (Matt. 16:18), and the reason the church has one mind and one heart is because the members have the one Holy Spirit. The only way Christians can actually be of one mind and one heart is to have the mind of Christ and yield to the mind of the Holy Spirit. This attitude of "one mind" can never be arrived at among human beings by getting folks to agree with each other. It is human nature for a person to set some things on the side that are his very own. The only thing two or more persons can agree on is a common project and this puts agreement on a limited basis. They will agree just so much, but they will not agree 100 per cent. The only One with whom we can agree 100 per cent is the Lord, who understands the individual Christian and overrules all his shortcomings and fills up all his deficiencies.

When thinking of the church as being not of this world, it is very important to remember that its origin is from God; because then we can realize that its nature, design, performance, and destiny will be from God. The life of the church, the actual, conscious fellowship and communion which the church has together, is not of this world. This means that it is not because these people all think the same human thoughts, have the same human ideas, have the same human values or the same human purpose, that they are members of the church. It can happen in the church that members belong to others with whom, humanly speaking, they could not associate at all. Sometimes Christians do not even seem to see the same things, yet in the Lord they will come together in one body. The basic communion in the church is communion with the Lord. The reason Christians have fellowship with each other is that they are "members one of another," they are members of the body of Christ, and they belong to Him.

Two men had been working in the office of a certain Christian institution. There had been some tension between them which had broken out into an open quarrel. One of the men was characteristically a German, and the other was characteristically a Jew. The one thought like a German and the other thought like a Jew. The manager of the agency called these two men in, and when he was talking to the young man who was a Jew he said, "You must remember that you are now a Christian and you are to act like a

Christian." In a very tense and frustrated way the man said, "Yes, I am a Christian. I believe in the Lord, and I want to act like a Christian. If only that other man would stop acting like a German. As long as he acts like a German, I have to act like a Jew. If he will act like a Christian, then I can act like a Christian." The manager then tried to show him that *he should be the one to start acting like a Christian.* This is the principle of the whole matter.

Think back to what has been said before about a Christian. The word *Christian* does not mean a certain advanced character of meekness, mildness, wisdom, or virtue. It would certainly be fine if every Christian had those attributes. But a person is a Christian when he believes in the Lord Jesus Christ for the salvation of his soul. He is a Christian the moment he believes. He may be only a babe in Christ and this will allow for a great many deficiencies. Among these deficiencies may be quarreling with each other, as the Corinthian church did. However, the ultimate fellowship and communion which wins out in the church is not a degree of human cordiality and friendliness. It is a communion in the Spirit, the Holy Spirit of God. Christians must remind themselves of this truth.

Not every congregation does what the church ought to do. It is possible that one congregation of people may be moved to do something no one else would feel right about. For example: A congregation of people might for several years devote themselves to, and absorb their whole interest in, the building of a particular type of building. When finished, they have simply built a sanctuary that cost twice as much as it needed to, because they wanted to have a big sanctuary to show off in the city where they were. That sort of action does not truly describe the church of the Lord Jesus Christ. True believers in the Lord Jesus Christ unite their hearts on the winning of the lost, and the promotion of good will among members. Wherever a Christian is found, these things will appeal to his heart and mind, because such things are of the Lord Jesus Christ and the Holy Spirit of God.

Service on the part of any church that is going out to do what the Lord Jesus Himself would do can expect to be inwardly sustained by the Holy Spirit of God. Such service will have to do with the winning of souls to God, because when the Lord Jesus was here on earth He went out to do one thing—"to seek and to save the lost" (Luke 19:10). While it may be allowed that the church may vary its procedure and do many different things, in whatever is done the ultimate purpose must be that it is going to act as the church of God. The Lord Jesus purchased the church with His own blood, built it in His own will, indwells it by His Holy Spirit, and directs it as His body, and we can be sure that whatever it does will be "not of this world."

SCRIPTURE REFERENCES

Genesis
1:1 31
1:2 150
1:3 150
1:4 24
1:27 ..... 12, 28, 30, 31
1:28 ..... 23, 36, 37, 38
2:7 .... 31, 32
2:17 59
2:18 .... 33, 210
2:20 34
2:21-22 34
2:24 .... 14, 186
3 58
3:9 .... 39, 60
3:13 ..... 39, 40, 41, 60
3:15 66
3:19 .... 31, 60
4:9 39
4:10 39
5:24 111
6:6 .... 20, 24
11:6 15
12:1 196
14:18-20 91
16:13 12
18:25 .... 23, 25
22:8 69

Exodus
1-14 196
3:14 19
11-12 70
12:13 70
15:20 90
20:8 .... 40, 137
20:12 53
20:13 53

20:15 .... 53, 56
20:16 .... 53, 56
21:24 61
26:33 75
29 81
40:34 .... 94, 212

Leviticus
1:9 76
16:5 89
16:8 89
17:11 67
20:7 .... 84, 85
20:26 85
23:27 89

Deuteronomy
6:4 .... 14, 15
6:15 83
29:29 112
32:36 23
33:27 21

Judges
4:4 90
6:34 150

I Samuel
10:1 90
10:9 151
15:29 20

I Kings
8:10-11 .... 94, 155
8:11 213
8:46 52

II Kings
2:11 111

Ezra
8:28 87

Job
5:7 49
23:10 12

Psalms
4:3 87
7:11 12
8:1 28
8:5 31
16:8 45
34:4 12
51:17 .... 22, 86
95:7 86
99:9 21
102:27 19
103:13 25
119:11 55
121:3 22
121:4 20
145:17 23
147:5 19

Proverbs
15:3 12
16:32 .... 37, 92
18:24 50

Isaiah
9:6 19
30:21 .... 138, 163
32:15 151
53 103
53:5 .... 71, 88
53:6 177
55:7 181
55:10 153
63:16 25

Jeremiah
18:2-4 24
31:33 152
31:34 79

Ezekiel
11:19 151
18:4 .... 24, 56

Joel
2:28 151

Jonah
3:10 20

Malachi
3:6 19

Matthew
1:23 101
3:16-17 14
3:17 98
4:4 .... 32, 49, 82
5:28 59
5:44 23
5:45 23
5:48 23
6:9 .... 17, 26, 215
6:10 115
6:11 215
6:24 83
9:16 128
9:17 129
9:36 50
9:37-38 50
11:5 22
11:19 122
11:27 26
11:28 50
11:29-30 50
12:50 199
14:15-21 104
16:18 220
16:24 197
16:26 82
17:2 101
17:5 98
18:20 .... 213, 215
19:5 .... 198, 200

19:21	23	23:34	171
19:26	18	24:37	16, 108
20:28	177	24:39	108
25:40	117	24:41	108
26:39	58, 106		
26:53	102	**John**	
28:19	14, 148	1:12	27, 130, 157
28:19-20	204	1:13	101, 219
28:20	174, 204	1:14	26, 100
		1:18	98, 99
Mark		1:29	44, 70, 71
1:15	123	1:32	153
3:1-5	203	1:34	98
4:39	104	2:19	105, 143
4:41	104	3:3	128, 133
5:28	104	3:8	32
5:30-31	105	3:13	17
6:34	36	3:16	26, 28, 107, 132
10:2	18		169, 216
10:45	105	3:35	99
15:34	106	4:14	153
		4:24	12
Luke		5:17	191, 204
1:13-15	152	5:19	191
1:15	152	7:17	131
1:35	98	7:39	146
2:36	90	8:29	47
2:44	102	10:30	98, 204
2:48	103	11:25-26	142, 145
2:49	103	11:41	204
3:16	153	14:1-2	17
4:8	101	14:1-3	141
4:18	22, 99	14:3	174
5:12	104	14:8	13, 57
5:13	104	14:9	13, 57
9:22	98	15:5	183
10:30-37	104, 169, 216	15:8	182
12:47-48	57	15:19	195, 219
15	45	16:7	146
15:7	45	16:8	160
18:27	18	16:13	147
19:10	42, 49, 221	17:2-3	143
22:27	191	17:5	99

17:11,14-16 . . 195,219,222
17:22 15
19:10 171
20:21 . . 203, 204, 205, 219
20:25 108
20:27 109
20:28 109

Acts
1-2 95
1:3 . . . . 111, 154
1:4-5 95
1:9 111
1:11 . . . . 116, 141
1:16 151
2 154
2:1 . . . . 154, 213
2:2 154
2:2-3 95
2:3 154
2:4 . . . . 95, 213
2:5-6 95
4:8 214
5:41 170
9:3-5 118
9:17 214
10:34 22
13:2 149
16:7 148
16:14 130
17:24 94
17:26 18
17:28 17
18:24 155
19:1-7 156
19:2 . . . . 156, 158
19:3 158

Romans
2:15 45
3:23 . . . . . . 52, 177, 178
3:24-25 65
3:26 69

5:5 168
5:11 90
5:20 52
5:20-21 61
6:11 197
6:23 . . . . 50, 51, 65
8:14-15 . . . . 26, 98
8:16 98
8:26 73
8:34 112
9:20 24
12:1 193
12:5 220
14:6 166
14:12 40
14:23 57

I Corinthians
1:2 181
3:6-8 15
3:16 94
5:7 70
6:19 174
9:22 192
9:27 37
12:22 211
12:26 206
12:27 209
15 . . . . 109, 144
15:20 154
15:21-22 25
15:22 42
15:44 16
15:50 127

II Corinthians
1:3-4 50
5:18-19 88
5:19 173
6:17 - 7:1 214
6:18 173
11:31 26
13:14 . . . . 14, 15

Galatians
- 2:20 176
- 3:13 66
- 3:28 15
- 4:4 219
- 4:6 157
- 5:22 ..... 164, 168, 171

Ephesians
- 1:3 26
- 1:11 18
- 2:1 110
- 2:12 87
- 2:20-22 211
- 2:21 ..... 211, 212, 213
- 2:22 ..... 212, 214, 155
- 4:11 210
- 4:12 211
- 4:13 188
- 4:18 88
- 4:30 149
- 6:17 174

Philippians
- 2:6 100
- 2:7 100
- 2:7-8 13
- 2:9-11 119
- 2:13 ..... 131, 152, 179
- 3:13-14 140
- 3:20 196
- 4:6 106

Colossians
- 1:3 26
- 1:18 186
- 1:28 133
- 3:17 ..... 136, 137, 139
- 3:23 136

I Thessalonians
- 4:13 112

II Thessalonians
- 2:14 11

II Timothy
- 1:12 126

Hebrews
- 1:3 13
- 4:15 ..... 59, 103
- 2:14-18 13
- 5:2 ..... 73, 91
- 5:6 91
- 7 91
- 7:21 91
- 7:25 ..... 26, 73, 93, 140, 157, 174
- 8:17 201
- 9:3 75
- 9:14 78
- 10:25 209
- 11:5 111
- 11:6 126
- 11:8 196
- 11:13 196
- 12:14 86
- 13:5 174
- 13:8 21

James
- 1:17 20
- 2:5 22
- 4:4 200
- 4:17 56
- 5:16 16

I Peter
- 1:5 96
- 1:18-19 68
- 1:23 175
- 2:5 ..... 211, 212
- 2:9 92
- 2:11 196
- 2:21 92
- 5:7 163

II Peter
  1:21 151
  3:18 .... 188, 189

I John
  1:9 66
  2:1 .... 72, 92
  2:16 .... 58, 219
  3:1 27
  3:2 110

  3:2-3 141
  4:4 129
  5:16 92

Revelation
  1:5 78
  1:17 118
  3:20 .... 86, 130, 131
  5:10 91
  22:17 .... 97, 174

INDEX

—A—

ABIDE — in Christ, 132-135
ABRAHAM—called out from the world, 196
ADAM — 33-34, 39
ADOPTION — into the family of God, 98, 173
ADULTERY — 59, 200
ADVENT — Second Coming of Christ, 116-119
ADVOCATE — in Christ, 72-73, 92
AGAPE — community of Love, 215-218
ALIENATE — 87, 106
ANGELS — do God's will, 18; man made lower than, 31; death angel, 70; Gabriel, 148
ANOINT — consecration of priests, 81; Jesus Christ, 99
APOSTLE — 210
APOSTLES' CREED — 11, 17, 185, 218
APPETITE — 58
ARK — of the covenant, 75
ASCENSION—of the Lord Jesus, 109, 110-113
ATONEMENT — the atonement, 69, 87-90; Day of Atonement, 68, 76, 89; through Jesus Christ, 67

—B—

BAPTISM — of Jesus of Nazareth, 14; receiving the Holy Spirit, 158
BARA — to create, 31
BELONGING — same as abiding in Christ, 133

BENEVOLENT — God is, 22
BELIEF—believing the Gospel, 123-126
BLOOD—the atonement, 67, 69; cleansed by the blood of Christ, 68, 77-80; the Passover, 70
BODY—(see Resurrection) material, 31-33; spiritual, 11-12, 16; resurrection of Jesus, 105, 107-110, 142-144; translated, 111; promise of God, 112
BORN AGAIN — second birth (regeneration), 26, 126-129, 175-177
BRIDE — the bride of Christ, 198-202

—C—

CALVARY — 70, 77, 89, 101, 141, 143, 163
CANDLESTICK — 76
CARNAL—opposite of spiritual, 164
CATECHISM — 55, 182
CHERUBIM — 75
CHIEF PRIEST (see Priest)
CHRIST (see Jesus Christ)
CHRISTIAN — 172-193; basic element, 97-98; members one of another, 205-209; being holy, 87, 92
CHURCH — 194-222; Christ the Head, 113-116; Holy Spirit works, 14, 165-168; officers, 72
CLEANSE — Holy Spirit persuades, 162; by the blood of

Christ, 77-80; the milk of the Word, 189
COMMANDMENT — Ten Commandments, 53
COMMISSION — sins of, 56
COMMUNION—of believers, 15, 33-36, 184-187; Communion Supper, 184, 218; of the Holy Ghost, 14; of love, 217
COMPASSIONATE — God is, 22; Christ has, 73
CONFESS — our sins, 65
CONSECRATION — 80-82
CONSCIENCE—man has, 45-48, 53; purge, 78
CONVERSION — regeneration, 175-177
COURSE — of sin, 58-61
COVENANT — the new, 151
CREATE — God created world, 21; man in image of God, 31; "Bara," 31
CREATION — God cares about, 23; the order of, 32
CREATOR — God is, 12, 39
CREED — (see Apostles' Creed)
CROSS — 70, 77, 89, 101, 107, 141, 143, 163
CRUCIFIXION — 107
CURSE — 60, 66

—D—
DEATH — of Jesus Christ, 77, 89, 101, 105-107, 141, 143, 163; angel, 70
DEMONS — 105
DEVIL — tempted Jesus, 32
DISCIPLES — with Christ, 147; early Church, 155; received the Holy Spirit, 156; Christ sent disciples, 219

—E—
EARTH — God manifests Himself, 14; God created, 21
ECCLESIA — 195-198
ETERNAL—God is eternal, 19-21; eternal life, 110, 143
EVOLUTION — 30
EXPIATION — 68

—F—
FAITH — 57; the Christian's faith, 173-175; the milk of the Word, 189
FAITHFUL — God is, 20-22
FATHER—baptized in the name of, 14; God is Father, 26-27; Son belongs to, 98-99
FELLOWSHIP — 177
FORGIVE — (also see giving) sins, 61-64, 160; milk of the Word, 189
FORM—Hebrew word "yatsar," 31
FRUIT — first fruits of God's work of salvation, 154; of the Spirit, 164, 168-171; bear fruit, 182-183

—G—
GENESIS — 34
GLORIFICATION — 181-184
GLORY — revealed, 101
GOD — 11-27; acts of God, 160; Creator, 12, 21, 39; Godhead, 14-15, 98, 147-148; a Person, 12; HIS ATTRIBUTES — Infinite, 16-19; eternal, 19-21, 101; omnipresent, 17; omnipotence, 17-18; holiness, 21-23, 67; faithfulness, 20; mercy, 22; jealous, 83; loves, 15, 22; unchangeable, 19; forgives, 61-64, 160; benevolent, 22;

compassion, 22; angry, 20 repent, 20; HIS CHARACTER—Activator, 14; Director, 14; Doer, 14; Judge, 16, 23-25, 40, 159; Performer, 14; Provider, 27, 210; Saviour, 25-26, 39; HIS NAMES — Jehovah, 19; Father, 26-27; Son, 13, 70, 97-99, 173-174; Holy Spirit, 11-13, 32, 46, 146-171, 174; Lamb of God, 67-71

GODHEAD (see Trinity)

GOSPEL — 120-145

GRACE — 15, 31; common grace, 47, 60-61; growing in grace, 187-190

GUILT — 60

—H—

HEAVEN — God manifests Himself, 13; home, where God is, 17; Jesus Christ has gone to, 73, 109; is real, 112; a Christian needs to think about, 189

HEIRS — of God, 201

HELL — 17, 189

HIGH PRIEST (see Priest) — 71-73

HOLY (also see whole) — God is, 21-23, 67, 160; keep Sabbath, 40; Holy place, 75; being holy, 85-87; to be holy, 181

HOLY GHOST — see Holy Spirit

HOLY OF HOLIES — 75-76

HOLY SPIRIT — 146-171; 11-13, 32, 46; in the New Testament, 151; in the Old Testament, 150-153; can feel, 149; brings men to Christ, 159-162; 174; has will, 149; to witness, 214; will guide, 163-164, milk of the Word, 189

HOPE — the Blessed, 139-142

—I—

IDOL — 11

IMAGE (also see shadow) — Christ, image of God, 12-13; man made in image of God, 23, 28-31, 87

INCARNATION — 13, 99-102

INCENSE — 76

—J—

JEHOVAH — 19

JEREMIAH — 24

JESUS CHRIST — 97-119; like God, 13-14; saves, 26, 38; our passover, 70; advocate, 72-73, 92; "anointed one," 99; Priest, 9; His compassion, 73; ascension, 109-113; abiding in, 132-135; believing in, 173-174; receiving, 129-132; serving, 135-139

JESUS OF NAZARETH (see Jesus Christ) — tempted of the devil, 32; always was the Son of God, 99

JONAH — 20

JOY — fruit of the Spirit, 170; a gift of God, 184

JUDGE — God is judge, 23-25; 40, 159

JUDGMENT — God's judgment not affected by size, 16; God's reaction to sin, 59-60, 65; repentance is, 122; sinners will come under God's, 159; Holy Spirit inclines people to be conscious of,

161; the milk of the Word, 189
JUSTIFICATION — in the Christian experience, 177-179
JUSTIFY — 178

—K—
KING — 90, 97

—L—
LAMB — Lamb of God, 69-71
LAVER — 75
LAW — conscience, 47; in the ark, 76; Law of God, 52-55, 152
LEAD — Holy Spirit will, 163; Christ will lead in the Church, 204
LORD JESUS CHRIST (see Jesus Christ)
LOST — man is, 42-45
LOVE — Love of God, 15, 22; Holy Spirit helps one to be aware of love of God, 163; Fruit of the Spirit, 168-178; Agape, community of love, 215-218

—M—
MAN — 28-51; made in God's image, 12; sanctified, 82
MANNA — 76
MARRIAGE — 33
MEMBER — relationship between Christians, 205-209
MERCY — God of Mercy, 22; Mercy seat, 76
MESSIAH — 97
MINISTRY—earthly ministry of Christ, 102-105
MOSES — Law of Moses, 54, 62; Moses received the Ten Commandments, 75

—N—
NATURE — subject to God, 18; nature of sin, 55-58; Jesus' power over nature, 104; old and new nature, 114; human nature, 127, 176; God shows Himself in, 159; nine aspects of the Christian's nature, 184; personal nature of belonging to the church, 199
NOAH — 195

—O—
OFFERING — sin offering, 66-69; burnt offering, 81
OMNIPOTENCE — God is infinitely powerful, 17, 18
OMNIPRESENT — 17
OMISSION — 56

—P—
PASSOVER — 70
PASTOR — 211
PAUL — 15, 40
PEACE—fruit of the Spirit, 170
PENTECOST—story of, 95; Holy Spirit came, 153-155, 213
PERSON — God is, 12
PHILIP — 13
PRAY — Jesus taught, 26; we know not how to, 73
PRAYER — 18; Holy Spirit reveals God, 163; Holy Spirit helps one be strong through effectual praying, 164
PRIEST — high priest, 71-73; office and function of, 90-93
PRIESTHOOD — 74-96
PROPHET — 90; watches over other people, 211
PROPITIATION — 65

—R—

RECEIVE—Christ, 129-132; the Holy Spirit, 156-159
RECONCILIATION — Gospel of reconciliation, 36; Christ effects, 69; meaning of, 71, 179
REDEEM — God sent Son to redeem, 157
REDEEMER — God is Redeemer, 25-26
REGENERATION (also see Born) — the Christian will experience spiritual renewal, 175-177
RELATED—Christians are, 207
REPENTANCE — 122-123; the milk of the Word, 189
RESPONSIBLE — man is, 39-42
REST — same as abiding, 133
RESURRECTION—Christ's body changed, 16; resurrection of Christ, 28, 107-110; unto eternal life, 142-145
RIGHTEOUSNESS — 61-62
RULE — man must, 36-39

—S—

SABBATH — 40, 87, 108
SACRAMENT — of the Lord's Supper, 185
SACRED — 80
SACRIFICE — for sins, 64-66; sin offering, 66-69; of Jesus Christ, 69; aspect of the work of the Lord Jesus Christ, 89; Jesus Christ was a vicarious sacrifice, 107; meaning of, 178
SAINT — 84; communion of, 184
SALVATION — 28
SANCTIFIED — being, 82-85
SANCTIFICATION — 83; of the Christian, 179-181
SANCTUARY — 87, 179
SATAN — subject to God's will, 18; does not have a body, 148
SAVIOUR — God is, 25-26; 39
SCAPEGOAT — the lot of, 89
SCIENCE — 38
SCRIPTURE — a Christian believes all things that the Scriptures teach, 174-175
SEPARATION—soul that sins is separated from God, 56; Christ experienced separation from God, 101
SERVE—serving the Lord, 135-139; Christians are to serve God and man, 214
SERVICE — of the Christian, 190-193
SHEKINAH GLORY — 93-96, 155, 213
SHEWBREAD — 76
SIN — 52-73; nature of sin, 55-58; course of sin, 58-61; forgiveness of sins, 61-64; sacrifice for sins, 64-66; sin offering, 66-69; must be confessed, 78; will remember their sin no more, 79; separates from God, 87; definition of, 132
SON (see God, Trinity) — God the Son, 13; baptized in the name of, 14; Son of God, 97-99
SOUL — of man, 28; man is, 31-33; man's emotional consciousness, 32; that sins, 56
SPIRIT (see Trinity, God, wind) —God is, 11-12; Holy Spirit, 13, 146-171; man is, 31-33;

manifests Himself in the Church, 14; baptized in the name of, 14; guides, 46; intellectual consciousness, 32; maketh intercession for us, 146-171

SPIRITUAL — man is, 31; spiritually lost, 43

SUBSTITUTE — 66

SUFFERING (see evil) — disobedience brings, 68; "Suffering Servant," 103

SUFFERS — man suffers, 48-51; He is willing to, 68

SUPPER (see communion)—the Communion Supper, 184; fellowship of believers, 218

—T—

TABERNACLE—72, 74-77, 154; dwelling place of God, 212

TEMPLE — 74, 76; "temple of His Body," 105; temple same as body, 143; dwelling place of God, 155; temple of the Holy Spirit, 212-215

TEMPTATION — 58, 60

TRANSFIGURATION—Mount of, 101

TRANSGRESSION — 60

TRINITY—three persons in one Godhead, 12-15, 98

TRI-THEISM — 15

TRUST—Holy Spirit leads, 162; 164

UNDERSTANDING — Holy Spirit will open eyes of, 162

UNITY — in the Godhead, 14; in function in Godhead, 15

—V—

VANITY — 59

VIRGIN BIRTH — 101, 219

—W—

WILL — will of God, 86; Holy Spirit has, 149

WITNESS — Holy Spirit leads people to, 161; Holy Spirit comes in heart of Christian to witness, 214

WORK — of the Holy Spirit, 160; empowers people to do specific work in the church, 166; God is working by His grace, 173; the Christian works, 191; God works, 192

WORLD — God created, 21; Christians called out of, 195; the Church — not of this world, 218-222

WORD—milk of the Word, 189

WORSHIP — 11; Holy Spirit moves people to worship, 167; communion is strengthened by worship, 186; Lord Jesus worshipped the Father, 187; the Christian is moved to worship, 214

—Y—

YAHWEH (see Jehovah) — 19

YIELD — a Christian yields in service to God, 191